DATE DUE

APR 2 7 2010	

DEMCO, INC. 38-2931

Getting the Job You Really Want

A Step-by-Step Guide to Finding a Good Job in Less Time

Fourth Edition

- Discover your best skills.

- Define and land your ideal job.

- Get the job you want in less time.

- Get ahead on your new job.

J. Michael Farr

Getting the Job You Really Want, Fourth Edition

A Step-by-Step Guide to Finding a Good Job in Less Time

© 2002 by JIST Publishing, Inc.

Published by JIST Works, an imprint of JIST Publishing, Inc.
8902 Otis Avenue
Indianapolis, IN 46216-1033

Phone: 1-800-648-JIST   Fax: 1-800-JIST-FAX
E-mail: info@jist.com   Web site: www.jist.com

Some Other Books by Michael Farr

The Very Quick Job Search   *Same-Day Resume*
The Quick Resume & Cover Letter Book   *America's 101 Fastest Growing Jobs*
Best Jobs for the 21st Century   *America's Top 101 Jobs for College Graduates*
Young Person's Guide to Getting &   *America's Top 101 Jobs for People Without a Four-Year Degree*
  Keeping a Good Job   *America's Top Resumes for America's Top Jobs*

Note to instructors. This book has substantial support materials, including a thorough instructor's guide, overhead and PowerPoint transparencies, a pocket data guide, and videos. Call 1-800-648-JIST or visit www.jist.com for details.

About career materials published by JIST. Our materials encourage people to be self-directed and to take control of their destinies. We work hard to provide excellent content, solid advice, and techniques that get results. If you have questions about this book or other JIST products, call 1-800-648-JIST or visit www.jist.com.

Quantity discounts are available for JIST products. Call 1-800-648-JIST or visit www.jist.com for a free catalog and for more information.

Visit www.jist.com. Find out about our products, get free book chapters, order a catalog, and link to other career-related sites. You can also learn more about JIST authors and JIST training available to professionals.

Visit CareerOINK.com. Get free information on 14,000 job titles.

Development Editor: Susan Pines
Cover and Interior Designer: Aleata Howard
Interior Layout: Carolyn J. Newland
Proofreaders: David Faust, Veda Dickerson

Printed in the United States of America

06 05 04   9 8 7 6 5 4

ISBN 1-56370-803-5

About This Book

A lmost everyone who looks for a job eventually finds one. This book, however, helps you find a better job or the one you really want—and find it in less time. These two points—how "good" the job is and how long it takes to find—are the only things that really matter in your job search.

My interest over many years has been to develop career planning and job search methods that get results. This book presents approaches that have been proven to help people identify career possibilities. It also presents proven methods that reduce the time it takes to find a job.

Career planning and job seeking are not easy. Luck plays a part, but you also have to work at it. The rewards are there if you do. This world holds an important place for you, and you will find it eventually if you try. Trust yourself. I wish you good "luck" in your career and your life.

Contents

Introduction

This is the fourth edition of this book. Earlier editions have been used by thousands of people, so you are in good company. I have made a variety of changes to this edition to keep up with the rapid changes in technology and our economy. For example, the Internet is an increasingly important source of career information and job leads, and I have added details throughout to assist you.

But the basics of finding and keeping a good job haven't changed all that much. You still need a clear sense of what you want to do, and you still need to convince an employer that you are worth hiring.

While career planning and job seeking can be complicated topics, only two things are truly important in planning your career and in looking for a job:

1. If you are going to work, you might as well do something you enjoy, are good at, and want to do.

2. If you want to find or change your job, you might as well do it in less time.

This book is about these topics—and about getting results.

Through examples and worksheets, it helps you identify a powerful new language to describe your skills and teaches you to use that language in interviews. If you don't have a job objective, it helps you define one. If you know what sort of job you want, you learn how to find out more about it and about other jobs that use similar skills.

The techniques you learn here have been proven to cut the time it takes to get a job—and help you get a better one. There is even a chapter on keeping the job once you get it that includes tips for moving up and leaving a job if you have to. I have tried to cover all the basic issues you should know in defining, getting, and keeping a good job.

In many ways, this is more than a job search book. It encourages you to learn more about yourself. It helps you identify what you enjoy and are good at—and to include these things in your search for meaningful work. This book asks you consider how you want to live your life. I hope that it helps you make better decisions and shows you techniques to be far more effective in your career planning and search for a job.

Getting the Job You Really Want is designed to be *used* and not just read. Make it your own by writing in it, jotting notes in margins, and completing the activities. I do hope that you enjoy it—and that it helps you get the job you really want in less time.

I wish you well.

Mike Farr

Mike Farr

CHAPTER 1

Getting the Life You Really Want

There Is More to Life Than Work

Most people work about 40 hours a week, but a week has 168 hours. Work takes up only about one-fourth of your time. While work is an important part of your life, it is just one way in which you spend your time. This chapter will help you put work in its place.

To prepare for the future, you need to think about more than the type of job you want. You need to consider what is important to you in your life. *The better you understand yourself, the more successfully you can plan your future.*

The following exercises will give you information about yourself. This insight will help you make better career and life plans and put you on the path to getting the job you want.

1

What Do You Want to Be Doing Ten Years from Now?

Imagine yourself ten years from now. If you could choose exactly what your life would be like, what would you be doing? Be realistic but positive. It's OK to dream! Take your time and answer the following questions. Use extra sheets of paper as needed.

1. Where would you be living, in what sort of area, in what sort of home?

_____

_____

_____

_____

2. How would you be making a living, doing what sorts of things?

_____

_____

_____

_____

3. Who or with what sorts of people would you be sharing your time?

_____

_____

_____

_____

4. How would you spend your leisure time, doing what sorts of things?

_____

_____

_____

_____

5. Any other important details?

_____

_____

_____

_____

An Inheritance from Uncle Harry

Imagine you've inherited $20 million dollars from an uncle you didn't know you had. Now, if you didn't want to, you would never have to work again. But there are a few catches! Harry put the money with a group of bankers. These people will give the money to you only after you have met certain conditions. Answer the following questions as honestly as you can.

1. For two years, the bankers will give you $75,000 annually for expenses. You can do anything you want, but you must spend your time learning about something that interests you. How would you spend this time, doing what sorts of things?

    _____

    _____

    _____

    _____

2. After the first two years, Uncle Harry requires you to spend half of your money ($10 million dollars) on a project that would help others. What would this project be?

    _____

    _____

    _____

    _____

3. What sort of lifestyle would you have after the two years are over? Where would you live, with whom, and how would you spend your time?

    _____

    _____

    _____

    _____

    _____

    _____

    _____

What Do You Want to Accomplish?

In ten or fifteen years from now, what three things would you most like to have accomplished? Don't think of all the reasons you might not succeed. Concentrate on the things you really would like to accomplish. You can list things from work or from your personal life.

1. _____
   _____
   _____
   _____
   _____

2. _____
   _____
   _____
   _____
   _____

3. _____
   _____
   _____
   _____
   _____

Setting Goals

The questions you just answered help you think about the future. They let you think about what you want to do or accomplish. These "dreams" can give you ideas for your work and your life goals.

While you may not be able to do everything you want, good planning can help you get closer. You need to ask yourself what you can do now to start making your dreams come true.

TIP

Take action! Be clear about your goals and set up steps you can take to meet them. The activities throughout this book will help you move closer to your dreams. The rest, of course, will be up to you.

Your Three Most Important Goals

Look over the exercises you just completed. Pick the three work or life achievements or goals that seem most important to you and write them here. Be realistic about what you could accomplish if you worked at it. Think in terms of ten years or more into the future.

Goal 1: _____

Goal 2: _____

Goal 3: _____

For each goal, complete the following.

Goal 1: _____

1. Give details about this goal. What would you like to accomplish? _____

_____

_____

_____

_____

_____

2. Within the next two years, what three things could you do to move closer to this goal?

✔ _____

_____

_____

✔ _____

_____

_____

(continues)

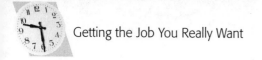

(continued)

✔ _____

_____

_____

3. List at least three things you could do in the next six months to begin working toward this goal.

✔ _____

_____

✔ _____

_____

✔ _____

_____

4. List at least three things you could do in the next thirty days to begin working toward this goal.

✔ _____

_____

✔ _____

_____

✔ _____

_____

Goal 2: _____

  1. Give details about this goal. What would you like to accomplish? _____

    _____

    _____

    _____

    _____

    _____

  2. Within the next two years, what three things could you do to move closer to this goal?

    ✔ _____

    _____

    _____

    ✔ _____

    _____

    _____

    ✔ _____

    _____

    _____

  3. List at least three things you could do in the next six months to begin working toward this goal.

    ✔ _____

    _____

    _____

    ✔ _____

    _____

    _____

    ✔ _____

    _____

    _____

    _____

(continues)

(continued)

4. List at least three things you could do in the next thirty days to begin working toward this goal.

    ✔ _____

    _____

    _____

    ✔ _____

    _____

    _____

    ✔ _____

    _____

    _____

Goal 3: _____

1. Give details about this goal. What would you like to accomplish? _____

    _____

    _____

    _____

    _____

    _____

2. Within the next two years, what three things could you do to move closer to this goal?

    ✔ _____

    _____

    _____

    ✔ _____

    _____

    _____

    ✔ _____

    _____

    _____

3. List at least three things you could do in the next six months to begin working toward this goal.

✔ _____

_____

_____

✔ _____

_____

_____

✔ _____

_____

_____

4. List at least three things you could do in the next thirty days to begin working toward this goal.

✔ _____

_____

_____

✔ _____

_____

_____

✔ _____

_____

_____

Dreams Can Come True If You Are Willing to Work at Them

Dreaming is not enough. While you could get lucky, planning to meet your goals is a far more effective way to get what you want from life. This chapter has helped you consider some of your long-term goals and get you working on them. You can often find ways to include these goals in your career planning. Then you can create a more meaningful and enjoyable future for yourself.

CHAPTER 2

Meeting an Employer's Expectations

An Employer's Point of View

To succeed as a job seeker and worker, you need to understand an employer's point of view. Many people believe that an employer thinks differently than they do. But employers are just like you and me. Try to think like an employer. Consider what you'd want your employees to do, and you can figure out what is expected of you as a worker. Knowing what employers want will help you present yourself successfully when you look for a job and help you get the job you want.

If You Were an Employer, How Would You Select People to Work for You?

This activity will help you learn to think like an employer. Imagine that you run a company. Give your company a name and decide whether you make products or provide a service. Then choose the products or services you offer. Next, imagine you have been asked to help others in your company decide which people to hire—or not hire.

Ten Reasons for Screening Job Applicants In or Out

In the following spaces, see how many reasons you can list for screening applicants in or out of a job. You can list negatives, such as "sloppy appearance," or positives, such as "good communication skills." Think of at least ten reasons.

1. _____
2. _____
3. _____
4. _____
5. _____
6. _____
7. _____
8. _____
9. _____
10. _____

Now go back and put check marks by the five reasons you think are the most important reasons to use when screening people in or out.

Your Top Three Reasons for Screening Job Applicants In or Out

From those five, choose the three reasons you think are most important to use in screening job applicants. List them below in order of importance. Put the most important one first.

1. _____
2. _____
3. _____

TIP

Your reasons are probably similar to those a real employer would list. Keep in mind, however, that different employers have different opinions about what is most important. Jobs, too, have different requirements. That is why different employers might include different and other reasons in their lists of points to consider in hiring someone.

What Employers Look For

Studies have been made to find out what employers look for in the people they hire. Check your list against the following findings. In deciding to hire one person over another, employers consider

1. First impressions

2. Dependability and other personality traits

3. Skills, experience, and training

Let's look at why this is true.

1. First Impressions

First impressions are important because negative ones are very hard to change. For example, employers in one survey said that more than 40 percent of the people they interviewed had a poor personal appearance. They were not dressed or groomed in a way that impressed the interviewer. It may not be fair, but it is a fact. First impressions can also include things like how you speak or whether you are friendly.

> **Did you put first impressions on your list?** You may have put something similar on your list. Why or why not? _____
>
> _____

2. Dependability

Most employers will not hire someone unless they think the person will be dependable. This is often true even if the person has good experience or training for the job. Being dependable means being on time, having good attendance, and working hard to meet deadlines. It also may mean that you are not likely to leave the job after a short time. If you convince an employer that you are dependable and hard working, you may get the job over someone with better credentials.

How do employers decide who will be dependable? They look at your past experience as well as your present situation. If you have been dependable in the past, they know you are likely to be dependable in the future. The information you or your references provide about previous jobs, schooling, and personal accomplishments will be very important in helping an employer decide if you will be dependable. If employers are not convinced they can depend on you, they will probably not hire you.

> **Did you put dependability on your list?** Why or why not? _____
>
> _____

3. Skills, Experience, and Training

Most employers will interview only those people who have at least the minimum requirements for a job. For example, they would quickly screen out applicants for an office job who could not use word-processing software. But employers often will hire a person with less training or experience over another applicant with more. Why? Many employers will hire the less experienced worker if that worker convinces the employer he or she will work harder or be more reliable.

In fact, most decisions are not based only on skills. If the employer thinks you can do the work or that you can quickly learn to do it, the employer may consider you for the job. If the employer thinks you will fit right in, be dependable, and work hard, you may get the job over someone with more experience!

Did you put skills, experience, and training on your list? Why or why not? _____
_____

Which Leads Me to This Conclusion

Farr's Rule of Job Seeking

It is not always the most qualified person who gets the job—it's the best job seeker!

Employers Are People, Too

Employers are people, just like you. Wouldn't you want to hire people who

- Look as if they could handle the job?

- Appear to be good, dependable workers?

- Convince you that they have enough job-related skills and training to handle the job or could learn them quickly?

Many employers *will* take a chance on hiring a less experienced worker *if* that worker convinces the employer that he or she can do the job. This is very good news for you because

- You can learn to create a positive first impression.

- You can emphasize why you can be counted on as a dependable worker.

- You can present your strengths in a way that convinces an employer that you can do the job.

You can learn to do all of these things as part of your job search preparation. You can learn to meet an employer's expectations. It is often the most prepared job seeker who gets the job, not the best qualified. This book will help you prepare. It will help you identify skills you have and enjoy using. It will help you decide what job you can do well and enjoy. And you will learn how to get and succeed on that job, even over more experienced workers.

CHAPTER 3

What Are You Good At?

Develop Your Skills Language

You have hundreds of skills. Most people do. You probably take for granted things you do well that others would find hard or even impossible to do. And no computer can yet handle simple things like riding a bike or getting across town.

Because we take our many skills for granted, most people are not good at explaining the skills they have. One study of employers found that three out of four people who interviewed for a job did not present the skills they had to do the job. Most people just don't have the language or interview training to spell out their skills.

In planning your career and in looking for a job, knowing what you can do well is very important. Knowing your skills can help you decide what kind of work is right for you. It makes a lot of sense to do the things you do best. If you do, you will probably be more successful.

It is also important to do things you enjoy. If you enjoy what you do and are good at it, your job and your life will be more satisfying.

This and the next chapter provide exercises to help you identify what you are good at and enjoy doing. Through these exercises, you will develop a powerful "skills language" that can help you plan your career and get the job you desire.

The Three Types of Skills

To help you identify your skills, let's begin by organizing them into the three groups shown in the triangle here. Each skill group is explained briefly in the following sections.

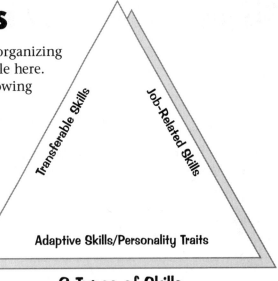

3 Types of Skills

Job-Related Skills

You need these skills for a specific job. An auto mechanic, for example, needs to know how to tune engines, repair brakes, and use a variety of tools. An office worker needs to know how to do word processing, use a spreadsheet, and do other office tasks. Most people think of job skills when they are asked what skills they have. While these skills are important, other skills are also important to have.

Adaptive Skills/Personality Traits

These skills can be defined as personality traits or personal characteristics. They help a person adapt to or get along in many situations. Examples of adaptive skills valued by employers include getting to work on time, honesty, enthusiasm, and being able to get along with others. While many job seekers do not emphasize these skills in an interview, they are very important to employers.

Transferable Skills

You can use these skills in many different jobs because they can transfer from one job to a very different one. For example, the ability to write clearly, speak clearly, and organize things would be desirable skills in many jobs.

TIP

Understanding that you have different types of skills is important. It is even more important to know what skills you have. Most job seekers think job-related skills are their most important skills. They are important. But employers often select job seekers with less experience who present their adaptive and transferable skills well in interviews. For this reason, knowing and being able to describe your adaptive and transferable skills can often give you a big advantage in getting the job you want.

Discover Your Adaptive Skills

This section will help you discover your many adaptive skills.

Your Good-Worker Traits

List five things about yourself that you think make you a good worker. Take your time. Think about what an employer might like about you or the way you work.

1. _____
2. _____
3. _____
4. _____
5. _____

Most people will list a variety of skills here. Often, one or more of these skills are adaptive, such as "get along with others" or "hard working." If you were an employer, would these skills be important for you to know about? Would knowing a job seeker's adaptive skills help you decide to hire one person over another?

In most cases, it would. Yet many people do not mention their adaptive skills in an interview! Use the checklist that follows to learn more about your adaptive skills.

Adaptive Skills Checklist

The following checklist shows the adaptive skills that most employers find important. Read each skill carefully. If you have or use that skill some of the time, put a check mark in the first column. If you have or use that skill most of the time, put a check mark in the second column. Don't mark either column if you don't use that skill very often.

Critical Skills

These are skills all employers value highly. They often won't hire a person who does not have or use some of these skills.

Skill	Some of the Time	Most of the Time
Arrive on time		
Follow instructions from supervisor		
Get along well with others		
Get things done		

Skill	Some of the Time	Most of the Time
Get to work every day		
Hard working, productive		
Honest		
Meet deadlines		

Other Adaptive Skills

Employers look for many other adaptive skills. Here are some of the more important ones. Use the spaces at the end to write adaptive skills that are important to you but that are not included in the list. Also write in adaptive skills you included in the "Your Good-Worker Traits" activity earlier.

Skill	Some of the Time	Most of the Time
Able to coordinate		
Ambitious		
Ask questions		
Assertive		
Capable		
Cheerful		
Competent		
Complete assignments		
Conscientious		
Creative		
Dependable		
Discreet		
Eager		
Efficient		

Skill	Some of the Time	Most of the Time
Energetic		
Enthusiastic		
Expressive		
Flexible		
Formal		
Friendly		
Good sense of humor		
Good-natured		
Helpful		
Highly motivated		
Humble		
Imaginative		
Independent		
Industrious		

(continues)

(continued)

Skill	Some of the Time	Most of the Time	Skill	Some of the Time	Most of the Time
Informal			Self-confident		
Intelligent			Self-motivated		
Intuitive			Sense of humor		
Leadership			Sincere		
Learn quickly			Solve problems		
Loyal			Spontaneous		
Mature			Steady		
Methodical			Tactful		
Modest			Take pride in work		
Motivated			Tenacious		
Natural			Thrifty		
Open-minded			Trustworthy		
Optimistic			Versatile		
Original			Well-organized		
Patient			Willing to learn new things		
Persistent			Other		
Physically strong					
Practice new skills					
Pride in doing a good job					
Reliable					
Resourceful					
Responsible					
Results-oriented					

Your Top Three Adaptive Skills

Review the "Adaptive Skills Checklist" carefully. Select three skills you checked that you think are most important to an employer. List these skills below.

1. _____

2. _____

3. _____

TIP

For you, the words you just listed are some of the most important in this book! Emphasize these adaptive skills, or personality traits, in job interviews. Employers will find them very important in deciding to hire you over someone else. Later in this book, you will learn to emphasize these skills in interviews, resumes, and other career planning and job search activities.

Discover Your Transferable Skills

Remember that transferable skills can be transferred from one job to another. You have *hundreds* of these skills. They have been learned and used at home and in school, hobbies, leisure activities, and volunteer and paid jobs.

The "Transferable Skills Checklist" that follows will help you identify some of these skills. It includes skills that are important to employers and job success.

Transferable Skills Checklist

Review each entry carefully. If you have that skill and are good at it, put a check mark in the first column. If you want to use the skill in your next job, put a check mark in the second column. Add any other skills you want to include in the "Other" sections. When you are finished, you should have checked ten to twenty skills in both columns.

Critical Skills

People who use these skills in their jobs tend to get higher levels of responsibility and pay. If you have these skills, they are worth emphasizing in an interview!

Skill	Strong Skill	Next Job		Skill	Strong Skill	Next Job
Accept responsibility				Plan activities or events		
Control budgets				Solve problems		
Deal with the public				Speak well in public		
Increase sales or efficiency				Supervise others		
Instruct others				Understand and control budgets		
Manage money or budgets				Work well as part of a group		
Manage people				Write well		
Meet deadlines				Other		
Meet the public						
Negotiate						
Organize or manage projects						

Other Transferable Skills
Using Your Hands/Dealing with Things

Skill	Strong Skill	Next Job		Skill	Strong Skill	Next Job
Assemble or make things				Operate or use tools and machinery		
Build, observe, inspect things				Repair things		
Construct or repair buildings				Use complex equipment		
Drive or operate vehicles				Use your hands		
Good with your hands				Other		

Dealing with Data

Skill	Strong Skill	Next Job	Skill	Strong Skill	Next Job
Analyze data or facts			Keep financial records		
Audit records			Locate answers or information		
Budget			Manage money		
Calculate, compute			Negotiate		
Check for accuracy			Observe or inspect		
Classify data or things			Record facts		
Compare, inspect, or record facts			Research		
Count, observe, compile			Set up budgets		
Detail-oriented			Synthesize		
Evaluate			Take inventory		
Investigate			Other		

Working with People

Skill	Strong Skill	Next Job	Skill	Strong Skill	Next Job
Administer			Patient		
Care for			Persuade		
Confront others			Pleasant		
Counsel people			Sensitive		
Demonstrate			Sociable		
Diplomatic			Supervise		
Help others			Tactful		
Insight			Teach		
Interview others			Tolerant		
Kind			Tough		
Listen			Trust		
Negotiate			Understand		
Outgoing			Other		

Using Words/Ideas

Skill	Strong Skill	Next Job	Skill	Strong Skill	Next Job
Articulate			Correspond with others		
Communicate verbally			Create new ideas		

(continues)

(continued)

Skill	Strong Skill	Next Job
Design		
Edit		
Ingenious		
Inventive		
Library research		
Logical		

Skill	Strong Skill	Next Job
Public speaking		
Remember information		
Research		
Speak in public		
Write clearly		
Other		

Leadership

Skill	Strong Skill	Next Job
Arrange social functions		
Competitive		
Decisive		
Delegate		
Direct others		
Explain things to others		
Get results		
Influence others		
Initiate new tasks		
Make decisions		
Manage or direct others		

Skill	Strong Skill	Next Job
Mediate problems		
Motivate people		
Negotiate agreements		
Plan		
Results-oriented		
Run meetings		
Self-confident		
Self-controlled		
Self-motivated		
Solve problems		
Take risks		

Creative/Artistic

Skill	Strong Skill	Next Job
Artistic		
Dance, body movement		
Drawing, art		
Expressive		
Music appreciation		

Skill	Strong Skill	Next Job
Paint		
Perform, act		
Play instruments		
Present artistic ideas		
Other		

Other

Skill	Strong Skill	Next Job

Skill	Strong Skill	Next Job

Your Top Five Transferable Skills

Carefully review your list of transferable skills. Then select the top five skills you want to use in your next job and list them below.

1. _____
2. _____
3. _____
4. _____
5. _____

TIP

It is important to use these transferable skills in your job. Doing so will allow you to use some of your best skills. Later, you will learn more about how to present these and other skills in interviews.

The Top Skills Employers Want

To illustrate that employers highly value adaptive and transferable skills, here is a list of the top skills that employers want in the people they hire. This information came from a study of employers conducted jointly by the U.S. Department of Labor and the American Association of Counseling and Development. Note that all skills are either adaptive or transferable.

1. Learning to learn
2. Basic academic skills in reading, writing, and computation
3. Listening and oral communication
4. Creative thinking and problem solving
5. Self-esteem and goal setting
6. Personal and career development
7. Interpersonal skills, negotiation, and teamwork
8. Organizational effectiveness and leadership

Continue Learning Your Skills Language

You have now learned the skills language for your adaptive and transferable skills. The next chapter will help you develop a skills language for your job-related skills. It will also help you emphasize accomplishments and identify your "power" skills—important steps in getting the job you want.

1" />

CHAPTER 4

Documenting Your Experience

Your Job-Related Skills

Knowing your adaptive and transferable skills is very important. But many jobs require skills that are specific to the occupation. For example, an airline pilot obviously needs to know how to fly an airplane. Being "good with people" or "well organized" would not be enough.

While it takes years to learn to be an airline pilot, you can learn the job-related skills for many jobs in just a few days, weeks, or months. You may have more job-related skills than you realize, and you may have other skills that will help you learn a job quickly.

This chapter will help you consider your accomplishments, identify job-related skills, and develop specific examples of when and where you used those skills. This thorough review of your history will prepare you to plan your career, answer interview questions, and write a good resume.

A series of forms will ask you for information on your education, training, work and volunteer history, and other life experiences. When completing the forms, include the key skills you identified in the previous chapter. Those skills, as well as your accomplishments and results, are of great interest to most employers.

When possible, give numbers to describe your activities and their results. For example, saying "organized a trip for thirty people" has more impact than "planned trip." Use an erasable pen or pencil on the worksheets to allow for changes.

Education and Training Worksheets

High School

For recent grads, this information is very important. The longer you are out of high school, the less important this experience is to employers. Even if you have been in the workforce for some time, complete this section since it will help you remember what you liked and did well in.

1. Name of school(s) and years attended _____

   _____

   _____

2. Subjects you did well in or that might relate to the job you want _____

   _____

   _____

3. Extracurricular activities/hobbies/leisure activities _____

   _____

   _____

   _____

   4. Accomplishments/things you did well (in and out of school)

   _____

   _____

   _____

   _____

   _____

   _____

   _____

(continues)

(continued)

College

If you graduated from college or took college classes, this will interest an employer. If you are a new graduate, these experiences are very important. Emphasize things that support your ability to do the job. For example, working your way through school supports being hard working. If you took job-related courses, include details on these as well.

1. Name of school(s) and years attended _____

   _____

   _____

2. Courses related to the job you want _____

   _____

   _____

3. Extracurricular activities/hobbies/leisure activities _____

   _____

   _____

   _____

4. Accomplishments/things you did well (in and out of school) _____

   _____

   _____

   _____

   _____

5. Specific things you learned and can do that relate to the job you want _____

   _____

   _____

   _____

   _____

   _____

   _____

   _____

Post High School Training

List any training that might relate to the job you want. Include military and on-the-job training, workshops, and informal training such as from a hobby.

1. Training/dates/certificates _____

   _____

   _____

   _____

   _____

2. Specific things you can do as a result _____

   _____

   _____

   _____

   _____

   _____

   _____

3. Specific things you learned and can do that relate to the

   job you want _____

   _____

   _____

   _____

   _____

   _____

   _____

   _____

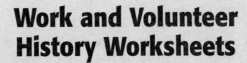

Work and Volunteer History Worksheets

Use these worksheets to list each major job you had and its related information. Begin with your most recent job, followed by previous ones. Include military experience and unpaid work here. Both count as work and are important if you do not have much paid civilian work experience. If you have been promoted, consider handling it as a separate job.

Try to include numbers to support what you did: number of people served over one or more years; number of transactions processed; percent sales increased; total inventory value you were responsible for; payroll of the staff you supervised; total budget you were responsible for; and other data. As much as possible, mention results using numbers too.

Photocopy additional worksheets to cover all of your significant jobs and unpaid experiences.

Job 1

1. Organization name _____

2. Address _____

   _____

3. Employed from _____ to _____

4. Job title(s) _____

5. Supervisor's name _____

6. Phone number with area code _____

7. Machinery and equipment you used _____

   _____

   _____

   _____

8. Data, information, and reports you created or used _____

   _____

   _____

   _____

9. People-oriented duties and responsibilities to coworkers, customers, others _____

   _____

   _____

   _____

10. Services you provided and products you produced _____
_____
_____
_____

11. If promoted or given pay increases, list reasons _____
_____
_____
_____
_____

12. Details on anything you did to help the organization, such as increase productivity, simplify or reorganize job duties, or decrease costs. Quantify results when possible—for example, "Increased order processing by 50 percent, with no increase in staff."
_____
_____
_____

13. Specific things you learned and can do that relate to the job you want _____
_____
_____

14. What would your supervisor say about you? _____
_____
_____

(continues)

(continued)

Job 2

1. Organization name _____

2. Address _____

_____

3. Employed from _____ to _____

4. Job title(s) _____

5. Supervisor's name _____

6. Phone number with area code _____

7. Machinery and equipment you used _____

_____

_____

_____

8. Data, information, and reports you created or used _____

_____

_____

_____

9. People-oriented duties and responsibilities to coworkers, customers, others _____

_____

_____

_____

10. Services you provided and products you produced _____

_____

_____

_____

11. If promoted or given pay increases, list reasons _____

_____

_____

_____

_____

12. Details on anything you did to help the organization, such as increase productivity, simplify or reorganize job duties, or decrease costs. Quantify results when possible—for example, "Increased order processing by 50 percent, with no increase in staff."

_____

_____

_____

13. Specific things you learned and can do that relate to the job you want _____

_____

_____

14. What would your supervisor say about you? _____

_____

_____

Job 3

1. Organization name _____

2. Address _____

_____

3. Employed from _____ to _____

4. Job title(s) _____

5. Supervisor's name _____

6. Phone number with area code _____

7. Machinery and equipment you used _____

_____

_____

_____

8. Data, information, and reports you created or used _____

_____

_____

_____

9. People-oriented duties and responsibilities to coworkers, customers, others _____

_____

_____

_____

(continues)

(continued)

10. Services you provided and products you produced _____

_____

_____

_____

11. If promoted or given pay increases, list reasons _____

_____

_____

_____

_____

12. Details on anything you did to help the organization, such as increase productivity, simplify or reorganize job duties, or decrease costs. Quantify results when possible—for example, "Increased order processing by 50 percent, with no increase in staff."

_____

_____

_____

13. Specific things you learned and can do that relate to the job you want _____

_____

_____

14. What would your supervisor say about you? _____

_____

_____

Job 4

1. Organization name _____

2. Address _____

_____

3. Employed from _____ to _____

4. Job title(s) _____

5. Supervisor's name _____

6. Phone number with area code _____

7. Machinery and equipment you used _____

_____

_____

_____

8. Data, information, and reports you created or used _____

_____

_____

_____

9. People-oriented duties and responsibilities to coworkers, customers, others _____

_____

_____

_____

10. Services you provided and products you produced _____

_____

_____

_____

11. If promoted or given pay increases, list reasons _____

_____

_____

_____

_____

12. Details on anything you did to help the organization, such as increase productivity, simplify or reorganize job duties, or decrease costs. Quantify results when possible—for example, "Increased order processing by 50 percent, with no increase in staff."

_____

_____

_____

13. Specific things you learned and can do that relate to the job you want _____

_____

_____

14. What would your supervisor say about you? _____

_____

_____

Other Life Experiences Worksheet

Use this worksheet to list accomplishments and information from hobbies, family responsibilities, recreational activities, travel, and other experiences. Write any that seem important to you and name the key skills you think were involved in doing them.

Situation 1

_____

_____

_____

Skills used _____

_____

_____

_____

Specific things you learned and can do that relate to the job you want _____

_____

_____

_____

Situation 2

_____

_____

_____

Skills used _____

_____

_____

_____

Specific things you learned and can do that relate to the job you want_____

_____

_____

_____

Situation 3

_____

_____

_____

Skills used _____

_____

_____

_____

Specific things you learned and can do that relate to the job you want_____

_____

_____

_____

TIP

The worksheets you just completed will help you identify many skills. The job-related ones to emphasize in your job search will depend on the work you want. If you don't know your job objective, Chapter 5 will help you determine it. Once your job objective is clear, you can review the worksheets for job-related skills that will best support your goal.

Your Power Skills

In your life, certain activities have given you a great sense of accomplishment. These could be things you did long ago—or yesterday—that may not mean much to anyone else. An example might be the first bike ride you made by yourself. Or the delicious bread you baked last week. Or that award you received. You may not have obtained recognition, but you did it well and enjoyed doing it.

The things you remember as accomplishments can be another source for discovering your skills. For example, riding a bike requires working by yourself, not giving up, and taking chances. To bake bread you need to plan ahead, organize and measure ingredients, and follow directions.

Skills that you use in your special accomplishments are "power skills." These are skills that you are good at and enjoy using. They can be adaptive, transferable, or job-related skills. If you can identify them—and use them in your next job—you will have a much better chance of career success and satisfaction.

List Your Accomplishments

To help identify your power skills, complete the following exercises.

1. List three accomplishments from the years before high school that are important to you.

   ✔ _____

   ✔ _____

   ✔ _____

2. List three accomplishments from your high school years.

   ✔ _____

   ✔ _____

   ✔ _____

3. List three accomplishments from your adult years.

   ✔ _____

   ✔ _____

   ✔ _____

Write a Story for Your Accomplishments

Select one accomplishment from each group on the facing page. Select those that mean the most to you—ones you truly enjoyed doing. Write a detailed story about each accomplishment on the following lines. Use your own paper if you need more space.

Here is one person's accomplishment story:

I wasn't the best student in high school and goofed off most of the time. But I took a class in political science with a teacher I really liked. I participated more in that class than in any other, and the teacher got me involved in the student elections. I used the existing rules to create a new political party. We even used the rules to block the dominant party from shutting us down. I learned to speak in public and work within the existing framework to make changes. We got a lot of people involved in school politics and in voting for the first time. We came close to winning the election. It was lots of fun, and I learned that I can lead. It helped me enormously with my self-confidence. I got one of the few A grades in my high school career and discovered that I could get good grades if I worked at them.

Story 1

_____

_____

_____

_____

_____

_____

Story 2

_____

_____

_____

_____

_____

_____

_____

(continues)

(continued)

Story 3

_____

_____

_____

_____

_____

_____

_____

Skills Used
in Accomplishments

Carefully review each story and circle the skills you mentioned. Also, look for skills you must have used or needed—even if you didn't mention them in your stories. Write those skills in the margin next to each story. If possible, have others listen to your accomplishments and add the skills they hear you using in each story.

When you are done, list all the skills from your three accomplishment stories in the spaces that follow. Put check marks by those skills that are mentioned in more than one story.

_____

_____

_____

_____

_____

_____

_____

_____

Your Top Five Power Skills

Now review the lists of top adaptive and transferable skills that you completed in the previous chapter. If any of those skills are not on the list you just made, add them now. From this combined list, select the five skills you would most enjoy using in your next job. List those five skills, in order of importance to you.

1. _____

2. _____

3. _____

4. _____

5. _____

TIP

These are your power skills. You are likely to enjoy and do well in a job that allows you to use all or most of these skills. It is important for you to look for jobs that allow you to use these skills. Mentioning your key skills in an interview can often help you get jobs over those with better credentials.

Key Accomplishments and Skills to Tell an Employer

Here are a few questions that can help you consider which items from your history are most important to mention in interviews, on resumes, and on applications.

1. What are the most important accomplishments and skills you can tell an employer in relation to your education and training? _____

   _____

   _____

   _____

2. What are the most important accomplishments and skills you can present to an employer in relation to your paid and unpaid work experiences? _____

   _____

   _____

   _____

3. What are the most important accomplishments and skills you can present to an employer in relation to your other life experiences? _____

   _____

   _____

   _____

Use Your Skills Language Throughout Your Job Search

You now have the basis for describing your key adaptive, transferable, and job-related skills. You have a new skills language. Like any new language, you need to use it. As you develop your skills language, you will get better at explaining what you are good at and how you can best use your skills. Later chapters will teach you to use your skills language in interviews, applications, resumes, and job advancement.

CHAPTER 5

Career Planning

A Career Is Different Than a Job

A career is long term, whereas a job is often short term. For example, you may work in a restaurant to earn money while going to school (a job) or to learn the restaurant business so you can eventually run your own place (a career). A job is what you do to earn money; a career is what you do with your life. A career is often made up of a variety of related jobs, each leading to another more responsible, challenging, or enjoyable job.

Sometimes your job and your career end up being the same thing, sometimes not. This chapter is about planning your career, as well as discovering the jobs you might seek as you move toward your longer-term career goal. It helps you explore career options based on your interests. While the emphasis is on exploring career and job options, it helps you consider education and training options too.

This chapter encourages you to define the job and career you really want. This issue is worth spending some time on, so let's begin.

Your Key Motivators Worksheet

Your life experiences are an important source of clues for planning your career path. The things you are good at, you enjoy doing, and that are important to you can help you identify career and job options. Your "ideal" career would include doing things you like to do and are good at. An enthusiasm for something often lasts your entire life and can form the basis for a career. I call these things your "motivators" because they motivate you to work toward a goal.

Let's do a quick review of life experiences that can help identify your key motivators. Use the lines to write your responses. Be specific about what you did and write why you liked each item or did well at it. You can use experiences from any time in your life, past or present. Some questions are similar to those asked in earlier chapters but are important to reconsider here.

1. What school subjects did you enjoy or were you good at? _____
   _____
   _____
   _____

2. What extracurricular activities did you enjoy or were you good at? _____
   _____
   _____
   _____

3. What hobbies or other leisure activities do you enjoy or do well in? _____
   _____
   _____
   _____

4. What family activities do you enjoy or are you good at? _____
   _____
   _____
   _____

5. What work and volunteer activities do you enjoy or are you good at? _____
   _____
   _____
   _____

6. What is really important to you or something you would like to make a difference in? This could be anything—such as saving the whales, helping the poor, or being very good at a particular thing. _____

_____

_____

_____

7. Look over your responses here. Do you see things you like to do and are also good at? Do any skills, abilities, or interests come up over and over? If so, list them here.

_____

_____

_____

8. The things you just wrote are your key motivators. Can you think of any careers or jobs that would allow you to use these skills and abilities—or let you make a difference in something that is very important to you? If so, write them here. _____

_____

_____

_____

What Are Your Interests?

Planning your career can be complicated. There are thousands of job titles and hundreds of training and education programs. Many people find it difficult to consider so many options. But don't give up. There is a simple way to explore career and job options. It is a system based on your interests. Your interests are based on life experiences and often include your skills, values, abilities, and other complex factors.

The most effective system for connecting interests to careers was developed by the U.S. Department of Labor. Its research found that

- Your interests are an important source of information to use in exploring career and learning options.

- You are more likely to be interested in things you are good at, you enjoy doing, or that are important to you.

- Your interests can accurately guide you to explore careers that are most likely to meet your needs.

Because exploring thousands of jobs is not practical, researchers organized all jobs into interest areas, which are explained in the following worksheet. The interest areas are from the *Guide for Occupational Exploration*, Third Edition, published by JIST Works. The *GOE* was originally developed by the Department of Labor to help people explore career and learning options. The third edition updates the original *GOE's* interest areas and other elements.

You learn more about specific job titles later. Let's begin by identifying your top interests in the "Career Interest Areas Worksheet."

Career Interest Areas Worksheet

Read each interest area carefully. For each area, put a check mark in the column to the right that best describes your interest level. The three columns are "Not Interested," "Somewhat Interested or Not Sure," and "Very Interested."

Interest Area	Not Interested	Somewhat Interested or Not Sure	Very Interested
Arts, Entertainment, and Media. *An interest in creatively expressing feelings or ideas, in communicating news or information, or in performing.* You can satisfy this interest in several creative, verbal, or performing activities. For example, if you enjoy literature, writing or editing might appeal to you. Do you prefer to work in the performing arts? If so, you could direct or perform in drama, music, or dance. If you especially enjoy the visual arts, you could become a critic of painting, sculpture, or ceramics. You may want to use your hands to create or decorate products. You may prefer to model clothes or develop sets for entertainment. Or you may want to participate in sports professionally as an athlete or coach.			
Science, Math, and Engineering. *An interest in discovering, collecting, and analyzing information about the natural world; in applying scientific research findings to problems in medicine, the life sciences, and the natural sciences; in imagining and manipulating quantitative data; and in applying technology to manufacturing, transportation, mining, and other economic activities.* You can satisfy this interest by working with the knowledge and processes of the sciences. You may enjoy researching and developing new knowledge in mathematics; or maybe solving problems in the physical or life sciences would appeal to you. You may want to study engineering and help create new machines, processes, and structures. If you want to work with scientific equipment and procedures, you could seek a job in a research or testing laboratory.			
Plants and Animals. *An interest in working with plants and animals, usually outdoors.* You can satisfy this interest by working in farming, forestry, fishing, and related fields. You may like doing physical work outdoors, such as on a farm. You may enjoy animals; perhaps training or taking care of animals would appeal to you. If you have management ability, you could own, operate, or manage a farm or related business.			
Law, Law Enforcement, and Public Safety. *An interest in upholding people's rights, or in protecting people and property by using authority, inspecting, or monitoring.* You can satisfy this interest by working in law, law enforcement, fire fighting, or related fields. For example, if you enjoy mental challenge and intrigue, you could investigate crimes or fires for a living. If you enjoy working with verbal skills, you might want to defend citizens in court or research deeds, wills, and other legal documents. You may prefer to fight fires and respond to other emergencies. Or, if you want more routine work, perhaps a job in guarding or patrolling would appeal to you. If you have management ability, you could seek a leadership position in law enforcement and the protective services. Many positions in the various military branches are related to this interest and give you the chance to learn technical and leadership skills while serving your country.			

Interest Area	Not Interested	Somewhat Interested or Not Sure	Very Interested
Mechanics, Installers, and Repairers. *An interest in applying mechanical and electrical/ electronic principles to practical situations by use of machines or hand tools.* You can satisfy this interest working with a variety of tools, technologies, materials, and settings. If you enjoy making machines run efficiently or fixing them when they break down, you could seek a job installing or repairing machines such as copiers, aircraft engines, automobiles, or watches. You may prefer to deal directly with certain materials, and could work cutting and shaping metal or wood. Or if electricity and electronics interest you, you could install cables, troubleshoot telephone networks, or repair videocassette recorders. If you prefer routine or physical work in settings other than factories, maybe repairing tires or batteries would appeal to you.			
Construction, Mining, and Drilling. *An interest in assembling components of buildings and other structures, or in using mechanical devices to drill or excavate.* If construction interests you, you can find fulfillment in the many building projects that are undertaken at all times. If you like to organize and plan, you can find careers in management. You can play a more direct role in putting up and finishing buildings by doing jobs such as plumbing, carpentry, masonry, painting, or roofing. You might like working at a mine or oilfield, operating the powerful drilling or digging equipment. There are also several other jobs that let you use your hands.			
Transportation. *An interest in operations that move people or materials.* You can satisfy this interest by managing a transportation service, by helping vehicles stay on their assigned schedules and routes, or by driving or piloting a vehicle. If you enjoy taking responsibility, maybe managing a rail line would appeal to you. If you work well with details and can take pressure on the job, you might consider being an air traffic controller. Or would you rather get out on the highway, on the water, or up in the air? If so, you could drive a truck from state to state, sail down the Mississippi on a barge, or fly a crop duster over a cornfield. If you prefer to stay closer to home, you could drive a delivery van, taxi, or school bus. You can use your physical strength to load freight and arrange it so that it gets to its destination in one piece.			
Industrial Production. *An interest in repetitive, concrete, organized activities most often done in a factory setting.* You can satisfy this interest by working in one of many industries that mass-produce goods, or for a utility that distributes electric power, gas, and so on. You may enjoy manual work, using your hands or hand tools. Maybe you prefer to operate machines. You might like to inspect, sort, count, or weigh products. Using your training and experience to set up machines or supervise other workers might appeal to you.			
Business Detail. *An interest in organized, clearly defined activities that require accuracy and attention to detail, primarily in an office setting.* You can satisfy this interest in a variety of jobs in which you take care of the details of a business operation. You may enjoy using your math skills; if so, maybe a job in billing, computing, or financial record keeping would satisfy you. If you prefer to deal with people, you may want a job in which you meet the public, talk on the telephone, or supervise other workers. You may like to do word processing on a computer, make copies on a photocopier, or work out sums on a calculator. Maybe a job in filing or recording would satisfy you. Or you might want to use your training and experience to manage an office.			
Sales and Marketing. *An interest in bringing others to a particular point of view by personal persuasion, using sales and promotional techniques.* You can satisfy this interest in a variety of sales and marketing jobs. If you like using technical knowledge of science or agriculture, you might enjoy selling technical products or services. Or maybe you are more interested in selling business-related services such as insurance coverage, advertising space, or investment opportunities. Real estate offers several kinds of sales jobs. Perhaps you'd rather work with something you can pick up and show to people. You might work in stores, sales offices, or customers' homes.			
Recreation, Travel, and Other Personal Services. *An interest in catering to the personal wishes and needs of others, so that they can enjoy cleanliness, good food and drinks, comfortable lodging away from home, and enjoyable recreation.* You can satisfy this interest by providing services for the convenience, feeding, and pampering of others in hotels, restaurants, airplanes, and so on. If you enjoy improving the appearance of others, perhaps working in the hair and beauty-care field would satisfy you. You might want to provide personal services such as taking care of small children, tailoring garments, or ushering. Or you may use your knowledge of the field to manage workers who are providing these services.			

(continues)

(continued)

Interest Area	Not Interested	Somewhat Interested or Not Sure	Very Interested
Education and Social Service. *An interest in teaching people or improving their social or spiritual well being.* You can satisfy this interest by teaching students, who may be preschoolers, retirees, or any age between. Or if you are interested in helping people sort out their complicated lives, you may find fulfillment as a counselor, social worker, or religious worker. Working in a museum or library may give you opportunities to expand people's understanding of the world. If you also have an interest in business, you might find satisfaction in managerial work in this field.			
General Management and Support. *An interest in making an organization run smoothly.* You can satisfy this interest by working in a position of leadership, or by specializing in a function that contributes to the overall effort. The organization may be a profit-making business, a nonprofit organization, or a government agency. If you especially enjoy working with people, you might find fulfillment from working in human resources. An interest in numbers may cause you to consider accounting, finance, budgeting, or purchasing. Or maybe you would enjoy managing the organization's physical resources (for example, land, buildings, equipment, or utilities).			
Medical and Health Services. *An interest in helping people be healthy.* You can satisfy this interest by working on a health-care team as a doctor, therapist, or nurse. You might specialize in one of the many different parts of the body or types of care, or you might be a generalist who deals with the whole patient. If you like technology, you might find satisfaction working with X rays, one of the electronic methods of diagnosis, or clinical laboratory testing. You might work with healthy people, helping them stay in condition through exercise and eating right. If you like to organize, analyze, and plan, a managerial role might be right for you.			

Your Top Interest Areas

Review each interest area from the previous list. Then write the names of the five areas that interest you the most. Don't worry for now whether your choices are practical. Just list five interest areas that you would like to know more about. You can put them in any order you want.

1. _____

2. _____

3. _____

4. _____

5. _____

Career Clues Worksheet

Knowing your top interest areas will give you some idea of career areas to explore more carefully. But you should also consider other things in exploring your career options. This worksheet helps you consider three important clues to support career decisions. These clues are "Education and Training," "Work Experience," and "Leisure Activities." Your interests or activities in each of these areas can help you identify career options.

Look at the worksheet that follows. Use the first column to write your top interest areas from "Your Top Interest Areas" on page 46.

Now look at the next three columns of the worksheet. At the top of each is one of the career clues. Use the blank space in each column to write notes related to each interest area you selected. Emphasize related activities you enjoyed or are good at. For example, people who select Plants and Animals as one of their top interest areas might write, in the "Education and Training Clues" column, that they liked and did well in biology and natural-science classes. In the "Work Experience Clues" column, they might write that they enjoyed a summer job working with horses at a riding stable. And in the "Leisure Activities Clues" column, they might write that they like camping and hiking. Here are some ideas to help you decide what to write for each clue:

- **Education and Training.** Do you have education or training related to this interest? Include formal learning and school course names, and informal learning such as reading or on-the-job learning.

- **Work Experience.** Do you have work experience related to this interest? List any paid or unpaid work related to this interest. This can include full- and part-time jobs, volunteer work, work you do at home, and working in a family business.

- **Leisure Activities.** Do you have hobbies or leisure activities related to this interest? Anything you do that is not "work" gives you clues to your real interests. For example, think of magazines you read, clubs and organizations you belong to, extracurricular activities, hobbies, and other related leisure activities.

After you finish with your first interest, do the same thing for the rest of your interest areas in the list. Instructions for filling in the empty circles come later.

Career Planning Clues

Write Your Top Interest Areas Here	For each clue, write in things you enjoy doing or are good at that relate to each interest area.			Score
	Education and Training Clues	Work Experience Clues	Leisure Activities Clues	
1.	○	○	○	
2.	○	○	○	
3.	○	○	○	
4.	○	○	○	
5.	○	○	○	

Score Each Interest Area

After you have written your notes in each clue box, total your scores for each interest area. Begin with your first interest area. Under the "Education and Training Clues" column, decide which of the following statements best describes the activities you wrote in that clue box:

1. Activities do not strongly support this interest.

2. Activities provide some support for this interest.

3. Activities provide strong support for this interest.

Now notice the small circles in the lower-right corner of each clue box. This is where you should write the number of the statement you selected. Do this for each clue box for your first interest area. Do the same thing for each clue for the other interest areas. When you are done, add up the numbers you wrote in the three circles for each interest area and put that total in the "Score" column on the right.

What Your Scores Mean

Higher scores usually mean that you have spent more time on or are very interested in that interest area. You may have taken more related classes, spent more leisure time in related activities, or have more directly related work experience. Interest areas with your highest scores are the ones you should consider more closely. They are likely to offer careers that interest you most.

Identify Specific Jobs Related to Your Interests

You now know more about your interests and the types of careers that relate to them. But what specific jobs should you consider? This can be hard to find out. Many jobs relate to an interest, but they are at different pay levels, require different training or education, and may have very different work situations.

For example, if Medical and Health Services appeals to you, you might consider being a medical doctor, an emergency medical technician, or a home health care worker. Each job is very different in training required, pay, and type of work, but all are related to the same interest area. For this reason, I include a chart that helps you identify specific jobs related to each interest area. Called the "Career Interests-to-Jobs Chart," it is explained next.

Tips on Using the Career Interests-to-Jobs Chart

The chart begins on page 57 and is organized to help you quickly find your top interest areas and then explore related jobs. Note that some jobs are repeated because they fit into more than one interest area. Here is more detail on the chart's structure:

- **Interest areas.** Jobs are organized within the 14 interest areas that appear in large, bold type. The interest areas were presented earlier in this chapter.

- **Work groups.** The *Guide for Occupational Exploration* divides each of the 14 interest areas into "work groups" of related jobs. The work group names are included in the chart under each interest area. You can use the work group names to find information on about 1,000 more specialized jobs in the *GOE*.

- **Job titles.** Specific job titles are listed in regular type. The chart provides lots of information about each job in the many columns it includes. The job titles are those used in the *Occupational Outlook Handbook (OOH)*, which is published by the Department of Labor and available from JIST Works. The *OOH* describes each job in detail and covers about 87 percent of the jobs in the labor market.

Information in the Chart's Columns

The chart provides 22 columns that give key information on the job titles. Here are details to help you understand and use the information in the chart's columns. Use the chart's information to help you identify jobs to explore in more detail later. The columns use simple codes to save space.

Education and Training

This column gives you information on the education and training typically required for entry into a job. It uses numbers from 1 to 11, with 1 as the highest level of education and training, and 11 for work that can be quickly learned on the job.

Some jobs that interest you may require more training or education than you had been considering. Don't eliminate these too quickly! If a job really interests you, learn more about it. If you really want to do that kind of work, you can often find ways to get the training or education needed. Here are what the numbers in this column mean:

- **1**—professional degree. Typically requires completion of a six-year academic program, including a bachelor's degree plus additional specialized education.

- **2**—doctoral degree. A two-to-three-year academic program beyond a bachelor's degree, often first requiring a master's degree.

- **3**—master's degree. A one-to-two-year academic program beyond a bachelor's degree.

- **4**—bachelor's degree plus related work experience.

- **5**—bachelor's degree. A four-year academic program beyond high school.

- **6**—associate degree. A two-year academic program beyond high school.

- **7**—postsecondary vocational training. Specific job-related training lasting from several months to several years. Some high schools provide substantial vocational training, although most is obtained after high school.

- **8**—work experience. Job-specific skills that are learned on the job.

- **9**—long-term, on-the-job training. More than one year of on-the-job training or a combination of training and formal classroom instruction.

- **10**—moderate-term, on-the-job training. One to twelve months of on-the-job training.

- **11**—short-term, on-the-job training. Up to one month of on-the-job training.

Median Earnings, Expected Job Openings, and Part-Time Availability

These columns use the following simple codes:

- **VH** means very high, in the top 25 percent of all jobs.

- **H** means high, in the top 50 percent to the top 25 percent of all jobs.

- **L** means low, in the lower 50 percent to the lower 25 percent of all jobs.

- **VL** means very low, in the bottom 25 percent of all jobs.

Median earnings means that half of all workers earn more and half earn less. Expected job openings refers to openings expected in the job each year from people leaving for any reason and from new positions. The part-time availability column helps you identify occupations that have more part-time jobs available.

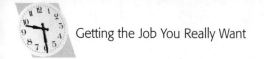

Skills and Abilities

Eight columns on specific skills and abilities appear for each job. A "0" in the column indicates that the skill or ability is either not important or requires only a basic level. Those with "1" in the column require you to have a practical level of that skill or ability to work in the job. Those with a"2" require more advanced skills or abilities that are an important part of the job. Here are brief notes on each skill and ability.

- **Math.** Includes the ability to perform calculations and manipulate data. Jobs that require math skills at level 1 involve algebra, geometry, and basic statistics. Level 2 jobs require linear algebra, calculus, or other higher levels of math.

- **English.** English skills at level 1 include a good command of vocabulary and grammar and the ability to read and prepare correspondence, observations, and instructions. Level 1 skills are required for most jobs. Level 2 English skills include the ability to comprehend and communicate complex instructions and ideas, as well as the ability to write clearly, persuasively, and creatively. In addition, workers with level 2 skills should have a vocabulary appropriate for understanding and expressing sophisticated subjects.

- **Science.** These skills refer to knowledge of the physical or life sciences. Science skills at level 1 require an understanding of the principles of the physical and life sciences, including biology, chemistry, geology, and physics. Level 2 science skills requires an in-depth, theoretical knowledge of one or more of the physical and life sciences.

- **Computer.** This refers to the ability to operate a computer and process data. Level 1 skills include the ability to use a computer to enter and manipulate data, make calculations, compose and print documents, access the Internet, or send electronic mail. Level 2 computer skills require a thorough understanding of computer hardware and software and how they interact.

- **Artistic or Creative.** These are the ability to form ideas to solve problems, communicate information, or express feelings, thoughts, and emotions. At level 1, they include devising original ways of approaching an issue or making progress. Level 2 skills are useful for accomplishing projects and dealing with problems in new and unique ways.

- **Interpersonal or Persuasive.** These skills allow positive interaction between people and the ability to sway the actions, opinions, or beliefs of others. Occupations requiring persuasive and interpersonal skills usually involve frequent contact with the public. Level 1 skills include the ability to deal with others courteously. Level 2 skills include the ability to sell products, ideas, or services convincingly.

- **Mechanical.** These skills involve an understanding of the relationships between moving parts. They involve knowledge of how objects connect and operate and the ability to diagnose and troubleshoot mechanical failures. Level 1 involves working with tools to assemble or repair equipment or machinery. Level 2 requires the ability to design or modify equipment or machinery.

- **Leadership or Management.** This is the ability to direct and organize others to achieve common goals. Effective communication skills are essential. Level 1 ability includes accepting responsibility for the work and actions of others. Level 2 includes motivating and inspiring others to achieve a common goal.

Working Conditions

These columns provide information on seven working conditions that are important on most jobs. A "0" in the column indicates that the condition is not an important part of the job. A "1" means the condition is an important or occasional part of the job. Those rated at "2" mean the condition is an essential or frequent part of the job. Here are some brief notes on each working condition.

- **Travel.** Requires workers to visit clients outside the regular workplace or travel away from home and stay overnight in a hotel. Level 1 jobs involve occasional but not constant travel between work sites or occasional overnight travel of short duration. Level 2 jobs involve frequent or daily travel between work sites or frequent overnight travel, usually several trips a month and/or trips for an extended number of days or weeks.

- **Hazardous.** Jobs having hazardous duties and conditions require following safety procedures to avoid injury or harmful exposure. Injury rates on these jobs may be higher than in others if workers fail to stay alert and take precautions. Level 1 jobs involve a minor degree of hazard, such as exposure to chemicals or unsafe working conditions. Level 2 jobs involve a major degree of hazard, involving potentially life-threatening situations.

- **Operates Machines or Equipment.** These jobs require daily operation of equipment, machinery, or motorized vehicles, such as cranes, tractors, and trucks, as well as saws, printing presses, and X-ray machines. Many of these jobs require workers to follow procedures to avoid property damage and personal injury. Level 1 jobs require occasional operation of equipment or machinery, while those rated level 2 require frequent operation.

- **Outdoors.** Jobs involving outdoor work expose workers to the elements. Level 1 jobs involve occasional outdoor work but also require that some work be performed indoors. Level 2 jobs require most of the work day be spent outside.

- **Irregular Schedule.** These jobs have schedules outside the standard 8 a.m. to 5 p.m. Monday-through-Friday workweek. This includes shift, weekend, split schedule, and seasonal work, as well as work requiring workers to be on call. Level 1 jobs have somewhat irregular schedules that may include hours that extend beyond 8 a.m. to 5 p.m. and include weekends. Level 2 jobs have extremely irregular schedules and are usually found in work settings that operate 24 hours a day.

- **Stress.** Stressful jobs involve either tremendous pressure to complete work on deadlines or concerns over safety or other work issues. Level 1 jobs involve a minor degree of stress, often jobs requiring constant attention to detail. Jobs rated level 2 involve a major degree of stress and may be due to responsibility for a large number of people or people in potentially dangerous situations.

- **Physically Demanding.** Jobs considered physically demanding may require moving, lifting, and handling materials; require workers to stand for long periods; or require manual dexterity and precise movement. Level 1 jobs require occasional lifting and movement while those rated level 2 require a considerable amount of heavy lifting or constant movement.

Top Values

The chart includes three columns for you to write in the top values you would like to include in your ideal job. While you can write in any three values you choose, following are 33 values that many people consider. Check those you would like to include in your ideal job. When you are done, go back and select the three you most want to include in your ideal job. Write the three you choose in the "Top Values" column on the chart. Then check mark the blank spaces on the chart if you think a job of interest would include the value.

- **Help society.** Contribute to the betterment of the world I live in.

- **Help others.** Help other people directly, either individually or in small groups.

- **Public contact.** Have a lot of day-to-day contact with people.

- **Work with others.** Have close working relationships with a group; work as a team toward common goals.

- **Affiliation.** Be recognized as a member of an organization whose type of work or status is important to me.

- **Friendship.** Develop close personal relationships with the people I work with.

- **Competition.** Pit my abilities against others where there are clear outcomes.

- **Make decisions.** Have the power to set policy and determine a course of action.

- **Work under pressure.** Work in a situation where deadlines and high-quality work are required by my supervisor.

- **Power and authority.** Control other people's work activities.

- **Influence people.** Be in a position to change other people's attitudes and opinions.

- **Work alone.** Do things by myself, without much contact with others.

- **Knowledge.** Seek knowledge, truth, and understanding.

- **Intellectual status.** Be regarded by others as a person of intellectual achievement or an expert.

- **Artistic creativity.** Do creative work in any of several art forms.

- **Creativity (general).** Create new ideas, programs, organizational structures, or anything else that has not been developed by others.

- **Aesthetics.** Have a job that involves sensitivity to beauty.

- **Supervision.** Have a job in which I guide other people in their work.

- **Change and variety.** Have job duties that often change or are done in different settings.

- **Precision work.** Do work that allows little tolerance for error.

- **Stability.** Have job duties that are largely predictable and not likely to change over a long period of time.

- **Security.** Be assured of keeping my job and getting a reasonable financial reward.

- **Fast pace.** Work quickly; keep up with a fast pace.

- **Recognition.** Be recognized for the quality of my work in some visible or public way.

- **Excitement.** Do work that is very exciting or that often is exciting.

- **Adventure.** Do work that requires me to take risks.

- **Profit, gain.** Expect to earn large amounts of money or other material possessions.

- **Independence.** Decide for myself what kind of work I'll do and how I'll go about it; not have to do what others tell me to.

- **Moral fulfillment.** Feel that my work is contributing to a set of moral standards that I feel are very important.

- **Location.** Find a place to live (town, geographic area) that matches my lifestyle and allows me to do the things I enjoy most.

- **Community.** Live in a town or city where I can get involved in community affairs.

- **Physical challenge.** Have a job whose physical demands are challenging and rewarding.

- **Time, freedom.** Handle my job according to my own time schedule; no specific working schedule.

- **Others** _____

_____

Career Interests-to-Jobs Chart

Find the interest areas (in bold letters) that appeal to you most. Then, review specific job titles. Put a check mark by any job title that interests you. Then go back and carefully review the key information provided in the columns for those jobs. Circle the five to ten job titles that you *most* want to learn more about. Do not eliminate any job that interests you based on its earnings, education, training requirements, or other factors. If it interests you, and you think you would enjoy it, plan to learn more about it. You can always eliminate it later.

TIP

It can take some time to thoroughly review the chart. But you should spend even more time before you make an important career decision. The reason is that the career decisions you make will affect your lifestyle for many years. You may decide to get additional training or education, which can be expensive in both time and money. So plan on spending more time learning about the career options you have identified. The information and worksheets that follow can help.

CAREER INTERESTS-TO-JOBS CHART

	Education and Training	Median Earnings	Expected Job Openings	Part-Time Availability	Math	English	Science	Computer	Artistic or Creative	Interpersonal or Persuasive	Mechanical	Leadership or Management	Travel	Hazardous	Operates Machines or Equipment	Outdoors	Irregular Schedule	Stress	Physically Demanding	1	2	3
					SKILLS AND ABILITIES										**WORKING CONDITIONS**					**TOP VALUES**		

Arts, Entertainment, and Media

GOE Work Groups—Managerial Work in Arts, Entertainment, and Media; Writing and Editing; News, Broadcasting, and Public Relations; Visual Arts: Studio Art; Visual Arts: Design; Performing Arts, Drama: Directing, Performing, Narrating, and Announcing; Performing Arts, Music: Directing, Composing and Arranging, and Performing; Performing Arts, Dance: Performing and Choreography; Craft Arts; Graphic Arts; Media Technology; Modeling and Personal Appearance; Sports: Coaching, Instructing, Officiating, and Performing

	Education and Training	Median Earnings	Expected Job Openings	Part-Time Availability	Math	English	Science	Computer	Artistic or Creative	Interpersonal or Persuasive	Mechanical	Leadership or Management	Travel	Hazardous	Operates Machines or Equipment	Outdoors	Irregular Schedule	Stress	Physically Demanding	1	2	3
Actors, Directors, and Producers	9	H	VL	H	0	2	0	0	2	2	0	1	2	0	0	1	2	1	1			
Advertising, Marketing, and Public Relations Managers	4	VH	L	VL	1	2	0	1	1	2	0	2	2	0	0	0	1	2	0			
Announcers	8	L	VL	VH	0	2	0	0	2	2	0	0	2	0	0	0	2	2	0			
Barbers, Cosmetologists, and Related Workers	7	VL	VL	VH	0	0	0	0	1	2	0	0	0	1	2	0	1	0	1			
Broadcast and Sound Technicians	7	H	VL	L	1	1	1	0	0	0	2	0	0	1	2	1	2	1	1			
Dancers and Choreographers	7	VH	VL	H	0	0	0	0	2	2	0	0	2	0	0	0	2	1	2			
Demonstrators, Product Promoters, and Models	11	L	H	H	0	1	0	0	1	1	0	0	2	0	0	1	2	1	0			
Designers	5	VH	VL	H	0	1	0	1	2	2	0	0	1	0	0	0	1	0	0			
Instructors and Coaches, Sports and Physical Training	8	L	H	H	0	1	1	0	1	0	0	1	1	1	0	1	2	1	2			
Jewelers and Precious Stones and Metal Workers	7	L	VL	H	0	0	1	1	2	2	1	0	0	0	1	0	1	0	0			
Musicians, Singers, and Related Workers	9	H	VL	VH	0	0	0	0	2	2	0	0	2	0	0	0	2	0	0			
News Analysts, Reporters, and Correspondents	5	H	VL	L	0	2	0	1	2	2	0	0	2	0	0	0	2	2	1			
Photographers and Camera Operators	10	L	VL	H	0	0	1	0	2	1	0	1	2	0	0	1	1	0	1			
Prepress Workers (example: Desktop Publishers)	9	H	VL	VL	0	1	0	1	0	0	0	0	0	0	2	0	2	0	0			
Public Relations Specialists	5	H	VL	L	0	2	0	1	2	2	0	2	2	0	0	0	1	1	0			
Visual Artists	4	H	VL	H	0	1	0	1	2	0	0	0	0	0	0	0	1	0	0			
Woodworking Occupations (examples: Woodcarvers, Furniture Designers)	9	L	VL	VL	0	0	0	0	0	0	0	0	0	0	2	2	0	0	1			
Writers and Editors, Including Technical Writers	5	VH	VL	L	0	2	0	1	2	0	0	0	0	0	0	0	2	1	0			

Science, Math, and Engineering

GOE Work Groups—Managerial Work in Science, Math, and Engineering; Physical Sciences; Life Sciences: Animal Specialization; Life Sciences: Plant Specialization; Life Sciences: Plant and Animal Specialization; Life Sciences: Food Research; Social Sciences: Psychology, Sociology, and Anthropology; Social Sciences: Economics, Public Policy, and History; Laboratory Technology: Physical Sciences; Laboratory Technology: Life Sciences; Mathematics and Computers: Data Processing; Mathematics and Computers: Data Analysis; Engineering: Research and Systems Design; Engineering: Industrial and Safety; Engineering: Design; Engineering: General Engineering; Engineering Technology: Surveying; Engineering Technology: Industrial and Safety; Engineering Technology: Design; Engineering Technology: General

	Education and Training	Median Earnings	Expected Job Openings	Part-Time Availability	Math	English	Science	Computer	Artistic or Creative	Interpersonal or Persuasive	Mechanical	Leadership or Management	Travel	Hazardous	Operates Machines or Equipment	Outdoors	Irregular Schedule	Stress	Physically Demanding	1	2	3
Accountants and Auditors	5	VH	L	L	2	1	0	1	0	1	0	0	0	1	0	0	1	1	0			
Actuaries	5	VH	VL	VL	2	1	0	1	0	0	0	0	0	0	0	0	0	0	0			
Aerospace Engineers	5	VH	VL	VL	2	2	2	2	0	0	2	0	0	0	1	0	0	0	0			
Agricultural and Food Scientists	5	VH	VL	VL	2	2	2	1	0	0	0	0	1	1	0	2	0	0	0			
Architects, Except Landscape and Marine	5	VH	VL	L	2	1	2	1	2	1	0	0	1	0	0	0	0	0	1	0		
Atmospheric Scientists	5	VH	VL	VL	2	2	2	2	0	0	0	0	0	0	1	0	1	1	0			
Biological and Medical Scientists	2	VH	VL	L	2	2	2	1	0	0	0	0	0	1	0	0	0	0	0			
Budget Analysts	5	VH	VL	L	2	1	0	1	0	0	0	0	0	0	0	0	0	1	0			

(continues)

(continued)

CAREER INTERESTS-TO-JOBS CHART

	Education and Training	Median Earnings	Expected Job Openings	Part-Time Availability	Math	English	Science	Computer	Artistic or Creative	Interpersonal or Persuasive	Mechanical	Leadership or Management	Travel	Hazardous	Operates Machines or Equipment	Outdoors	Irregular Schedule	Stress	Physically Demanding	1.	2.	3.
Chemical Engineers	5	VH	VL	VL	2	2	2	2	0	0	1	0	0	0	1	0	0	0	0			
Chemists	5	VH	VL	VL	2	2	2	1	0	0	0	0	0	1	1	0	0	0	0			
Civil Engineers	5	VH	VL	VL	2	2	2	2	0	0	2	0	1	0	1	1	0	0	0			
Computer Programmers	5	VH	VL	VL	2	0	0	2	0	1	0	0	0	0	0	0	0	0	0			
Computer Systems Analysts, Engineers, and Scientists	5	VH	L	VL	2	1	2	2	0	1	0	1	0	0	0	0	0	0	0			
Conservation Scientists and Foresters	5	VH	VL	VL	2	2	2	1	0	1	0	0	2	1	0	2	0	0	1			
Construction and Building Inspectors	8	VH	VL	L	1	1	1	1	0	1	0	0	2	1	0	1	0	0	1			
Drafters	7	H	VL	VL	1	1	1	1	1	1	0	0	0	0	0	0	0	0	0			
Economists and Marketing Research Analysts	5	VH	VL	L	2	2	0	1	0	1	0	0	1	0	0	0	0	1	0			
Electrical and Electronics Engineers	5	VH	VL	VL	2	2	2	2	0	0	1	0	0	0	1	0	0	0	0			
Engineering, Natural Science, and Computer and Information Systems Managers	4	VH	VL	VL	2	2	2	2	0	2	1	2	0	0	0	0	1	0	0			
Engineering Technicians	6	VH	L	VL	2	1	1	1	0	0	1	0	0	1	2	0	0	0	1			
Geologists, Geophysicists, and Oceanographers	5	VH	VL	VL	2	2	2	1	0	0	0	0	2	0	2	1	0	0	1			
Industrial Engineers, Except Safety Engineers	5	VH	VL	VL	2	2	2	2	0	0	2	0	2	0	1	0	0	0	0			
Landscape Architects	5	VH	VL	L	2	1	2	1	2	1	0	0	1	0	0	1	0	0	0			
Machinists and Numerical Control Machine Tool Programmers	8	H	VL	VL	1	0	1	1	0	0	2	0	0	1	2	0	0	0	1			
Materials Engineers	5	VH	VL	VL	2	2	2	2	0	0	1	0	0	0	2	0	0	0	0			
Mathematicians	2	VH	VL	VL	2	1	0	1	0	0	0	0	0	0	0	0	0	0	0			
Mechanical Engineers	5	VH	VL	VL	2	2	2	2	0	0	2	0	0	0	2	0	0	0	0			
Mining Engineers, Including Mine Safety Engineers	5	VH	VL	VL	2	2	2	2	0	0	1	0	1	1	1	1	0	0	0			
Nuclear Engineers	5	VH	VL	VL	2	2	2	2	0	0	1	0	0	0	1	0	0	0	0			
Operations Research Analysts	3	VH	VL	VL	2	2	0	2	0	1	0	0	0	0	0	0	0	1	0			
Petroleum Engineers	5	VH	VL	VL	2	2	2	2	0	0	1	0	2	0	1	1	0	0	0			
Physicists and Astronomers	2	VH	VL	VL	2	2	2	2	0	0	0	0	1	0	2	0	0	0	0			
Psychologists	3	VH	VL	H	1	2	2	1	1	2	0	0	1	0	0	0	1	1	0			
Science Technicians	6	H	VL	L	2	1	1	1	0	1	1	0	1	1	2	0	0	0	1			
Social Scientists, Other	3	VH	H	L	2	2	2	1	1	1	0	1	1	1	0	0	0	1	0			
Statisticians	5	VH	VL	VL	2	1	0	1	0	0	0	0	0	0	0	0	0	0	0			
Surveyors, Cartographers, Photogrammetrists, and Surveying Technicians	7	H	VL	L	1	1	1	1	0	0	0	0	2	0	1	2	0	0	1			
Urban and Regional Planners	3	VH	VL	L	1	2	2	1	2	2	0	0	1	0	0	0	0	1	0			

Plants and Animals

GOE Work Groups—Managerial Work: Farming and Fishing; Managerial Work: Nursery, Groundskeeping, and Logging; Animal Care and Training; Hands-on Work: Farming; Hands-on Work: Forestry and Logging; Hands-on Work: Hunting and Fishing; Hands-on Work: Nursery, Groundskeeping, and Pest Control

	Education and Training	Median Earnings	Expected Job Openings	Part-Time Availability	Math	English	Science	Computer	Artistic or Creative	Interpersonal or Persuasive	Mechanical	Leadership or Management	Travel	Hazardous	Operates Machines or Equipment	Outdoors	Irregular Schedule	Stress	Physically Demanding	1.	2.	3.
Conservation Scientists and Foresters	5	VH	VL	VL	2	2	2	1	0	1	0	0	2	1	0	2	0	0	1			
Farmers and Farm Managers	4	VL	L	H	1	1	1	1	0	0	2	1	0	1	2	2	2	1	2			
Fishers and Fishing Vessel Operators	10	L	VL	L	0	0	0	0	0	0	0	0	2	1	2	2	1	0	2			
Forestry, Conservation, and Logging Occupations	11	H	VL	L	0	0	1	0	0	0	0	0	2	2	2	2	1	0	2			
Landscape Architects	5	VH	VL	L	2	1	2	1	2	1	0	0	1	0	0	1	0	0	0			

CAREER INTERESTS-TO-JOBS CHART

	Education and Training	Median Earnings	Expected Job Openings	Part-Time Availability	Math	English	Science	Computer	Artistic or Creative	Interpersonal or Persuasive	Mechanical	Leadership or Management	Travel	Hazardous	Operates Machines or Equipment	Outdoors	Irregular Schedule	Stress	Physically Demanding	1.	2.	3.
					SKILLS AND ABILITIES										**WORKING CONDITIONS**					**TOP VALUES**		
Landscaping, Groundskeeping, Nursery, Greenhouse, and Lawn Service Occupations	10	L	L	H	0	0	1	0	1	0	0	0	2	1	2	2	1	0	2			
Veterinarians	1	VH	VL	VL	1	2	2	1	0	1	0	0	1	1	2	0	1	2	1			
Veterinary Assistants and Nonfarm Animal Caretakers	11	VL	VL	VH	0	0	1	0	0	0	0	0	0	1	1	0	2	0	1			

Law, Law Enforcement, and Public Safety

GOE Work Groups—Managerial Work in Law, Law Enforcement, and Public Safety; Law: Legal Practice and Justice Administration; Law: Legal Support; Law Enforcement: Investigation and Protection; Law Enforcement: Technology; Law Enforcement: Security; Public Safety: Emergency Responding; Public Safety: Regulations Enforcement

	Education and Training	Median Earnings	Expected Job Openings	Part-Time Availability	Math	English	Science	Computer	Artistic or Creative	Interpersonal or Persuasive	Mechanical	Leadership or Management	Travel	Hazardous	Operates Machines or Equipment	Outdoors	Irregular Schedule	Stress	Physically Demanding	1.	2.	3.
Adjusters, Investigators, and Collectors	10	H	H	L	1	1	0	1	0	1	0	0	2	0	0	1	1	0	0			
Correctional Officers	9	H	VL	VL	0	0	0	0	0	2	0	1	0	2	0	1	2	2	2			
Emergency Medical Technicians	7	L	VL	H	1	1	1	0	0	2	0	0	2	2	2	2	2	2	2			
Fire Fighting Occupations	8	H	VL	VL	0	0	1	0	0	1	0	1	2	2	2	2	2	2	2			
Guards	11	L	L	H	0	0	0	0	0	1	0	1	0	2	0	0	2	2	2			
Inspectors and Compliance Officers, Except Construction	8	H	VL	VL	0	0	1	1	0	1	0	0	2	0	0	0	1	0	0			
Lawyers and Judicial Workers	1	VH	VL	L	0	2	0	1	1	2	0	2	2	0	0	0	1	2	0			
Paralegals and Legal Assistants	6	H	VL	L	0	1	0	1	0	2	0	0	0	0	0	0	0	1	0			
Police and Detectives	8	VH	VL	VL	0	1	0	0	0	2	0	1	2	2	0	2	2	2	2			
Private Detectives and Investigators	10	L	VL	H	0	0	0	0	0	2	0	0	2	0	0	1	2	2	1			
Science Technicians (example: Crime Lab Technicians)	6	H	VL	L	2	1	1	1	0	1	1	0	1	1	2	0	0	0	1			

Mechanics, Installers, and Repairers

GOE Work Groups—Managerial Work in Mechanics, Installers, and Repairers; Electrical and Electronic Systems: Installation and Repair; Electrical and Electronic Systems: Equipment Repair; Mechanical Work: Vehicles and Facilities; Mechanical Work: Machinery Repair; Mechanical Work: Medical and Technical Equipment Fabrication and Repair; Mechanical Work: Musical Instrument Fabrication and Repair; Hands-on Work in Mechanics, Installers, and Repairers

	Education and Training	Median Earnings	Expected Job Openings	Part-Time Availability	Math	English	Science	Computer	Artistic or Creative	Interpersonal or Persuasive	Mechanical	Leadership or Management	Travel	Hazardous	Operates Machines or Equipment	Outdoors	Irregular Schedule	Stress	Physically Demanding	1.	2.	3.
Aircraft Mechanics and Service Technicians	7	VH	VL	VL	1	0	1	0	0	0	2	0	0	1	2	1	1	0	2			
Automotive Body Repairers	9	H	VL	VL	1	0	1	0	1	0	1	0	0	1	2	0	0	0	2			
Automotive Mechanics and Service Technicians	7	H	L	VL	1	0	1	1	0	0	2	0	0	1	2	1	0	0	2			
Blue-Collar Worker Supervisors	8	VH	L	VL	0	0	0	0	0	2	0	2	1	0	0	0	1	0	1			
Coin and Vending, and Amusement Machine Servicers and Repairers	9	L	VL	L	1	0	0	0	0	0	2	0	2	2	1	0	0	0	2			
Computer, Automated Teller, and Office Machine Repairers	7	H	VL	VL	1	0	1	2	0	0	1	0	2	1	2	0	0	0	1			
Diesel Mechanics and Service Technicians	9	H	VL	VL	1	0	1	1	0	0	2	0	0	1	2	1	0	0	2			
Electric Power Generating Plant Operators and Power Distributors and Dispatchers	9	VH	VL	VL	1	0	1	1	0	0	2	0	0	1	2	0	2	0	1			
Electronic Home Entertainment Equipment Repairers	7	VH	VL	VL	1	0	1	0	0	0	1	0	1	1	2	0	0	0	1			
Electronics Repairers, Commercial and Industrial Equipment	7	H	VL	VL	1	0	1	2	0	0	2	0	2	1	2	0	1	0	1			
Elevator Installers and Repairers	9	VH	VL	VL	1	0	1	0	0	0	2	0	2	1	2	0	1	0	2			

(continues)

(continued)

CAREER INTERESTS-TO-JOBS CHART

	Education and Training	Median Earnings	Expected Job Openings	Part-Time Availability	SKILLS AND ABILITIES										WORKING CONDITIONS					TOP VALUES		
					Math	English	Science	Computer	Artistic or Creative	Interpersonal or Persuasive	Mechanical	Leadership or Management	Travel	Hazardous	Operates Machines or Equipment	Outdoors	Irregular Schedule	Stress	Physically Demanding	1.	2.	3.
Farm Equipment Mechanics	9	L	VL	VL	1	0	1	0	0	0	2	0	2	2	2	2	1	0	2			
Handlers, Equipment Cleaners, Helpers, and Laborers	11	L	VH	H	0	0	0	0	0	0	0	0	0	0	0	1	0	0	2			
Heating, Air Conditioning, and Refrigeration Mechanics and Installers	9	H	VL	VL	1	0	1	0	0	0	2	0	2	2	2	1	1	0	2			
Home Appliance and Power Tool Repairers	9	H	VL	VL	1	0	0	0	0	0	2	0	2	2	2	0	1	0	2			
Industrial Machinery Repairers	9	H	VL	VL	1	0	1	0	0	0	2	0	2	2	2	0	1	0	2			
Line Installers and Repairers	9	VH	VL	VL	0	0	0	0	0	0	1	0	2	2	2	2	1	0	2			
Maintenance Mechanics, General Utility	11	L	L	L	0	0	1	0	0	0	2	0	0	2	2	0	1	0	2			
Millwrights	9	VH	VL	VL	1	0	1	0	0	0	2	0	1	2	2	0	1	0	2			
Mobile Heavy Equipment Mechanics	9	VH	VL	VL	1	0	1	0	0	0	2	0	2	2	2	1	0	0	2			
Motorcycle, Boat, and Small-Engine Mechanics	9	L	VL	VL	1	0	1	0	0	0	2	0	0	2	2	1	0	0	2			
Musical Instrument Repairers and Tuners	9	L	VL	VL	0	0	1	0	1	0	1	0	2	0	0	0	0	0	1			
Telecommunications Equipment Mechanics, Installers, and Repairers	7	VH	VL	VL	1	0	1	1	0	0	1	0	2	1	2	0	1	0	1			

Construction, Mining, and Drilling

GOE Work Groups—Managerial Work in Construction, Mining, and Drilling; Construction: Masonry, Stone, and Brick Work; Construction: Construction and Maintenance; Construction: General; Mining and Drilling; Hands-on Work: Construction, Extraction, and Maintenance

	Education and Training	Median Earnings	Expected Job Openings	Part-Time Availability	Math	English	Science	Computer	Artistic or Creative	Interpersonal or Persuasive	Mechanical	Leadership or Management	Travel	Hazardous	Operates Machines or Equipment	Outdoors	Irregular Schedule	Stress	Physically Demanding	1.	2.	3.
Blue-Collar Worker Supervisors	8	VH	L	VL	0	0	0	0	0	2	0	2	1	0	0	0	1	0	1			
Boilermakers	9	VH	VL	VL	0	0	1	0	0	0	2	0	2	1	2	0	0	0	2			
Bricklayers and Stonemasons	9	VH	VL	VL	0	0	0	0	1	0	0	0	2	0	1	2	0	0	2			
Carpenters	9	H	L	L	1	0	1	0	0	0	2	0	2	2	2	2	0	0	2			
Carpet, Floor, and Tile Installers and Finishers	10	H	VL	L	0	0	0	0	0	0	0	0	2	0	1	0	0	0	2			
Cement Masons, Concrete Finishers, and Terrazzo Workers	9	H	VL	VL	0	0	0	0	1	0	0	0	2	0	2	1	0	0	2			
Construction and Building Inspectors	8	VH	VL	L	1	1	1	1	0	1	0	0	2	1	0	1	0	0	1			
Construction Equipment Operators	10	H	L	VL	0	0	0	0	0	0	0	0	2	2	2	2	0	0	2			
Construction Managers	5	VH	VL	VL	1	1	1	1	0	2	1	2	2	1	0	1	1	2	1			
Drywall Installers and Finishers	10	H	VL	VL	0	0	0	0	1	0	0	0	2	0	1	0	0	0	2			
Electricians	9	VH	VL	VL	1	0	1	0	0	0	1	0	2	2	1	1	0	0	2			
Glaziers	9	H	VL	VL	0	0	0	0	1	0	0	0	2	1	2	2	0	0	2			
Handlers, Equipment Cleaners, Helpers, and Laborers	11	L	VH	H	0	0	0	0	0	0	0	0	0	0	0	1	0	0	2			
Hazardous Materials Removal Workers	8	H	H	H	1	0	1	0	0	0	1	0	2	2	1	1	2	1	2			
Insulation Workers	10	H	VL	VL	0	0	0	0	0	0	0	0	2	1	1	1	0	0	2			
Material Moving Equipment Operators	10	H	L	VL	0	0	0	0	0	0	0	0	2	2	2	2	0	0	2			
Painters and Paperhangers	9	H	VL	L	0	0	0	0	1	0	0	0	2	1	0	2	0	0	2			
Plasterers and Stucco Masons	9	H	VL	VL	0	0	0	0	1	0	0	0	2	1	0	1	0	0	2			
Plumbers, Pipefitters, and Steamfitters	9	VH	VL	VL	1	0	1	0	0	0	2	0	2	0	1	1	1	0	2			
Roofers	10	H	VL	L	0	0	0	0	0	0	0	0	2	2	2	2	0	0	2			
Sheet Metal Workers and Duct Installers	10	H	VL	VL	1	0	0	0	0	0	0	0	2	2	2	0	0	0	2			
Structural and Reinforcing Metal Workers	9	VH	VL	VL	0	0	1	0	0	0	1	0	2	2	2	1	0	0	2			

CAREER INTERESTS-TO-JOBS CHART

	Education and Training	Median Earnings	Expected Job Openings	Part-Time Availability	Math	English	Science	Computer	Artistic or Creative	Interpersonal or Persuasive	Mechanical	Leadership or Management	Travel	Hazardous	Operates Machines or Equipment	Outdoors	Irregular Schedule	Stress	Physically Demanding	1.	2.	3.
Transportation																						

GOE Work Groups—Managerial Work in Transportation; Vehicle Expediting and Coordinating; Air Vehicle Operation; Water Vehicle Operation; Truck Driving; Rail Vehicle Operation; Other Services Requiring Driving; Support Work in Transportation

	Education and Training	Median Earnings	Expected Job Openings	Part-Time Availability	Math	English	Science	Computer	Artistic or Creative	Interpersonal or Persuasive	Mechanical	Leadership or Management	Travel	Hazardous	Operates Machines or Equipment	Outdoors	Irregular Schedule	Stress	Physically Demanding	1.	2.	3.
Aircraft Pilots and Flight Engineers	5	.VH	VL	L	2	1	2	1	0	0	1	0	2	2	2	1	2	2	1			
Air Traffic Controllers	9	VH	VL	L	1	1	0	1	0	2	0	1	0	0	2	0	2	2	0			
Blue-Collar Worker Supervisors	8	VH	L	VL	0	0	0	0	0	2	0	2	1	0	0	0	1	0	1			
Busdrivers	10	L	L	VH	0	0	0	0	0	1	0	0	2	2	2	1	2	1	1			
Dispatchers	10	H	VL	L	0	0	0	1	0	2	0	1	0	0	0	0	2	1	0			
Flight Attendants	9	VH	VL	VH	0	0	0	0	0	2	0	0	2	0	0	0	2	1	1			
Handlers, Equipment Cleaners, Helpers, and Laborers	11	L	VH	H	0	0	0	0	0	0	0	0	0	0	0	1	0	0	2			
Material Moving Equipment Operators	10	H	L	VL	0	0	0	0	0	0	0	0	2	2	2	2	0	0	2			
Rail Transportation Occupations	8	H	VL	VL	0	0	0	0	0	1	1	0	2	1	2	1	2	0	1			
Taxi Drivers and Chauffeurs	11	L	VL	H	0	0	0	0	0	1	0	0	2	2	2	1	2	1	1			
Truckdrivers	11	H	VL	VL	1	0	1	0	0	0	1	0	2	2	2	2	2	0	2			
Water Transportation Occupations	8	H	VL	VL	1	0	1	0	0	0	1	0	2	2	2	2	2	0	2			

Industrial Production

GOE Work Groups—Managerial Work in Industrial Production; Production Technology: Machine Set-up and Operation; Production Technology: Precision Hand Work; Production Technology: Inspection; Production Work: Machine Work, Assorted Materials; Production Work: Equipment Operation, Assorted Materials Processing; Production Work: Equipment Operation, Welding, Brazing, and Soldering; Production Work: Plating and Coating; Production Work: Printing and Reproduction; Production Work: Hands-on Work, Assorted Materials; Metal and Plastics Machining Technology; Woodworking Technology; Systems Operation: Utilities and Power Plant; Systems Operation: Oil, Gas, and Water Distribution; Hands-on Work: Loading, Moving, Hoisting, and Conveying

	Education and Training	Median Earnings	Expected Job Openings	Part-Time Availability	Math	English	Science	Computer	Artistic or Creative	Interpersonal or Persuasive	Mechanical	Leadership or Management	Travel	Hazardous	Operates Machines or Equipment	Outdoors	Irregular Schedule	Stress	Physically Demanding	1.	2.	3.
Apparel Workers	9	VL	L	L	0	0	0	0	0	0	0	0	0	2	2	0	0	0	1			
Bindery Workers	10	L	VL	VL	0	0	0	0	0	0	0	0	0	0	2	0	0	0	1			
Blue-Collar Worker Supervisors	8	VH	L	VL	0	0	0	0	0	2	0	2	1	0	0	0	1	0	1			
Butchers and Meat, Poultry, and Fish Cutters	10	L	VL	VL	0	0	0	0	0	0	0	0	0	2	2	0	0	0	2			
Dental Laboratory Technicians	9	H	VL	H	1	0	1	0	1	0	0	0	0	0	2	0	0	0	1			
Electric Power Generating Plant Operators and Power Distributors and Dispatchers	9	VH	VL	VL	1	0	1	1	0	0	2	0	0	1	2	0	2	0	1			
Electronic Semiconductor Processors	10	L	VL	VL	1	0	1	1	0	0	1	0	0	0	2	0	2	0	0			
Forestry, Conservation, and Logging Occupations	11	H	VL	L	0	0	1	0	0	0	0	0	2	2	2	2	1	0	2			
Handlers, Equipment Cleaners, Helpers, and Laborers	11	L	VH	H	0	0	0	0	0	0	0	0	0	0	0	1	0	0	2			
Industrial Production Managers	5	VH	VL	VL	2	1	0	2	0	2	1	2	0	1	0	0	1	2	0			
Inspectors, Testers, and Graders	8	H	L	VL	1	0	0	0	0	0	0	0	0	0	1	0	1	0	1			
Jewelers and Precious Stones and Metal Workers	7	L	VL	H	0	0	1	1	2	2	1	0	0	0	1	0	1	0	0			
Machinists and Numerical Control Machine Tool Programmers	8	H	VL	VL	1	0	1	1	0	0	2	0	0	1	2	0	0	0	1			
Material Moving Equipment Operators	10	H	L	VL	0	0	0	0	0	0	0	0	2	2	2	2	0	0	2			
Metalworking and Plastics-Working Machine Operators	10	L	L	VL	0	0	0	1	0	0	1	0	0	2	2	0	2	0	1			

(continues)

(continued)

CAREER INTERESTS-TO-JOBS CHART

	Education and Training	Median Earnings	Expected Job Openings	Part-Time Availability	SKILLS AND ABILITIES										WORKING CONDITIONS					TOP VALUES		
					Math	English	Science	Computer	Artistic or Creative	Interpersonal or Persuasive	Mechanical	Leadership or Management	Travel	Hazardous	Operates Machines or Equipment	Outdoors	Irregular Schedule	Stress	Physically Demanding	1.	2.	3.
Ophthalmic Laboratory Technicians	9	L	VL	L	1	0	0	0	0	0	0	0	0	0	2	0	0	0	1			
Painting and Coating Machine Operators	10	H	VL	VL	0	0	0	0	0	0	0	0	0	2	2	0	2	0	1			
Photographic Process Workers	10	L	VL	H	0	0	0	0	1	0	0	0	0	2	2	0	1	0	0			
Precision Assemblers	8	VH	VL	VL	0	0	0	0	0	0	2	0	0	0	2	0	1	0	1			
Prepress Workers	9	H	VL	VL	0	1	0	1	0	0	0	0	0	0	2	0	2	0	0			
Printing Press Operators	10	H	VL	VL	0	0	0	0	0	0	1	0	0	0	2	0	2	0	1			
Shoe and Leather Workers and Repairers	9	L	VL	H	0	0	0	0	1	0	0	0	0	2	2	0	0	0	1			
Stationary Engineers	9	VH	VL	VL	1	0	1	1	0	0	2	0	0	2	2	0	2	0	1			
Textile Machinery Operators	10	L	VL	L	0	0	0	0	0	0	0	0	0	2	2	0	2	0	1			
Tool and Die Makers	9	VH	VL	VL	1	0	1	1	0	0	2	0	0	1	2	0	0	0	1			
Upholsterers	9	L	VL	L	0	0	0	0	1	0	0	0	0	1	2	0	0	0	2			
Water and Wastewater Treatment Plant Operators	9	H	VL	VL	1	0	1	1	0	0	2	0	0	2	2	1	2	0	1			
Welders, Cutters, and Welding Machine Operators	10	H	VL	VL	0	0	1	0	0	0	1	0	0	2	2	0	0	0	2			
Woodworking Occupations (example: Wood Lathe Operators)	9	L	VL	VL	0	0	0	0	0	0	0	0	0	2	2	0	0	0	1			

Business Detail

GOE Work Groups—Managerial Work in Business Detail; Administrative Detail: Administration; Administrative Detail: Secretarial Work; Administrative Detail: Interviewing; Bookkeeping, Auditing, and Accounting; Material Control; Customer Service; Communications; Records Processing: Verification and Proofing; Records Processing: Preparation and Maintenance; Records and Materials Processing; Clerical Machine Operation

	Education and Training	Median Earnings	Expected Job Openings	Part-Time Availability	Math	English	Science	Computer	Artistic or Creative	Interpersonal or Persuasive	Mechanical	Leadership or Management	Travel	Hazardous	Operates Machines or Equipment	Outdoors	Irregular Schedule	Stress	Physically Demanding	1.	2.	3.
Adjusters, Investigators, and Collectors	10	H	H	L	1	1	0	1	0	1	0	0	2	0	0	1	1	0	0			
Administrative Services and Facility Managers	8	VH	VL	VL	1	1	0	1	0	2	0	2	0	0	0	0	0	1	0			
Bank Tellers	11	L	L	VH	0	0	0	1	0	1	0	0	0	0	0	0	0	0	0			
Billing Clerks and Billing Machine Operators	11	L	VL	L	0	0	0	1	0	0	0	0	0	0	0	0	0	0	0			
Bookkeeping, Accounting, and Auditing Clerks	10	L	H	VH	0	0	0	1	0	0	0	0	0	0	0	0	0	0	0			
Brokerage Clerks and Statement Clerks	11	H	VL	L	0	0	0	1	0	0	0	0	0	0	0	0	0	0	0			
Cashiers	11	VL	VH	VH	0	0	0	0	0	1	0	0	0	0	0	0	2	1	1			
Communications Equipment Operators	10	L	VL	H	0	0	0	1	0	2	0	0	0	0	0	0	1	2	0			
Computer Operators	11	L	L	VH	0	0	0	1	0	1	0	0	0	0	0	0	0	0	0			
Counter and Rental Clerks	11	VL	L	VH	0	0	0	0	0	1	0	0	0	0	0	0	2	0	1			
Court Reporters, Medical Transcriptionists, and Stenographers	7	H	VL	H	0	2	0	1	0	0	0	0	1	0	0	0	0	1	0			
Dispatchers	10	H	VL	L	0	0	0	1	0	2	0	1	0	0	0	0	2	1	0			
Employment Interviewers, Private or Public Employment Service	5	H	VL	VL	0	1	0	1	0	2	0	0	0	0	0	0	0	0	0			
File Clerks	11	L	L	VH	0	0	0	1	0	0	0	0	0	0	0	0	0	0	1			
Health Information Technicians	6	L	VL	H	1	1	1	1	0	0	0	0	0	0	0	0	0	0	0			
Hotel, Motel, and Resort Desk Clerks	11	VL	VL	H	0	0	0	1	0	2	0	0	0	0	0	0	2	1	0			
Human Resources Clerks, Except Payroll and Timekeeping	11	H	VL	VL	0	0	0	1	0	1	0	0	0	0	0	0	0	0	0			
Interviewing and New Account Clerks	10	L	VL	VH	0	0	0	1	0	2	0	0	0	0	0	0	0	0	0			
Library Assistants and Bookmobile Drivers	11	L	VL	VH	0	1	0	1	0	1	0	0	1	0	0	0	1	0	1			
Loan Clerks and Credit Authorizers, Checkers, and Clerks	11	L	VL	L	0	0	0	1	0	1	0	0	0	0	0	0	0	0	0			

CAREER INTERESTS-TO-JOBS CHART

	Education and Training	Median Earnings	Expected Job Openings	Part-Time Availability	Math	English	Science	Computer	Artistic or Creative	Interpersonal or Persuasive	Mechanical	Leadership or Management	Travel	Hazardous	Operates Machines or Equipment	Outdoors	Irregular Schedule	Stress	Physically Demanding	1.	2.	3.
Mail Clerks and Messengers	11	L	VL	H	0	0	0	0	0	0	0	0	0	0	1	2	0	0	2			
Office and Administrative Support Supervisors and Managers	8	H	L	VL	0	0	0	1	0	2	0	2	0	0	0	0	0	0	0			
Office Clerks, General	11	L	VH	VH	0	0	0	1	0	0	0	0	0	0	0	0	0	0	0			
Order Clerks	11	L	VL	L	0	0	0	1	0	1	0	0	0	0	0	0	0	0	0			
Payroll and Timekeeping Clerks	11	H	VL	L	0	0	0	1	0	1	0	0	0	0	0	0	0	0	0			
Postal Clerks and Mail Carriers	11	H	H	L	0	0	0	1	0	0	0	0	2	0	2	2	1	1	2			
Prepress Workers	9	H	VL	VL	0	1	0	1	0	0	0	0	0	0	2	0	2	0	0			
Receptionists	11	L	H	VH	0	0	0	1	0	2	0	0	0	0	0	0	0	0	0			
Reservation and Transportation Ticket Agents and Travel Clerks	11	L	VL	H	0	0	0	1	0	2	0	0	0	0	0	0	2	1	1			
Secretaries	7	H	H	H	0	0	0	1	0	2	0	0	0	0	0	0	0	1	0			
Shipping, Receiving, and Traffic Clerks	11	L	L	L	0	0	0	0	0	0	0	0	0	0	0	0	0	0	2			
Stock Clerks	11	VL	H	L	0	0	0	0	0	0	0	0	0	0	1	0	1	0	2			
Word Processors, Typists, and Data Entry Keyers	7	L	L	H	0	0	0	1	0	0	0	0	0	0	0	0	0	0	0			

Sales and Marketing

GOE Work Groups—Managerial Work in Sales and Marketing; Sales Technology: Technical Sales; Sales Technology: Intangible Sales; General Sales; Personal Soliciting

	Education and Training	Median Earnings	Expected Job Openings	Part-Time Availability	Math	English	Science	Computer	Artistic or Creative	Interpersonal or Persuasive	Mechanical	Leadership or Management	Travel	Hazardous	Operates Machines or Equipment	Outdoors	Irregular Schedule	Stress	Physically Demanding	1.	2.	3.
Advertising, Marketing, and Public Relations Managers	4	VH	L	VL	1	2	0	1	1	2	0	2	2	0	0	0	1	2	0			
Cashiers	11	VL	VH	VH	0	0	0	0	0	1	0	0	0	0	0	0	2	1	1			
Counter and Rental Clerks	11	VL	L	VH	0	0	0	0	0	1	0	0	0	0	0	0	2	0	1			
Demonstrators, Product Promoters, and Models	11	L	H	H	0	1	0	0	1	1	0	0	2	0	0	1	2	1	0			
Economists and Marketing Research Analysts	5	VH	VL	L	2	2	0	1	0	1	0	0	1	0	0	0	0	1	0			
Insurance Sales Agents	5	VH	VL	L	1	1	0	1	0	2	0	0	1	0	0	0	1	1	0			
Manufacturers' and Wholesale Sales Representatives	10	VH	L	L	1	1	0	1	0	2	0	0	2	0	0	0	1	1	0			
Public Relations Specialists	5	H	VL	L	0	2	0	1	2	2	0	2	2	0	0	0	1	1	0			
Real Estate Agents and Brokers	8	VH	VL	L	1	1	0	1	0	2	0	0	2	0	0	0	1	1	0			
Retail Salespersons	11	VL	VH	VH	0	0	0	0	0	2	0	0	0	0	0	0	2	1	1			
Retail Sales Worker Supervisors and Managers	11	VL	VH	VH	0	0	0	0	0	2	0	0	0	0	0	0	2	1	1			
Securities, Commodities, and Financial Services Sales Representatives	5	VH	VL	L	1	1	0	1	0	2	0	0	0	0	0	0	0	2	0			
Services Sales Representatives	10	VH	VH	L	1	1	0	1	0	2	0	0	2	0	0	0	1	1	0			
Travel Agents	7	L	VL	H	0	1	0	1	0	2	0	0	0	0	0	0	0	1	0			

Recreation, Travel, and Other Personal Services

Managerial Work in Recreation, Travel, and Other Personal Services; Recreational Services; Transportation and Lodging Services; Barber and Beauty Services; Food and Beverage Services: Preparing; Food and Beverage Services: Serving; Apparel, Shoes, Leather, and Fabric Care; Cleaning and Building Services; Other Personal Services

	Education and Training	Median Earnings	Expected Job Openings	Part-Time Availability	Math	English	Science	Computer	Artistic or Creative	Interpersonal or Persuasive	Mechanical	Leadership or Management	Travel	Hazardous	Operates Machines or Equipment	Outdoors	Irregular Schedule	Stress	Physically Demanding	1.	2.	3.
Barbers, Cosmetologists, and Related Workers	7	VL	VL	VH	0	0	0	0	1	2	0	0	0	1	2	0	1	0	1			
Busdrivers	10	L	L	VH	0	0	0	0	0	1	0	0	2	2	2	1	2	1	1			
Chefs, Cooks, and Other Kitchen Workers	10	VL	VH	VH	0	0	1	0	1	1	0	0	0	1	1	0	2	1	1			

(continues)

CAREER INTERESTS-TO-JOBS CHART

	Education and Training	Median Earnings	Expected Job Openings	Part-Time Availability	SKILLS AND ABILITIES										WORKING CONDITIONS					TOP VALUES		
					Math	English	Science	Computer	Artistic or Creative	Interpersonal or Persuasive	Mechanical	Leadership or Management	Travel	Hazardous	Operates Machines or Equipment	Outdoors	Irregular Schedule	Stress	Physically Demanding	1.	2.	3.
Flight Attendants	9	VH	VL	VH	0	0	0	0	0	2	0	0	2	0	0	0	2	1	1			
Food and Beverage Service Occupations	11	VL	VH	VH	0	0	0	0	0	2	0	0	0	0	1	0	2	1	1			
Home Health and Personal Care Aides	11	VL	L	H	0	0	0	0	0	2	0	0	2	1	0	0	1	0	1			
Hotel Managers and Assistants	7	VH	H	VL	0	1	0	1	0	2	0	2	2	0	0	0	2	2	0			
Hotel, Motel, and Resort Desk Clerks	11	VL	VL	H	0	0	0	1	0	2	0	0	0	0	0	0	2	1	0			
Janitors and Cleaners and Institutional Cleaning Supervisors	8	VL	VH	H	0	0	0	0	0	0	0	0	0	0	1	0	1	0	1			
Pest Controllers	10	L	VL	L	0	0	1	0	0	1	0	0	2	2	2	2	1	0	1			
Private Household Workers	11	VL	L	VH	0	0	0	0	0	1	0	0	0	0	1	1	0	0	1			
Recreation Workers	5	VL	VL	H	0	1	0	0	1	2	0	0	1	0	0	2	1	0	1			
Reservation and Transportation Ticket Agents and Travel Clerks	11	L	VL	H	0	0	0	1	0	2	0	0	0	0	0	0	2	1	1			
Restaurant and Food Service Managers	8	H	L	L	0	1	0	1	1	2	0	2	0	0	0	0	2	2	0			
Retail Salespersons	11	VL	VH	VH	0	0	0	0	0	2	0	0	0	0	0	0	2	1	1			
Taxi Drivers and Chauffeurs	11	L	VL	H	0	0	0	0	0	1	0	0	2	2	2	1	2	1	1			
Travel Agents	7	L	VL	H	0	1	0	1	0	2	0	0	0	0	0	0	0	1	0			

Education and Social Service

GOE Work Groups—Managerial Work in Education and Social Service; Social Services: Religious; Social Services: Counseling and Social Work; Educational Services: Counseling and Evaluation; Educational Services: Postsecondary and Adult Teaching and Instructing; Educational Services: Preschool, Elementary, and Secondary Teaching and Instructing; Educational Services: Library and Museum

	Education and Training	Median Earnings	Expected Job Openings	Part-Time Availability	Math	English	Science	Computer	Artistic or Creative	Interpersonal or Persuasive	Mechanical	Leadership or Management	Travel	Hazardous	Operates Machines or Equipment	Outdoors	Irregular Schedule	Stress	Physically Demanding	1.	2.	3.
Adult and Vocational Education Teachers	8	VH	L	VH	1	2	1	1	1	2	0	1	0	0	1	0	2	0	0			
Archivists, Curators, Museum Technicians, and Conservators	3	H	VL	H	1	2	2	1	2	1	0	0	1	0	0	0	0	0	1			
College and University Faculty	2	VH	L	VH	2	2	2	2	2	2	0	1	0	0	0	0	1	0	0			
Counselors	3	VH	VL	L	0	2	1	0	1	2	0	1	0	0	0	0	1	1	0			
Education Administrators	4	VH	VL	L	1	2	0	1	0	2	0	2	0	0	0	0	1	1	0			
Human Resources Clerks, Except Payroll and Timekeeping	11	H	VL	VL	0	0	0	1	0	1	0	0	0	0	0	0	0	0	0			
Human Service Workers and Assistants	10	L	L	VH	0	1	0	0	0	2	0	0	2	0	0	0	1	1	0			
Instructors and Coaches, Sports and Physical Training	8	L	H	H	0	1	1	0	1	0	0	1	1	1	0	1	2	1	2			
Librarians	3	VH	VL	H	0	2	0	1	0	2	0	0	0	0	0	0	1	0	1			
Library Assistants and Bookmobile Drivers	11	L	VL	VH	0	1	0	1	0	1	0	0	1	0	0	0	1	0	1			
Library Technicians	11	L	VL	H	0	1	0	1	0	2	0	0	0	0	0	0	1	0	1			
Preschool Teachers and Child-Care Workers	5	VL	H	VH	0	0	0	0	1	2	0	1	0	0	0	0	0	1	1			
Protestant Ministers	1	H	VL	L	0	2	0	0	1	2	0	2	1	0	0	0	1	1	0			
Psychologists	3	VH	VL	H	1	2	2	1	1	2	0	0	1	0	0	0	1	1	0			
Rabbis	1	H	VL	L	0	2	0	0	1	2	0	2	1	0	0	0	1	1	0			
Recreation Workers	5	VL	VL	H	0	1	0	0	1	2	0	0	1	0	0	2	1	0	1			
Roman Catholic Priests	1	H	VL	L	0	2	0	0	1	2	0	2	1	0	0	0	1	1	0			
School Teachers-Kindergarten, Elementary, and Secondary	5	VH	VH	L	1	2	1	1	1	2	0	1	0	0	0	0	1	1	1			
Social Workers	5	H	L	L	0	2	1	0	1	2	0	0	2	0	0	1	1	1	0			
Special Education Teachers	5	VH	VL	L	1	2	1	1	1	2	0	1	0	0	0	0	1	1	1			
Teacher Assistants	11	VL	H	VH	1	1	0	0	1	2	0	0	0	0	0	0	0	0	0			

CAREER INTERESTS-TO-JOBS CHART

		Education and Training	Median Earnings	Expected Job Openings	Part-Time Availability	SKILLS AND ABILITIES										WORKING CONDITIONS					TOP VALUES		
						Math	English	Science	Computer	Artistic or Creative	Interpersonal or Persuasive	Mechanical	Leadership or Management	Travel	Hazardous	Operates Machines or Equipment	Outdoors	Irregular Schedule	Stress	Physically Demanding	1.	2.	3.

General Management and Support

General Management Work and Management of Support Functions; Management Support: Human Resources; Management Support: Purchasing; Management Support: Accounting and Auditing; Management Support: Investigation and Analysis

Accountants and Auditors	5	VH	L	L	2	1	0	1	0	1	0	0	0	1	0	0	1	1	0			
Adjusters, Investigators, and Collectors	10	H	H	L	1	1	0	1	0	1	0	0	2	0	0	1	1	0	0			
Administrative Services and Facility Managers	8	VH	VL	VL	1	1	0	1	0	2	0	2	0	0	0	0	0	1	0			
Budget Analysts	5	VH	VL	L	2	1	0	1	0	0	0	0	0	0	0	0	0	1	0			
Cost Estimators	5	VH	VL	L	2	1	1	1	0	0	0	0	2	0	0	1	0	0	0			
Economists and Marketing Research Analysts	5	VH	VL	L	2	2	0	1	0	1	0	0	1	0	0	0	0	1	0			
Employment Interviewers, Private or Public Employment Service	5	H	VL	VL	0	1	0	1	0	2	0	0	0	0	0	0	0	0	0			
Financial Managers	4	VH	L	VL	2	1	0	1	0	2	0	2	1	0	0	0	0	0	0			
General Managers and Top Executives	4	VH	H	VL	1	2	0	1	0	2	0	2	2	0	0	0	1	2	0			
Government Chief Executives and Legislators	4	VH	VL	VL	1	2	0	1	0	2	0	2	2	0	0	0	1	2	0			
Human Resources, Training, and Labor Relations Specialists and Managers	4	VH	L	VL	0	1	0	1	0	2	0	1	1	0	0	0	0	0	0			
Insurance Underwriters	5	H	VL	VL	2	0	0	1	0	0	0	0	1	0	0	0	0	0	0			
Loan Officers and Counselors	5	VH	VL	L	1	0	0	1	0	2	0	0	1	0	0	0	0	1	0			
Management Analysts	4	VH	VL	L	1	2	0	1	1	2	0	2	2	0	0	0	1	1	0			
Office and Administrative Support Supervisors and Managers	8	H	L	VL	0	0	0	1	0	2	0	2	0	0	0	0	0	0	0			
Property, Real Estate, and Community Association Managers	5	VH	L	VL	1	1	0	1	0	2	0	0	1	0	0	0	1	1	0			
Purchasing Managers, Buyers, and Purchasing Agents	5	VH	L	VL	1	1	0	1	0	2	0	0	1	0	0	0	1	1	0			
Receptionists	11	L	H	VH	0	0	0	1	0	2	0	0	0	0	0	0	0	0	0			
Secretaries	7	H	H	H	0	0	0	1	0	2	0	0	0	0	0	0	0	1	0			

Medical and Health Services

Managerial Work in Medical and Health Services; Medicine and Surgery; Dentistry; Health Specialties; Medical Technology; Medical Therapy; Patient Care and Assistance; Health Protection and Promotion

Cardiovascular Technologists and Technicians	6	H	VL	H	1	1	1	1	0	1	0	0	0	2	2	0	1	2	0			
Chiropractors	1	HV	VL	L	1	2	2	1	0	2	0	0	0	0	2	0	1	0	1			
Clinical Laboratory Technologists and Technicians	5	H	VL	H	1	1	2	1	0	0	0	0	0	2	2	0	1	0	0			
Dental Assistants	10	L	VL	VH	0	0	1	0	0	1	0	0	0	1	1	0	0	0	1			
Dental Hygienists	6	VH	VL	VH	0	1	1	0	0	1	0	0	0	2	2	0	1	0	1			
Dentists	1	VH	VL	H	1	2	2	1	0	2	0	0	0	2	2	0	0	0	0			
Dietitians and Nutritionists	5	H	VL	H	1	2	2	0	0	2	0	0	0	0	0	0	0	0	0			
Emergency Medical Technicians	7	L	VL	H	1	1	1	0	0	2	0	0	2	2	2	2	2	2	2			
Health Information Technicians	6	L	VL	H	1	1	1	1	0	0	0	0	0	0	0	0	0	0	0			
Health Service Managers	4	VH	L	VL	1	1	1	1	0	2	0	2	1	0	0	0	1	0	0			
Home Health and Personal Care Aides	11	VL	L	H	0	0	0	0	0	2	0	0	2	1	0	0	1	0	1			
Licensed Practical Nurses	7	H	VL	H	1	1	1	0	0	2	0	0	0	2	1	0	2	0	1			

(continues)

(continued)

CAREER INTERESTS-TO-JOBS CHART

	Education and Training	Median Earnings	Expected Job Openings	Part-Time Availability	Skills and Abilities										Working Conditions					Top Values		
					Math	English	Science	Computer	Artistic or Creative	Interpersonal or Persuasive	Mechanical	Leadership or Management	Travel	Hazardous	Operates Machines or Equipment	Outdoors	Irregular Schedule	Stress	Physically Demanding	1.	2.	3.
Medical Assistants	10	H	VL	H	0	1	1	1	0	1	0	0	0	1	0	0	0	0	0			
Nuclear Medicine Technologists	6	VH	VL	H	1	1	1	1	0	1	0	0	0	2	2	0	1	0	0			
Nursing and Psychiatric Aides	11	L	H	H	0	0	1	0	0	2	0	0	0	1	0	0	2	1	2			
Occupational Therapists	5	VH	VL	H	0	2	2	0	1	2	0	0	0	0	2	0	1	0	2			
Occupational Therapy Assistants and Aides	10	H	VL	H	0	0	1	0	0	2	1	0	0	0	1	0	1	0	1			
Opticians, Dispensing	9	L	VL	L	1	1	1	0	0	1	1	0	0	0	2	0	1	0	0			
Optometrists	1	VH	VL	L	1	2	2	1	0	2	0	0	0	0	2	0	0	0	0			
Pharmacists	5	VH	VL	L	1	2	2	1	0	2	0	0	0	0	0	0	2	1	0			
Pharmacy Technicians and Assistants	10	L	VL	H	1	1	1	0	0	1	0	0	0	0	0	0	2	1	0			
Physical Therapist Assistants and Aides	10	L	VL	H	0	0	1	0	0	2	0	0	0	0	1	0	1	0	1			
Physical Therapists	5	VH	VL	H	0	2	2	0	0	2	0	0	0	0	2	0	1	0	2			
Physician Assistants	5	VH	VL	H	1	2	2	1	0	2	0	0	1	2	1	0	2	2	1			
Physicians	1	VH	VL	VL	1	2	2	1	0	2	0	0	1	2	2	0	2	2	1			
Podiatrists	1	VH	VL	L	1	2	2	1	0	2	0	0	0	0	2	0	1	0	0			
Psychologists	3	VH	VL	H	1	2	2	1	1	2	0	0	1	0	0	0	1	1	0			
Radiologic Technologists	6	H	VL	H	1	1	1	1	0	1	0	0	1	2	2	0	2	0	0			
Recreational Therapists	5	H	VL	H	0	2	2	0	1	2	0	0	0	0	0	1	1	0	1			
Registered Nurses	6	VH	L	H	1	2	2	1	0	2	0	0	0	2	1	0	2	2	1			
Respiratory Therapists	6	H	VL	H	1	2	2	0	0	2	0	0	1	2	2	0	1	1	0			
Speech-Language Pathologists and Audiologists	3	VH	VL	H	1	2	2	1	0	2	0	0	1	0	1	0	1	0	0			
Surgical Technologists	7	H	VL	H	1	1	1	0	0	1	0	0	0	2	2	0	2	2	1			

Your Top Jobs List

Go over the "Career Interests-to-Jobs Chart" and select the five job titles that most interest you. List those, in order of your interest, below (where 1 is the job that interests you most). Then list another five job titles or groupings that interest you greatly. List these in the second section, in any order you want.

Your Top Five Job Titles

1. _____
2. _____
3. _____
4. _____
5. _____

Your Next Five Job Titles

6. _____
7. _____
8. _____
9. _____
10. _____

Sources of Additional Information

Now that you have identified possible career options, you'll want to explore them further. Many good information sources exist for career, education, and training options. Here are some of the most-used print, Internet, and other resources. Use these materials to help you complete the worksheet that follows. All books are available from JIST Works.

- *Occupational Outlook Handbook.* If you use only one reference book, this should be it. Published by the Department of Labor and updated every two years, it provides descriptions for the jobs listed in the "Career Interests-to-Jobs Chart." Descriptions give detailed, up-to-date information on pay, working conditions, training or education required, related jobs, projected growth, and more. Most libraries have the *OOH* or the bookstore version of it, titled *America's Top 300 Jobs.*

- *Guide for Occupational Exploration,* **Third Edition.** The *GOE* is based on solid research by the Department of Labor to help people explore career options based on interests. It provides lots of information on career, training, and education options based on the 14 interest areas used in this chapter. Thorough overviews are provided for each interest area, plus information on related jobs, education and training needed, and more. It also includes descriptions for about 1,000 jobs. This edition of the *GOE* also provides useful "crosswalks" to jobs based on values, leisure and home activities, school subjects, work settings, skills, abilities, and knowledge.

- *Enhanced Occupational Outlook Handbook.* A good all-in-one reference to identify the many jobs related to the major ones in the "Career Interests-to-Jobs Chart." It includes all the job descriptions from the *OOH,* plus descriptions of related jobs from the Department of Labor's O*NET database (about 800 jobs) and from the *Dictionary of Occupational Titles* (about 1,700 descriptions). O*NET stands for Occupational Information Network.

- *O*NET Dictionary of Occupational Titles.* Provides thorough descriptions for almost 1,000 jobs in the U.S. Department of Labor's O*NET database. These jobs cover a very high percentage of the job market, and this book is the most thorough printed source of the O*NET job information. Descriptions include details on related skills, earnings, abilities, education, projected growth, and more.

- *Best Jobs for the 21st Century.* Emphasizes jobs with fast growth, high pay, or large numbers of openings. It includes over 500 descriptions plus many useful lists such as highest paying, best overall, and best at various levels of education.

- *Career Guide to Industries.* Similar to the *Occupational Outlook Handbook* but reviews trends, jobs, and earnings in major industries. While most people think in terms of jobs, the industry you work in is often just as important.

- *Quick Guide to College Majors Careers.* If you are considering college, this book presents highly reliable information on over 100 college majors and the jobs related to the majors.

- **Other research options.** You can find career information at libraries, at school career centers, through professional associations (which are listed in the *OOH*), and from people you know who work in jobs that interest you. The Internet offers a multitude of career sites. Start with the Department of Labor's site at www.stats.bls.com, which includes access to the job descriptions in the *OOH* and other labor market information. And the site at www.jist.com lists recommended sites with information on career, education, and related topics.

Job Exploration Worksheet

The "Career Interests-to-Jobs Chart" has helped you identify job titles that interest you most. Now it is time to look more closely at these options. This worksheet helps you collect additional information on specific jobs. Make one photocopy of the worksheet for each job title you research. Start by getting more information on the jobs you listed in "Your Top Five Job Titles" at the end of the "Career Interests-to-Jobs Chart." Use the reference sources listed in the previous section to do your research.

Basic Information on This Job

Job title _____

Interest area _____

Source(s) of information used to research this job _____

_____

More Information on This Job

What do people in this job do? _____

_____

_____

_____

_____

_____

Key skills and abilities this job requires _____

_____

_____

Training, education, other qualifications needed _____

_____

Projected growth rate _____

Average earnings (national)_____

(continues)

(continued)

Working conditions _____

_____

Is this job likely to include your most important values? _____

Related jobs _____

_____

Your Observations

What are the negatives about this job? _____

_____

On a scale of 1 to 10, how interested are you in this job in relation to others? _____

What more do need to know about this job before you can make a decision? _____

_____

_____

_____

What barriers do you face in getting this job, and how might you overcome them? _____

_____

_____

_____

What could you do now to begin preparing for this job? _____

_____

_____

_____

Other Points to Consider in Your Planning

Planning your career is complicated. There are many things you should consider, and you will probably change your career plans in the future. This chapter can't cover everything you might consider, but I hope it helps. Here are some other things to consider:

- **Self-employment.** While much of this book teaches you how to find a job, many of its techniques can help you become self-employed or start a business. The Small Business Administration at www.sba.gov offers reading materials and courses, the library has many books and magazines, and the Internet features a great amount of related information.

- **Military careers.** Many people make their careers in the military, since it offers excellent training, education benefits, and other advantages. A good book titled *America's Top Military Careers* reviews each service branch plus gives information on 197 military occupations, training and education options, pay, advancement, and more.

- **Education and training.** Better-paying jobs typically (but not always) require higher levels of training or education. As you explore career options, you are likely to consider additional training or education to reach your goals. Look to your school counseling office, the library, or the Internet for information.

- **Volunteer work.** Volunteer jobs can give you excellent work experience and "employers" who can provide recommendation letters. Once again, a variety of good books and Internet sites discuss the many opportunities available.

- **All jobs teach you something.** Don't ignore the learning opportunities that part-time, summer, and "survival" jobs can offer. For example, someone working as a waiter must (to do well) work quickly, get along with difficult people, be pleasant, and handle stress. These skills are needed in many other jobs and can be emphasized to help you get them. If you are in a situation where you need "a" job, consider looking for one related to your interests. The experience and the contacts can help you land a more desirable, related job in the future.

What Do You Want to Do Next?

I hope this chapter helps you decide on both short-term and long-term goals. As I said earlier, you will never be finished with your career and life planning. You will probably need to keep revising your plans as you learn and experience more.

In fact, most people are not at all positive about what they want to do long term. That's OK. For example, I have different interests now than I did ten years ago and am likely to have different ones ten years from now. If you are not certain about what you want to do for the rest of your life, relax. A better career-planning question for you to consider might be "What do I want to do next?" Think about it. Then develop a plan to move in that direction.

CHAPTER 6

Some Job Search Methods Work Better Than Others

Finding a Job Is a Job

Finding a good job often takes longer than most people think. The average adult spends two to three months looking for a new job. In some cases, luck helps someone get hired quickly. For most people, however, finding a job takes more than luck.

The truth is that almost everyone who wants one will eventually find a job. Since this is so, your task in the job search is to accomplish two simple things:

1. Reduce the time it takes to find a job.
2. Get a better job than you might otherwise.

In this chapter and the next one, I review all major job search methods. While any job search method can work well for some people, certain methods have been proven to reduce the time it takes to find a job. Other methods help you find openings that are a better match to what you want to do. These more effective methods tend to be active rather than passive and help you find jobs that are not advertised or widely known about. As a result, people using these methods often face less direct competition and are more likely to find jobs that closely match their skills.

List All the Job Search Methods You Can Think of

People use many different methods to find jobs. List as many as you can think of in the spaces below.

_____	_____
_____	_____
_____	_____
_____	_____
_____	_____

Which Methods Do You Think Are Most Effective?

Some job search techniques are used by more people than others. Some methods work better than others. Think about your own experiences and those of people you know. Which five job search techniques do you think work best? List them here, beginning with the most effective method, followed by the second most effective method, and so on. The answers appear at the end of the chapter on pages 87–88.

1. _____

2. _____

3. _____

4. _____

5. _____

What We Know About the Job Market and How People Find Jobs

Before reviewing specific job search methods, consider the following important points about the job market and the job search.

At Any One Time, There Are Lots of Openings

According to the U.S. Department of Labor, the United States has about 150 million workers. During the course of a year, there will be about 30 million job openings due to growth and replacement needs. While no one knows how many jobs are available on any given day, the numbers are huge.

And this counts only formally open jobs. Employers without a formal opening may hire someone if they like the person and see a need for the person's skills. These potential openings are not counted anywhere.

There Is No Organized System for People to Find Jobs—or for Employers to Hire People

Although millions of jobs are open today, the problem is that you don't know where they are. Yes, you can find some openings in the want ads. Public and private employment agencies list others. Many openings are posted on the Internet. Still, if you put all these advertised sources together, they list less than 35 or so percent of the jobs available.

No one place exists for finding out about all—or even most—job openings. This is an obvious problem for you, the job seeker.

Why Most Jobs Are Never Advertised

Most jobs are never advertised. Why not? Think about it for a bit. Then write three reasons below.

1. _____

2. _____

3. _____

Employers Don't Like to Advertise and Often Don't Need To

It would be nice if you could find out about all job openings from one source. Unfortunately, no such resource exists. One reason is that this is a free country. Employers can find their employees in any way they want. Employers don't advertise openings for many reasons. The most common ones are

- They don't like to.

- They often don't need to.

Why don't employers like to advertise job openings? When employers put an ad in the paper or post an opening on the Internet, they end up interviewing strangers. Plus, most employers are not trained interviewers and don't enjoy it. Finally, the screening and interviewing process takes lots of time and can be very expensive.

A few thoughts on interviewing strangers: Research suggests that hiring strangers is not the best way to find good employees. John Wanous, a researcher at Ohio State University, analyzed data from 28 studies of 39,000 employees. He found that new hires are more likely to stay on a job if recruited through inside sources instead of ads and employment agencies. Long-term success increases by 25 percent or more when new employees are referred by former employees, current employees, or internal postings.

While most employers don't know about this research, they know that hiring strangers is not the best way to find good people. They have learned that interviews and background checks are not very reliable.

When unemployment is low, employers will use any method to find the people they need. This is most true for jobs that are hard to fill, such as entry-level, technical, and high-skills openings. Even in these situations, employers prefer to hire people recommended by someone they trust.

And why don't employers often need to advertise? It makes sense that employers would rather hire people they know. This is why most jobs are filled before advertising is needed. The employer may know someone who seems to be right for the job. Or someone hears about an opening through someone else and gets an interview before the job is advertised.

The point to remember is that about 65 percent of all job openings are never advertised. These unadvertised jobs are often the best jobs, and knowing how to find them can make a big difference to you.

Most People Work for Small Employers, Yet Most Job Search Methods Were Developed by or for Large Employers

Years ago, most people worked for large employers. Many traditional job search methods were developed by these large employers to make it easier for them to screen applicants. For example, application forms collect information to help large personnel departments review applicants more quickly. In job search books written by people who worked in corporate personnel departments, the authors recommend techniques such as writing an attention-getting resume to help it stand out in a pile of boring resumes.

But things have changed. Most people now work for smaller employers. These employers don't have human resources departments! What this means is that job seekers need very different techniques to find openings in smaller organizations.

Small employers are even more important when you consider that they create most new jobs. The U.S. Small Business Administration found that very small employers, those with twenty or fewer workers, created about half of all new jobs. Small employers are too important to ignore in your job search.

Most People Work in Small Organizations

Almost two-thirds of all nongovernment workers are employed by small organizations!

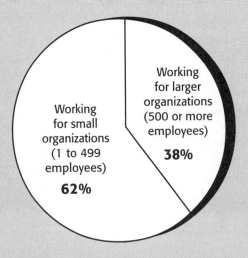

Working for small organizations (1 to 499 employees) **62%**

Working for larger organizations (500 or more employees) **38%**

Source: U.S. Department of Labor, Current Population Survey. Includes workers in private firms plus self-employed workers.

The Clearer You Are About What You Want, the More Likely You Are to Find It

Job seekers often look for any job. They look through want ads and other sources and will apply for anything they think they might get. Instead, as I say in earlier chapters, I recommend that you be clear about the job you would most like to have. Then look for employers who are most likely to have that kind of work.

Most Job Seekers Don't Spend a Lot of Time Looking

Past research found that few unemployed people spend more than fifteen to twenty hours a week looking for work. As a result, they get relatively few interviews and are unemployed longer than they need to be. Instead, looking for a job should be your full-time job when you are unemployed! It's a simple idea: The more time you spend looking, the more likely you are to get job offers.

Job Seekers Don't Use the Most Effective Methods

Looking for work is not easy. Looking for a job using traditional job search methods can be discouraging. Traditional methods include responding to want ads, mailing resumes to employers, and answering want ads. Traditional methods don't work all that well, and most people get discouraged after using them and not getting results.

"Friction" Affects the Job Market

The U.S. Department of Labor found that many jobs are available at the same time that many qualified applicants are looking for them. The problem is that the job seeker and the employer have not yet found each other. This time between a job becoming open and being filled is responsible, they found, for about 40 percent of total unemployment. They called this inefficiency in the labor market "frictional unemployment." What this means is that, today, an employer wants to hire someone with your skills. All you have to do is find that employer. That is where more effective job search methods can help.

Frictional Unemployment Happens When Job Seekers Cannot Find a Job Match for Their Skills

Frictional unemployment adds thirty-plus days to the job search. Other types of unemployment also affect a job search. "Cyclical unemployment" occurs in a sluggish business cycle. "Structural unemployment" happens during the restructuring of work performed in the U.S.

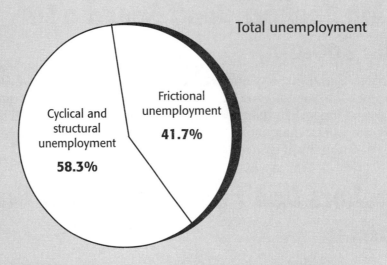

Total unemployment

Frictional
unemployment
41.7%

Cyclical and
structural
unemployment
58.3%

Based on Department of Labor data used in *The Job Market* by Richard Lathrop, National Center for Job Market Studies, Washington, D.C.

Job Search Methods People Actually Use

Earlier in this chapter, I asked you to write down all the job search methods you could think of. The U.S. Department of Labor conducts a regular survey of unemployed people who are actively looking for work. The results of this survey are presented on the next page. The survey shows the percentage of job seekers who used each method listed.

Survey Results Showing Percentage of Unemployed Using Various Job Search Methods

- Contacted employers directly: 64.5%

- Sent out resumes/filled out applications: 48.3%

- Contacted public employment agency: 20.4%

- Placed or answered help wanted ads: 14.5%

- Contacted friends or relatives: 13.5%

- Contacted private employment agency: 6.6%

- Used other active search methods: 4.4%

- Contacted school employment center: 2.3%

- Checked union or professional registers: 1.5%

Source: U.S. Department of Labor, Current Population Survey

Compare Your List to Actual Job Search Methods

Look over the information above and compare it to the job search methods you listed in the first worksheet on page 73. Did you list methods not given in the survey above? What are your observations on the differences between your list and the survey answers? Write your observations.

_____

_____

_____

_____

_____

_____

Some Observations on the Survey

The information from the survey is interesting but limited. Here are some of my observations:

- **The survey collected information on just nine job search methods.** The people in the survey were asked if they had used each method listed. They either did or did not. They may have used other methods, but that information was not collected.

- **What about the Internet?** The survey did not ask if people had used the Internet to look for job openings. This is an important question, since many people use the Internet—and many job-seeking resources are available there. I say more about using the Internet in your job search in just a bit.

- **What about the results of each method?** The survey only tells you that job seekers used certain job search methods. It does not say if a method worked in finding job leads or in getting job offers. Unfortunately, there has not been much recent research on the effectiveness of various job search methods. Most of what we know is based on older research and the observations of people who work with job seekers. I share information on the effectiveness of various techniques in the pages that follow.

Some Job Search Methods Work Better Than Others

As the survey of job search methods shows, most people use more than one job search technique. For example, one person might read want ads, fill out applications, and ask his friends for job leads. Another might post her resume on Web sites, contact everyone she knows from professional contacts, and sign up at one or more employment agencies. Other job seekers use different methods and in different combinations.

While job seekers usually use a variety of job search methods, some methods are more likely to result in interviews and offers. Studies show that the more effective methods include contacting friends and relatives and contacting employers directly. These two methods will be covered in more detail in the next chapter.

Which methods are best for you? The truth is, every job search method works for some people. But experience and research show that some methods are more effective than others. The best approach is to understand the different job search methods as described next and in Chapter 7, and to use a variety of methods during your job search.

Job Seeking on the Internet

The "Survey Results Showing Percentage of Unemployed Using Various Job Search Methods" did not include information on the Internet. But it is obvious that more and more people are using the Internet to find job leads. Thousands of Internet sites are devoted to the job search, and more are launched each week. In many ways, the Internet has adapted many of the traditional job search methods. Here are some examples.

- **Traditional way:** Mail out resumes to employers and hope they call you for an interview. **Internet way:** Post your resume on an Internet resume site and hope employers contact you.

- **Traditional way:** Visit an employer's office, and then ask for an application to fill out or drop off a resume. **Internet way:** Visit an employer's Web site and e-mail your resume for consideration.

- **Traditional way:** Call an employer and ask to speak with the person in charge. **Internet way:** Visit a targeted employer's Web site and e-mail a request for the name of the best person to contact about your interest in a job.

- **Traditional way:** Ask friends and relatives for names of people to contact who might know of an opening. **Internet way:** E-mail friends and relatives rather than call. In addition, some interest group e-mail lists may allow you to post a request for job referrals. Or you may get leads from chat group members.

But how many people get jobs through the Internet? No one knows for sure. In a study detailed in an article titled "Jobseeking on the Internet," the U.S. Department of Labor found that

- About 60 percent of unemployed job seekers who used the Internet from a home computer also used the Internet to look for jobs.

- About 7 percent of people who are currently employed had recently used the Internet to look for jobs.

- Unemployed people who use the Internet are more likely to use a variety of job search methods. They had higher rates of use in all but two of the job search methods listed in the "Survey Results Showing Percentage of Unemployed Using Various Job Search Methods" presented earlier. The only methods they used less were "contacted employers directly" and "contacted friends or relatives."

While this study did not report how effective the Internet was in finding jobs, it does show that job seekers are using the Internet more and more. And it indicates that many are using it to replace or partly replace the nine methods traditionally measured by the Department of Labor.

Overall, job seekers increased their use of only two of the nine traditional job search methods, "sending resumes" and "other active methods," during a five-year period when use of the Internet grew rapidly. They decreased their use of all other methods during this time. For example, there was a 25 percent reduction in users of public employment agencies during the study period.

My conclusion is that many people are using the Internet to replace the traditional methods measured by the Department of Labor. That is why,

(continues)

(continued)

for example, "other active methods" increased. Job seekers are using the Internet to send resumes and make direct contacts with employers. It's logical.

Like the telephone, the Internet can be an important tool in the job search. As with other job search methods, the Internet should be one of several methods used and not the only one.

While thousands of Internet sites exist, my concern is that many encourage a passive approach. Simply posting your resume on Web sites works for some, but a more active approach will work better.

Listing Internet job sites is not practical here, since there are so many and they change so often. I do list some sites throughout this book. A source of helpful Internet resources appears at www.jist.com, which lists sites for job search, education, training, and career information.

Get the Most Out of Less Effective Job Search Methods

You should consider using the less effective job search methods. Each of these methods works for some people, and I provide tips here to increase their effectiveness.

Newspaper Help Wanted Ads

Only about 15 percent of all people get their jobs through the want ads. This means that 85 percent find their jobs using other methods. Everyone who reads the paper knows about these job openings, so competition for advertised jobs is fierce. Still, some people get jobs this way, so go ahead and apply. Just be sure to spend most of your time using more effective methods.

Tips

- **Read the want ads on a regular basis.** Sunday and Wednesday newspaper editions usually have the most ads. Look at every ad. Jobs of interest may not be listed in an obvious way. For example, an accounting job could be listed under "bookkeeper," "accountant," "controller," or some other heading.

- **Respond to any ad that sounds interesting, even if you don't have all qualifications listed.** Employers sometimes list skills they do not require to find the most ideal candidates.

- **If possible, contact the employer directly.** Instead of sending a resume or completing an application, call and ask for the person who supervises the position you want. Ask for an appointment to discuss the position. This sometimes works and can reduce your chances of being screened out.

- **Look at old want ads.** Organizations that are hiring often have openings they have not yet advertised. Also, jobs advertised in past weeks may still be open, and you could be the only candidate at this point!

- **Read want ads during the evenings and weekends.** Save weekdays for making direct contacts with employers.

Internet Tips

- **Many company sites have want ads.** In addition, these sites sometimes provide details on pay, benefits, and working conditions, and even allow you to interact with current employees via e-mail.

- **Numerous sites post job openings from many employers.** Employers provide a brief want ad and frequently give additional details not often available in a newspaper, such as a job description.

- **Most Internet job listings ask you to send a resume in electronic form.** Electronic resumes are covered Chapter 13.

- **Be careful and formal in the e-mail you send to an employer who lists a job on the Internet.** Errors in spelling and grammar will hurt you, so be careful about what you say and how you say it.

- **As with newspaper want ads, don't hold your breath waiting for a response.** You will never hear from many employers.

The Employment Service and One-Stop Centers—Free Employment Help Available to All

There are two basic types of employment agencies. One is operated by the government and is free. The other is run as a for-profit business and charges a fee. There are advantages and disadvantages to each. I'll start with the employment agency run by the government.

Each state has a network of local offices to pay unemployment compensation, provide job leads, and offer other services. These services are given without charge to you and to employers. The service's name varies by state, and it may be called "Job Service," "Department of Labor," "Unemployment Office," "Workforce Development," or another name. Many states now provide a variety of employment services through "One-Stop Centers." These centers may provide career reference books, computerized career information systems and job listings, and other resources. You may even see the service's computer screens in malls and other public places, listing jobs and offering information.

Nationally, only about 5 to 6 percent of job seekers get their jobs here. The service typically lists only 5 to 10 percent of the openings in a region. But, in some areas, the local office may list as many as 30 percent of the jobs in an area.

Tips

- **Most offices require you to go to their physical location to apply for unemployment compensation.** But many of their resources, such as job listings and career information, are available online or through computer systems at the offices.

- **Visit your local office early in your job search.** Find out if you qualify for unemployment compensation and learn more about its services. Look into it—the price is right.

- **Employment service offices list local openings and have computer access to details on openings nationwide.** Ask for referrals to jobs you qualify for, and the office will send you to employers with openings.

- **Some states provide substantial help.** Assistance comes in the form of job search workshops, career reference materials, computer and Internet access, and more. Ask about various services and use any that might help you.

- **Look into special services.** You may be eligible for programs that help people with disabilities, veterans, laid-off workers, youth, older workers, women, the economically disadvantaged, and other groups.

Internet Tips

- **Check out a Web site run by the federal government.** It's at www.doleta.gov/uses/ and gives lots of information on the various programs provided by the employment service. It also provides links to many useful sites.

- **Jobs listed with each local office are posted on the Internet for America's Job Bank at www.ajb.dni.us.** The site lists approximately a million openings on any given day and many millions during the year. You can search for jobs by region and other criteria.

Private Employment Agencies

Private employment agencies are businesses that charge a fee either to you or to the employer who hires you. You often see their ads in the help wanted section of the newspaper, and many have Web sites. Fees can be from less than one month's pay to 15 percent or more of your annual salary.

Be careful about using fee-based employment agencies. Recent research indicates that more people use and benefit from fee-based agencies than in the past. But you need to realize that relatively few people who register with private agencies get a job through them.

Tips

- **If your skills are in demand and you have a clear job objective, an agency is more likely to help you.** For example, an experienced accountant, medical technician, or carpenter is more likely to get good results than a teacher or someone wanting to change careers.

- **Ask for job leads where the employer pays the fee.** Unless the employer pays the fee, using a private employment agency can be very expensive and is not a good idea for most people.

- **Do not sign an agreement until you take it home and read it carefully.** If you are pressured to sign anything during your first visit, refuse to sign it and leave.

- **Many agency workers find their clients jobs by calling employers.** The agencies ask employers if they have any job openings and use methods you can use yourself. So consider doing the work and saving a bundle.

- **Some agencies will pressure you to accept any job they can talk you into to collect their fee.** If pressured to take a job, say you want to think about it overnight. Do not accept a job you do not want!

- **Watch want ads placed by these agencies.** The advertised position may not be available, and the agency may refer you to a less desirable job.

- **If you decide to use a private agency, continue to look for jobs on your own.** Any agreement you sign should not require you to pay a fee for a job that you find yourself or limit your job search in any way.

- **Understand that executive search firms are specialized fee-based agencies.** Sometimes call "headhunters," these agencies are paid by employers to find already employed people with excellent work histories. With few exceptions, they are not interested in unemployed people who are looking for jobs.

Internet Tips

- **Most private employment agencies have Web sites.** These sites often list their openings and provide other information. You can also find these agencies in the yellow pages.

- **A Web site run by the federal government lists many of these agencies.** Go to www.ajb.dni.us.

Temporary Agencies Can Make Sense

Temporary agencies offer jobs lasting from several days to many months. They charge the employer a bit more than you are paid and keep the difference, so you pay no direct fee. Many private employment agencies now provide temporary jobs as well. Temp agencies have grown rapidly in recent years for good reason. They provide employers with short-term help, and employers often use them to find people they may want to hire later. Temp agencies can help you survive between jobs, get experience in different work settings, and may lead to a long-term job offer. They provide a very good option while you look for a long-term job, and you may get a job offer while working in a temp job.

Mailing Resumes and Posting Them on the Web

Many job search "experts" suggest that sending out lots of "powerful" resumes is a great job search technique. That advice probably helps sell their resume books, but mailing out resumes to people you do not know has never been an effective approach. Every so often it works, but a 5 percent or lower response rate and few interviews are the more common outcome. Posting your resume on one or more Internet employment sites makes a bit more sense; more on this later.

Tips

- **Very few people get a job by sending resumes to people they do not know.** It is almost always better to contact the employer in person, by phone, or by e-mail first. Then send your resume before the interview.

- **Make sure you have a presentable resume as soon as you start your job search.** Do a simple one at first. You can always do a better one later. See Chapter 13 for help.

- **Give your resume to friends, relatives, and anyone else you can think of.** Ask them to pass it along to anyone they think might know of an opening for someone with your skills.

Internet Tips

- **Mailing your resume to people you don't know does not make much sense, but posting it on the Internet might.** Putting your resume into an Internet database allows it to be accessed by many potential employers. The posting does not take much time, and it saves the cost of stamps. The chapter on resumes gives you more advice on this topic.

- **People with in-demand technical and other skills are most likely to get responses from posting their resumes.**

- **You can do a variety of things to increase your resume's effectiveness on the Internet.** I cover these points in Chapter 13.

Filling Out Applications

Most employers require you to complete an application. But you need to know that employers use applications to screen people out. This is why you need to fill them out carefully.

Tips

- **Application forms are designed to collect negative information.** For example, forms ask for your education and training history. If yours is not the best, you will often be screened out, even if you can do the job.

- **Employers filling entry-level jobs rely heavily on applications as a hiring tool.** This is why young people have more success in using applications to find jobs than more experienced workers do.

- **Many employers require that you complete an application before you are hired.** The form collects information that employers need and that is usually not on a resume. So you need to know how to complete applications carefully. Chapter 8 covers this topic.

- **When you fill out an application, make it neat and error-free and do not include anything that could get you screened out.** If necessary, leave a problem section blank. It can always be explained after you get an interview.

- **Your best approach is to ask to talk to the person who will make the hiring decision.** If you are required to fill out an application first, you should still ask for an interview. It is always better to ask to see the person in charge. Fill out an application if you are asked to, but don't expect it to get you an interview.

Internet Tip

Some employers now require you to complete an application on a computer at their office or at a Web site before you get an interview. The forms usually ask questions similar to those on paper application forms. Chapter 8 gives lots of tips to help you complete electronic and paper applications.

School and Other Employment Centers

Contacting the school employment center is one of the job search methods included in the survey presented earlier in this chapter. Only a small percentage of people said they used this method. This is probably because very few people in the survey had a school employment center available to them. If you do, find out about its services. Some school employment centers have many resources, including resume-writing software, job opening lists, career interest tests, and career reference books.

Similar employment center programs are available to veterans, people with disabilities, welfare recipients, union members, professional groups, and many others. Some programs are excellent, and some provide valuable resources such as child-care assistance to job seekers, education and training assistance, individual counseling, and medical benefits. If you qualify for employment assistance from your school or other source, consider using it.

How People Find Jobs

Various studies have been done to find out how people find jobs. There are a number of ways to approach this topic, and many of the studies don't come up with the same data. One of the biggest surveys of unemployed people is part of the Current Population Survey. The Census Bureau gives this survey to thousands of U.S. households on a regular basis. The survey asks the employment status of those surveyed and, if unemployed, what job search methods were used by the them. Unfortunately, the survey does not ask which approaches worked.

On one occasion, special questions were added to the survey that asked which job search techniques resulted in the unemployed finding their most recent job. At that time, the two most effective methods were contacting an employer directly and getting leads from friends or relatives. Since then, a variety of studies have been done on how people find jobs, but none surveyed as large a group. One study conducted by the U.S. Department of Labor, titled "Jobseeking on the Internet," included data on those using the Internet in their job search. Once again, though, they did not measure the effectiveness of the Internet in landing a job.

So, having looked at the available research on how people actually find jobs, I present the following data on the major techniques. These figures are approximate, but they are supported by a variety of research findings.

How People Find Jobs

- Heard about opening from someone they know (including friends, relatives, and acquaintances): 35%

- Contacted employer directly: 30%

- Answered a want ad: 14%

(continues)

(continued)

- Referred by private employment agency: 6%
- Referred by the public employment service: 5%
- Other methods (referred by school, took civil service test, referred by union, placed ads in journals, and so on): 10%

P.S. We know that some people are getting their jobs from leads they obtain on the Internet. Each method listed here most likely includes job seekers who used the Internet. For example, of those who "contacted an employer directly" to get their jobs, some mailed in a resume, and others knocked on the door, completed an application, used the phone, or made an Internet contact of some kind. People use the Internet as another tool in their job search. Some Internet users go directly to an employer's site and submit their resumes online. Others use e-mail to contact people they know and ask for job leads. Still others go to Internet resume banks or sites listing openings and then post their resumes or search for jobs.

So the Internet's effect on the job search is hidden somewhat. I will continue to look for more data and, if you find any, please consider forwarding it to me via editorial@jist.com. Thanks!

Active Job Search Methods Work Better Than Passive Ones

I say earlier that any job search method will work for some people some of the time. I also said that the best approach is to use a variety of job search methods. When planning which methods to use, the wise thing to do is to try those that are most effective.

One thing that separates more effective job search methods from less effective ones is that effective methods tend to be active rather than passive. For example, filling out an application is passive, since it requires the employer to contact you back. A more active approach is to contact the employer directly and ask for an interview. You could do this by walking in and asking for the manager, using the phone and asking for an appointment, or sending an e-mail requesting an interview. Those are active methods. Later, you can complete the application.

Passive job search methods are more likely to result in an employer not contacting you at all. Think about it. If you fill out an application and leave, you may not hear from that employer. But if you drop in and ask to talk to the person who does the hiring, you are more likely to get an interview right then.

In the next chapter, you learn about more active job search methods. These approaches are designed to help you find the two out of three or so of all openings that are never advertised. An effective job search will use both passive and active techniques, with an emphasis on active methods. It just makes sense.

CHAPTER 7

How to Find Jobs in the Hidden Job Market

Traditional Job Search Methods Won't Uncover Most Jobs

The last chapter reviewed several traditional job search methods. These include answering want ads, getting job leads from public and private employment agencies, and getting leads from school employment centers. While many people use those methods, relatively few people get their jobs through them. There are two good reasons for this:

- Those methods concentrate on the 35 percent or so of all jobs that are advertised.

- Almost anyone who is looking can find out about them.

If you use only traditional job search methods, you are unlikely to find out about the 65 percent or so of the jobs that are never advertised. These jobs are in what is called the "hidden job market." These jobs are available, and people get hired for them, but they are hidden from someone looking for a job using conventional methods. This chapter is about using job search methods to help you find this hidden job market.

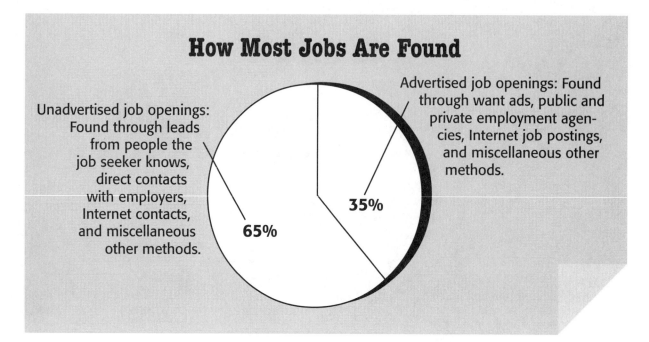

How Most Jobs Are Found

Unadvertised job openings: Found through leads from people the job seeker knows, direct contacts with employers, Internet contacts, and miscellaneous other methods.

Advertised job openings: Found through want ads, public and private employment agencies, Internet job postings, and miscellaneous other methods.

65%

35%

Look for Jobs *Before* They Open

The job search, for most people, is a search for open positions. That makes sense, and all conventional job search methods take that approach. The problem is that this results in your missing many of the best opportunities. Instead, I suggest that

Your job search should be a search for employers who need your skills, whether or not a job is open now.

This is a *very* different approach to the job search. It allows you to talk to employers *before* a job is available. You can, of course, also look for openings that exist now.

The fact is that jobs are always available, but getting them depends on the methods you use. In the last chapter, I mention that two job search methods work better than others. They are getting leads from people you know (friends, relatives, and others) and making direct contact with employers. I cover these approaches in this chapter.

The Four Stages of a Job Opening

If you look just for advertised jobs, you will never know about the good jobs that are not advertised. Someone else will get them. But how do you find these openings if they're not advertised? You have to learn to find employers *before* they advertise the job you want.

Most jobs don't simply pop open. They are created over time. Carefully study the graphic that follows. It shows how most jobs open up and get filled. Notice that about 65 percent of all jobs get filled by the third stage. That is why so few jobs are advertised—most are filled before they need to be.

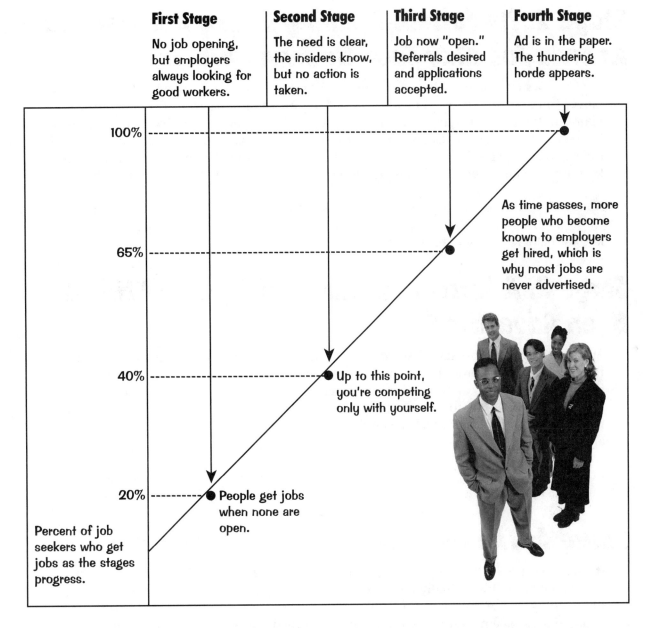

First Stage	Second Stage	Third Stage	Fourth Stage
No job opening, but employers always looking for good workers.	The need is clear, the insiders know, but no action is taken.	Job now "open." Referrals desired and applications accepted.	Ad is in the paper. The thundering horde appears.

100% ●

As time passes, more people who become known to employers get hired, which is why most jobs are never advertised.

65% ●

40% ● Up to this point, you're competing only with yourself.

20% ● People get jobs when none are open.

Percent of job seekers who get jobs as the stages progress.

All jobs open up in stages, creating opportunities for those who contact employers before a job is advertised. Your task in this chapter is to learn how to find job opportunities before they are advertised. The graphic presents an important idea—that a job opening happens in stages. Let's look at the four stages in more detail.

Stage 1: There Is No Opening Now

If you contact an employer at this stage and ask if the company has any openings, the employer will say no. If you go about your job search in the traditional way, you would not even talk to this employer. Yet, should an opening come up in the future, this employer will first consider people he or she knows.

About 20 percent of all people get their jobs by becoming known to employers during this stage, before an opening exists.

Stage 2: No Formal Opening Exists, But Insiders Know a Job May Soon Be Available

As time goes on, someone inside an organization knows that a need exists for a new employee in the future. Perhaps business is picking up. Or a new product or marketing plan is in the works. Maybe someone is getting ready to leave or will be fired. If you ask the boss if a job opening exists at this stage, you will probably be told no once again—unless you happen ask the right person in that organization. And most job seekers will keep looking elsewhere, not seeing the job that was about to open up right before them.

About 40 percent of all jobs are filled by people who come to know an employer before the end of this stage, when no job is formally open but someone in the organization knows that a job is likely to become available soon.

Stage 3: A Formal Opening Exists, But It Has Not Been Advertised

At some point, the boss says that, yes, there is a job opening. Maybe someone suddenly resigned or that big order just arrived. People who work for the company know about the opening, but it is often days or weeks before it is advertised. If you happen to ask if there is a job opening now, you will finally be told that, yes, there is. If you are fortunate to be at this place at this time (and with the right credentials), you will probably get an interview.

But the problem is that, for those who see the job search as a search for advertised openings, most jobs get filled before or at this stage. Those jobs never need to be advertised.

Stage 4: The Position Is Finally Advertised

If a job does not get filled by insider referrals, by someone the boss knows, or by other informal means, it will finally be made known to the public. An employer might post the opening on the Internet or run an ad in the newspaper. A sign may be hung in the window, and the employment service may be notified. Since anyone looking for a job can now find out about it, dozens or hundreds of people apply for it. That is why the competition for these relatively few advertised jobs is so fierce.

But relatively few jobs make it this far. All the others, including many of the best ones, are filled before they need to be advertised.

Your Job Search Should Seek Employers at All Stages of an Opening

To succeed in your job search, you should get to employers at all stages of an opening. This means contacting employers in the first, second, and third phases, before the position is publicly available.

Of course, you should also go after advertised openings—those in the fourth stage. But you must realize that most jobs will not be advertised. The job search methods presented in this chapter have proven to work better than more traditional approaches. They can help you find better jobs, and they can help you find them in less time.

The Two Job Search Methods That Work Best

The two job search methods that work for most people are getting leads from someone they know and contacting employers directly.

A variety of job search methods fall under these general types. To help you understand the different methods, I've come to call them "warm contacts" and "cold contacts." When you ask for help or advice from people you know, you are using warm contacts. When you contact people you don't know, you are talking to cold contacts.

Both methods can be very effective if used properly. Since it is often easier to contact people you know, I begin with warm contacts. Cold contact methods are covered later in this chapter.

Get Leads from People You Know—Your Warm Contacts

The people you know form a support network. A network is an informal group of people who have something in common. As a job seeker, your network is made up of all the people who can help you—and the people they know. Networking is the process you use in contacting these people. You may be surprised at how many people you can meet this way. Let's look at how networking works.

Start with the People You Know

Your friends and relatives are the people most willing to help you find a job. And they can provide valuable leads to the people they know. To see how networking can work for you, begin by writing the names of three friends or relatives on the following lines.

1. _____

2. _____

3. _____

Networking Can Result in Thousands of Contacts

Now take the first person on the list as an example. If you ask that person for the names of two people, you will have two new contacts. Continue the process, and your network will look like the following:

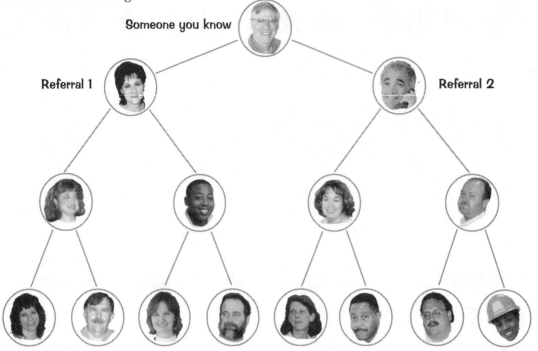

Someone you know

Referral 1

Referral 2

If you ask each referral for two names and follow through, your network will soon look like this:

The number of people you could contact this way is amazing. For example, if you kept getting two referrals from each person, you would have 1,024 people in your network after the tenth level of contact. And that is starting with only one person!

You can network using the phone, making face-to-face contact, and via e-mail. Networking is a simple idea, and it works. It helps you meet potential employers you would not find through any other method. These potential employers are a friend of a friend of a friend. And they will be willing to see you for this reason.

Effective Networking Requires Clear Goals

Networking is a very effective job search method. If you do it well, networking will help you contact many potential employers. To be effective, your networking must begin with clear goals. Think in advance what you want to accomplish when you contact someone in your network. Write your networking goals below.

_____

_____

_____

_____

Three Important Networking Goals

Following are three goals that experience shows are very important to keep in mind for each networking contact.

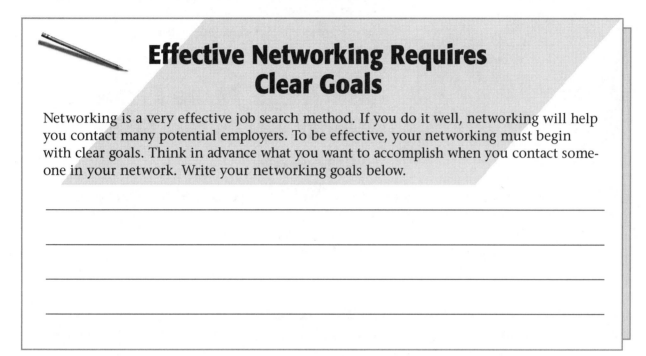

1. **Select good contacts.** It is possible to begin networking with anyone who knows people and is willing to talk to you. But people who know and like you are often the best ones to use as your first contacts. Select friends and relatives who are likely to have good contacts or who know something about the type of work you want. The people they refer you to are likely to know even more about the job you want, or have better contacts. As each person in your network refers you to others, your contacts will more and more likely be those who hire people with your skills or those who know someone who does.

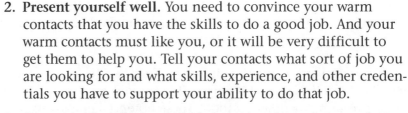

2. **Present yourself well.** You need to convince your warm contacts that you have the skills to do a good job. And your warm contacts must like you, or it will be very difficult to get them to help you. Tell your contacts what sort of job you are looking for and what skills, experience, and other credentials you have to support your ability to do that job.

3. **Get two referrals.** Sometimes a warm contact knows of an opening for someone with your interests. But more often, the contact will not. Your objective is to get the names and contact information of two people who could help you in your search.

Ask These Three Essential Questions to Get Good Referrals

To expand your network, it is important that you get names of other people to contact from each person in your network. Based on many years of experience, the three questions below are most likely to get you good referrals. Ask one question after another until you get the names of two more people to contact.

Three Essential Questions to Get Referrals

1. Do you know of anyone who might have a job opening in my field? If no, then ask…

2. Do you know of anyone who might know of someone who would? If still no, then ask…

3. Do you know someone who knows lots of people?

Even without job search training, most job seekers get leads from friends, relatives, and other people they know. But most job seekers do not use their contacts with people they know in an organized way. They get job leads in spite of not asking the three essential questions!

Even with training, most people don't ask the second and third questions. Because they don't ask, they do not get the good referrals that many people would otherwise give them. So ask the three questions throughout your job search. They work!

Networking Worksheet— Groups of People You Know

You already know many people who can help you. To identify them, it is helpful to think about the groups of people that have something in common with you. I list some of the groups most often listed by other job seekers. Look over the list of groups and put a check mark to the left of each group you are part of. Then add other groups not on the list. Use the listed groups for ideas and add others that make sense to you. Be specific. For example, write "people in my aerobics class" or "members of the association of collectible jelly jars." Finally, when you finish your list, go back and write in the number of people that might be in each group.

✓	Check If You Are in This Group	Other Groups You Are Part of
	Friends	
	Relatives	
	Friends of parents	
	Former coworkers	
	Members of my church or religious group	
	People who sell me things (store clerks, insurance agent, real estate agent, and so on)	
	Neighbors	
	People I went to school with	
	Former teachers	
	Members of social clubs	
	People who provide me with services (hair stylist, counselor, mechanic, and so on)	
	Former employers	
	Members of sports or hobby groups	
	Members of a professional organization I belong to (or could quickly join)	

Create a List of Networking Contacts for Each Contact Group

Most people never guess they have as many potential warm contacts as they do. The worksheet on the previous page can help you identify many people you might overlook. Yet most of these people will be willing to help you in your job search if you ask them nicely.

You may not know some of these people well or at all. But you have something in common with them. It is enough to allow you to talk to them. This takes some courage, but you will find that most people are willing to help if you ask them.

Each group on the previous worksheet can be used to create a list of names for your network. And these people can give you the names of others to contact. Following is a sample worksheet for just one of the groups on your list. Go ahead and complete it now. Later, you can do a similar list for each group you listed.

Networking Worksheet—Friends List

How many friends do you have? Don't limit yourself to close friends. Include anyone who is friendly to you. Think hard and guess how many friends' names you might be able to list.

Write the number here _____

Now list as many names of friends as you can think of below. You can use additional sheets later if you need more space. You also can add phone numbers and e-mail addresses later.

Name	Phone Number and/or E-Mail Address

Networking allows you to begin with people you know. They, in turn, will lead you to others you did not know previously. As each person refers you to others, you are more and more likely to get the names of people who are employers. Often very quickly, some of your referrals will supervise people with skills similar to yours, or give you names of others who do.

If you create lists for each group on your "Networking Worksheet—Groups of People You Know" list, you could end up with hundreds of names. Each person knows other people who will refer you to still others. If you keep at it, you will eventually meet someone who needs a worker with your skills. That might very well lead to a job offer. Networking that begins with your warm contacts may be the only job search method you need. It is very effective for finding unadvertised jobs.

Make Direct Contacts with Employers—Your Cold Contacts

Another effective job search technique is contacting employers directly. As you learned in the previous chapter, many job seekers use this method. It is also one of the two most effective job search methods.

Contacting people you don't know is called "cold contacting." The most common methods for making cold contacts are calling an employer on the phone without a referral and dropping in without an appointment. Both methods are covered here, along with tips to adapt these approaches for use on the Internet.

Use the Yellow Pages to Develop a Prospects List and Contact Employers

In any community, the best listing of organizations that might hire you appears in the phone book's yellow pages. The yellow pages provide an easy way to find potential employers and contact them by phone. In one hour, you could call ten to twenty employers. With the right approach, you could set up one or more interviews in a short time. The yellow pages are also available on the Internet, allowing you to get contact information for organizations anywhere in the country or the world.

You might be surprised at how many types of organizations could be job sources for you: small and large employers of all kinds and government employers, which are listed in a special section. Here is how to use the yellow pages to find potential employers.

Step 1. Find the index. The yellow pages have an index in the front that lists the types of organizations in general groupings. The groupings are arranged in alphabetic order.

Step 2. Select likely targets. Go through the index and, for each entry, ask yourself this question:

Could this type of organization use a person with my skills?

If the answer is yes or maybe, put a check by that type of organization.

Step 3. Prioritize those targets. For the types of organizations you checked, put a number next to each type based on how interesting it sounds to you. Use the following scale:

1 = Sounds very interesting

2 = Not sure if interested

3 = Does not sound interesting at all

Step 4. Call specific organizations. Once you have identified target groups, you can turn to the section of the yellow pages where those organizations are listed. Once there, you can use the phone numbers provided to call directly and ask for an interview.

Many Internet sites allow you to do the same research as with the printed yellow pages. Most allow you to sort by organization type and by city or region. If you want to relocate to another area, this can be a big help! Most major Internet providers, including America Online and MSN, have this feature.

Sample of a Completed Yellow Pages Index Section

I include part of a real page from a yellow pages index to show you how this process works. The person using it is looking for a job as computer-based graphic designer or desktop publishing professional. The check marks are for those organization types that might need these skills, and the numbers refer to the job seeker's interest level.

As you can see, this is a very good process for identifying opportunities you might otherwise overlook—and this is only one page from the index!

12 Hand-Hygienists

Yellow Pages Prospects Worksheet

Get your hands on the yellow pages and use the index to identify at least twenty types of organizations you might contact. Then use this worksheet to write them down, along with your interest level.

Type of Target Organization	Level of Interest*
1.	
2.	
3.	
4.	
5.	

(continues)

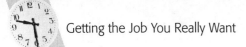
(continued)

Type of Target Organization	Level of Interest*
6.	
7.	
8.	
9.	
10.	
11.	
12.	
13.	
14.	
15.	
16.	
17.	
18.	
19.	
20.	

* Level of interest codes: 1 = Sounds very interesting. 2 = Not sure if interested. 3 = Does not sound interesting at all.

You now have a list of types of organizations you can contact. All you need to do is turn to the section of the yellow pages for each type of organization, business, and service. There you will find specific names of organizations and their phone numbers. You can call these places and ask to speak with the person in charge of the department or function you're interested in.

Although this sounds easy, making effective phone calls takes practice. You will learn much more about how to make effective phone calls to these cold contacts in Chapter 10.

Many organizations listed in the yellow pages have Web sites that provide additional information. Call and ask for a company's Web address, particularly before an interview. You can also do a search for the company or organization's name.

Drop in on Employers Without an Appointment

If you look, you have many opportunities to make direct contacts with employers during your job search. For example, on your way home from an interview, look for other places that might use someone with your skills. Stop in and ask to see the person in charge. In smaller organizations, this will usually be the manager or owner. In larger organizations, ask for the person in charge of the department where you are most likely to work.

Many times you can speak with the person in charge without an appointment. If so, tell the person you are looking for a position and would like to speak briefly about your qualifications. If you're told the company has no openings, say you would still like to talk about the possibility of future openings. If the boss seems busy, it is often best to set up a time when you can come back. Get his or her business card or name and set a day and time for your appointment.

While this approach takes courage, it often works. If you make a good impression, you are likely to be considered for a future job—before it is advertised!

Nothing works all the time. Sometimes dropping in without an appointment will get you an interview. At other times, you will have to be more creative to overcome an initial rejection. For example, if the person you want is not in, ask if someone else can help you. Make friends with that person and ask him or her to tell the boss you will follow up by phone. Leave a JIST Card (see Chapter 9) for the boss and your new contact. Then call the boss later and ask for an interview. Your new contact, if he or she likes you, will probably put in a good word for you. Be creative! Learn to follow up and don't take an initial no as a final answer.

The Importance of Follow Up

Following up is an important part of the job search. Send a thank-you note after you talk with an employer. Mention that you will call back at a certain date and time to answer any other questions and to check on your status as an applicant. Send a thank-you note after a helpful phone conversation with someone in your network. Stay in touch in a friendly, polite way with everyone on your network list. Following up and thanking people who help you is good manners. And it is also likely to help you in your job search.

Other Job Search Methods

I have covered the major methods used to find jobs. But there are many other creative ways you can find job leads. Here are just a few, to give you some ideas.

- **Volunteer.** If you lack experience or are not getting job offers, consider volunteering to work for free. Perhaps you could offer your services for a day or a week to show an employer what you can do. Promise that if things don't work out, you will leave with no hard feelings. This really does work, and many employers will give you a chance because they like your attitude.

- **School employment assistance.** This is mentioned in the previous chapter but deserves emphasis again. If you are lucky enough to attend a school that offers help in career planning or job search, find out what is available. If the school offers job listings, follow the counselor's advice and go to any interviews he or she sets up. Never miss an interview the school sends you to.

- **Professional associations.** Many professions have associations for people who work in that field. They are often a good source of information and networking contacts. The *Occupational Outlook Handbook* lists major professional associations for each job it covers and gives contact information, including Web addresses.

- **Civil service jobs.** Jobs with government agencies are a major part of our labor market. Applying for them often requires special tests and other procedures. It often takes a long time to get an interview for one of these jobs and even longer before you get an offer. Even so, they may be worth looking into. Find out about local, state, and federal jobs by contacting the personnel divisions for each. State and local government agencies are often listed in the yellow pages, and many have Internet sites that provide information. Two sites providing government job information are www.ajb.dni.us and www.opm.gov. *America's Federal Jobs* from JIST Works is another good information source.

- **Self-employment.** Self-employment is an option you might consider. If you want to join the growing number of people who work for themselves, start by learning more about self-employment options. Libraries offer many helpful books and resource materials. The Small Business Administration provides free resources for entrepreneurs. You can find it in the phone book or at www.sba.gov. Another good idea is to work in a business like the one you want to start. There is no better way to learn how to run a similar business.

- **Start at the bottom.** If you are being told you do not have enough experience to get the job you want, take an entry-level job in the field that interests you. Look for ways to work your way up as quickly as possible. Learn as much as you can, let the boss know you want to move up, and take on difficult tasks.

- **Consider additional training or education.** If a job interests you, it is often worth getting the education it requires. Additional training and education often quickly pay off in earnings and advancement opportunities. For example, the average annual pay of a college graduate is about $15,000 more than that of a high school graduate. Many of the fastest growing jobs require education or training beyond the high school level. These jobs often pay better and have more potential for the future than jobs that do not require special training. While a college degree is required for more and more jobs, many good-paying jobs require training or education that lasts from six months to two years. Look into financial aid that is available through many schools. Even if you can't afford to go to school full time, you can often go to night classes or work an evening job that allows you to take classes during the day. Once you are sure about what you want to do long term, find a way to get the education or training it requires. Few people regret it.

You Have Already Learned a Lot!

You already know more about job seeking than most people do. The last two chapters cover a variety of basic job search methods. Some key points to remember include

- Most jobs are not advertised.

- Use a variety of job-seeking methods.

- Some of your best leads will come from people you know.

- You don't have to wait for a job opening before contacting a potential employer.

- Always try to make direct contact with the person who will hire you.

- Follow up!

The chapters that follow build on what you have learned. You are off to a good start!

CHAPTER 8

Filling Out Applications—Without Burying Yourself

What Is a Job Application?

Most employers want you to fill out an "application for employment" when you apply for a job. These forms collect information that a company needs before deciding to hire you.

Most employers use paper application forms. Some ask you to answer questions on a computer screen or through the Internet. These are also applications, but in an electronic format.

Some Reasons Employers Use Applications

Why do employers want you to complete an application? List some of the reasons below.

1. _____

2. _____

3. _____

4. _____

5. _____

Employers Use Applications for a Good Reason

You probably listed several good reasons above. But did you write that most employers use applications to help them screen out unqualified job seekers?

The major purpose of applications is to help employers screen people out. If your qualifications are not "right," you will not get an interview.

Even a qualified candidate often gets screened out based on his or her application. Maybe it was incomplete, had bad handwriting, or was messy. Some applicants get screened out because they do not have as much experience or credentials as good as others. Some employers screen out those who got paid more than other applicants on their last job. Companies have many reasons for rejecting applicants. You might be able to do that job, but you may never have the chance.

Completing an Application Is Often Not the Best Way to Get an Interview

Some people do get interviews by filling out applications. Many young people, for example, get their jobs in this way. This is because employers are often less selective for the entry-level and lower-paying jobs many young people apply for.

But, for most people, filling out applications is not an effective way to get an interview. As you have learned, it is almost always better to ask an employer directly for an interview.

Even so, there are reasons for knowing how to successfully complete applications. Employers often require them. Even when you have set up an interview in advance, some employers will ask you to fill out an application before the interview. Government jobs often require an application. And knowing how to respond on an application can help you prepare to answer interview questions.

Tips for Completing Applications

Here are some general suggestions for completing applications. These tips are for paper applications, but most are also important when filling out electronic applications. Keep these simple points in mind when you apply for jobs.

Follow Directions

Carefully read and complete all sections of the application. Follow the directions! If you are asked to print all responses, do not write! You can make a negative impression quickly if you don't follow directions.

Be Neat and Complete

Carefully answer all sections of the application. A messy or incomplete application gives a negative impression. It will make you look as if you don't care. Carry an erasable black or blue ink pen with you for completing applications. It gives a more professional look than a pencil and allows you to correct errors.

Provide Only Positive Information

Most application forms are designed to collect negative information about you. But if you provide such information, it will be used to screen you out. Leaving a space blank is better than giving information that will keep you from being considered.

Try to include all of your positive information on an application. For example, list any unpaid (volunteer) experience in the work experience section. List training you received in school or in the military that relates to the job you want.

Find a spot to write down your skills and accomplishments, even if the application does not ask for this information. This is an exception to my earlier advice to follow the application's instructions. Look for a place to put positive facts, even if it is the margin!

Tips for Overcoming Problem Questions on Applications

Applications ask some difficult questions. How you answer them could get you screened out. Remember that you should never give negative information. Doing so will often result in your being screened out. But you should never lie on an application. That could get you fired later.

Several laws limit the types of questions employers can ask on application forms and in interviews. Even so, some employers may not know about these laws or may still use old applications. Or they may create their own forms. These forms may include "illegal" questions. If so, you can leave illegal questions blank.

Let's review typical problem questions and ways to handle them.

Gaps in Employment

Employers want your complete employment history. They will wonder what you did during the times you were not employed. If you have a good reason for an employment gap, be sure to list it. Examples include "raising children," "returned to school," and "helped uncle start a new business." If you did any work for money during a gap, list yourself as "self-employed."

Did your activities during an employment gap relate in any way to the job you want? If so, present the skills you used and the accomplishments you achieved that support your job objective.

TIP

You can downplay a gap by showing the start and finish dates of your employment as complete years. For example, "2000 to 2001" does not show that you were unemployed from January through June 2000 before finding a job in July 2000.

Arrest Record

Applications used to ask, "Have you ever been arrested?" Laws today allow an employer to ask only if you have ever been *convicted* of a serious crime, such as a felony. Companies can also inquire about crimes that could affect your ability to do the job. For example, an employer can ask accounting clerks and warehouse workers if they have ever been arrested for theft.

These laws are designed to keep you from being screened out of a job for arrests (when you were not found guilty) and minor crimes that would not affect your work. So, if you were arrested but not convicted of a felony, write "no" on applications.

Disabilities or Physical or Emotional Problems

Unless your problem prevents you from doing the job safely, it is probably not an employer's business. You should write "no" in almost all cases when asked for this information.

Reason for Leaving Last Job

Give the reason for leaving your last job, and make it sound positive. Don't write "fired" if you were laid off because of a business slowdown or similar situation. If you didn't leave on the best of terms but didn't do anything illegal, it is often best to list a legitimate excuse. Use something neutral, such as "returned to school" or "decided on a career change." You can always explain the details in an interview.

Too Little Experience

If you don't have much experience for the job you want, emphasize your other strengths. Present volunteer jobs in the work section and leave the wages paid blank. You can also give lots of details for related training, education, and skills used in other jobs.

Pay and Position Desired

Don't list a specific pay rate. It is often best to write "open" or "negotiable." This approach will not get you screened out.

If possible, list a broad career field. For example, write down "general office" rather than a specific title such as "file clerk." Titles and duties are rarely the same from place to place. Listing a narrow job title may keep you from being considered for other jobs you could do.

Too Much or Too Little Education

If you are overqualified or your credentials are strong but in another field, consider leaving out some of your unrelated education. If a job usually requires a degree but you did not graduate, write that you "attended" certain institutions. Don't say whether you graduated. You can explain the details in the interview.

Let Your Conscience Be Your Guide

Many people are tempted to lie on an application. This is not a good idea. Many employers will later fire you if they find out you lied on your application. A better approach is to leave a sensitive question blank. If you have a serious problem that an application would reveal, you're better off looking for job openings that don't require an application.

Remember that an application is more likely to do you harm than good. When you fill one out, be sure that it is truthful but also as good as you can make it. Include nothing on your application that could get you screened out. Remember that your goal is to get interviews, not complete applications.

Employment Tests and Background Checks

Some employers may ask you to take one or more tests as part of the application process. The tests can be paper-and-pencil tests or given on a computer screen. Some tests are designed to measure how honest you are. Other tests measure your personality, friendliness, and whether you are likely to get along with coworkers and supervisors. Tests can measure how quickly you work and other job-related skills. Before you are employed, some employers may require you to take a drug test or go to a medical screening. Some tests have been found to be illegal, but others can be used by employers to help them select employees. If you want the job, you will probably have to take the tests. Do your best on whatever tests you are asked to complete.

Many employers will ask you to sign an agreement that will let them check your background. This agreement is sometimes included at the end of an application. A background check will usually allow an employer to check your criminal and credit history, collect information from previous employers, and verify your education, training, or other details presented on your application. Again, if you want the job, you will probably have to cooperate.

Sample Applications

I've included two sample applications in this chapter. Albert C. Smith has completed the first one. Albert is not a real person, and his application includes many errors. Some of his errors are funny, but many come from things real people did on real applications. Find as many errors as you can on poor Albert's application and circle them. Then don't make the same mistakes on your own applications!

The second application is a blank one. This is a very thorough application, and it shows most of the details you'll see on real applications. For practice, use a pencil or erasable pen to fill in the blank application. Complete it as carefully and as neatly as you can. Make sure all your dates, addresses, and other information are complete and correct. When you are done, you can tear out the finished application and take it with you on your job search. You can then refer to it when filling in applications.

Date *April 1*

APPLICATION FOR EMPLOYMENT

PLEASE PRINT INFORMATION REQUESTED IN INK.

BROWN'S IS AN EQUAL OPPORTUNITY EMPLOYER and fully subscribes to the principles of Equal Employment Opportunity. Brown's has adopted an Affirmative Action Program to ensure that all applicants and employees are considered for hire, promotion and job status, without regard to race, color, religion, sex, national origin, age, handicap, or status as a disabled veteran or veteran of the Vietnam Era.

To protect the interests of all concerned, applications for certain job assignments must pass a physical examination before they are hired.

Note: This application will be considered active for 90 days. If you have not been employed within this period and are still interested in employment at Brown's, please contact the office where you applied and request that your application be reactivated.

Name *Albert C. Smith*
Last / First / Middle

Social Security Number *411-76-2614*
(Please present your Social Security Card for review)

Address *1526 No Otter*
Number / Street / City / State / Zip Code

County *Marion*

Current phone or nearest phone _____

Previous Address *Same*
Number / Street / City / State / Zip Code

Best time of day to contact *any*
(Answer only if position for which you are applying requires driving)

If hired, can you furnish proof of age? ✔ Yes ____ No

Licensed to drive car? ____ Yes ✔ No

If hired, can you furnish proof that you are legally entitled to work in U.S. ____ Yes ✔ No

Is license valid in this state? ____ Yes ✔ No

Have you ever been employed by Brown's? Yes ____ No X If so, when _____ Position *any thing*

Have you a relative in the employment of Brown's Department Store? Yes ____ No X

A PHYSICAL OR MENTAL DISABILITY WILL NOT CAUSE REJECTION IF IN BROWN'S MEDICAL OPINION YOU ARE ABLE TO SATISFACTORILY PERFORM IN THE POSITION FOR WHICH YOU ARE BEING CONSIDERED. Alternative placement, if available, of an applicant who does not meet the physical standards of the job for which he/she was originally considered is permitted.

Do you have any physical or mental impairment which may limit your ability to perform the job for which you are applying? *Yes, I have a back problem & was in Central State Hospital for 6 months.*

If yes, what can reasonably be done to accommodate your limitation? _____

	School Attended	No. of Years	Name of School	City/State	Graduate?	Course or College Major	Average Grades
EDUCATION	Grammar	10	PS 93	Scranton	Yes	General	B C
	Jr. High	3	Crestview	"	"	"	C
	Sr. High	3	WCHS	"	"		C-
	Other	1		"	"		
	College	3	State U	Scranton	NO		some C's

	Branch of Service	Date Entered Service	Date of Discharge	Highest Rank Held	Service-Related Skills and Experience Applicable to Civilian Employment
MILITARY SERVICE	USA	2000 6 months	I can explain this	E-2	radio stuff

What experience or training have you had other than your work experience, military service and education? (Community activities, hobbies, etc.)

I am interested in the type of work I have checked:

Sales X Office X Mechanical ✔ Warehouse X Other (Specify): ✔ _____

Or the following specific Job *whatever*

I am seeking (check only one):
✔ Temporary employment (6 days or less)
✔ Seasonal employment (one season, e.g. Christmas)
✔ Regular employment (employment for indifinite period of time)

If temporary, indicate dates available *now*

I am available for (check only one)
✔ Part-Time
✔ Full-Time Work

If part-time, indicate maximum hours per week and enter hours available in block to the right.

HOURS AVAILABLE FOR WORK	
Sunday	To
Monday	To
Tuesday	To
Wednesday	To
Thursday	To
Friday	To
Saturday	To

anytime - but don't like too early in morning

Have you been convicted during the past seven years of a serious crime involving a person's life or property?

NO X YES ____ If yes, explain: *drunk in public*

REFERENCES

LIST BELOW YOUR FOUR MOST RECENT EMPLOYERS, BEGINNING WITH THE CURRENT OR MOST RECENT ONE. IF YOU HAVE HAD LESS THAN FOUR EMPLOYERS, USE THE REMAINING SPACES FOR PERSONAL REFERENCES. IF YOU WERE EMPLOYED UNDER A MAIDEN OR OTHER NAME PLEASE ENTER THAT NAME IN THE RIGHT HAND MARGIN. IF APPLICABLE, ENTER SERVICE IN THE ARMED FORCES ON THE REVERSE SIDE.

NAMES AND ADDRESSES OF FORMER EMPLOYERS BEGINNING WITH THE CURRENT OR MOST RECENT	Nature of Employer's Business	Name of your Supervisor	What kind of work did you do?	Starting Date	Starting Pay	Date of Leaving	Pay at Leaving	Why did you leave? Give details
NOTE: State reason for and length of inactivity between present application date and last employer.								
Name: *Don't know* Address: *Walnut St* Tel. No. Zip Code City: *Scranton* State:	*School*	*Eric Burgess*	*Clean up*	Month *7* Year *99*	$7 an hr Per Week	Month ▓▓ Year		*Fired but not my fault*
NOTE: State reason for and length of inactivity between present application date and last employer.								
Name: *Fred Willis* Address: Tel. No. Zip Code City: *Scranton* State: *PA*	*Houses*	*Rafael*	*Electrician helper labor*	Month *7* Year *98*	$6.50 an hr Per Week	Month ▓▓ Year	$11.00 Per Week	*worked for a couple of months a year. Boss always picked on me.*
NOTE: State reason for and length of inactivity between present application date and last employer.								
Name: *Wayne Const.* Address: *4432 N. Anderson* Tel. No. *555-9911* City: *Scranton* State: *PA*	*Construction*	*Kim Lewski*	*Jack hammer wiring*	Month *2001* Year	$6 an hr Per Week	Month Year	$10.00 Per Week	*Company went broke.*
NOTE: State reason for and length of inactivity between present application date and last employer.								
Name: *Central Hospital* Address: *Washington St.* Tel. No. Zip Code City: *Scranton* State: *PA*	*mental hospital*	*Lynn Donovan*	*Clean up*	Month *2001* Year	$5.50 hr Per Week	Month Year	*same* Per Week	*I got better + was discharged.*

I certify that the information in this application is correct to the best of my knowledge and understand that any misstatement or omission of information is grounds for dismissal in accordance with Brown's policy. I authorize the references listed above to give you any and all information concerning my previous employment and any pertinent information they may have, personal or otherwise, and release all parties from all liability for any damage that may result from furnishing same to you. In consideration of my employment, I agree to conform to the rules and regulations of Brown's, and my employment and compensation can be terminated with or without cause, with or without notice, at any time, at the option of either the Company or myself. I understand that no unit manager or representative of Brown's other than the President or Vice-President of the company, has any authority to enter into any agreement for employment for any specified period of time, or to make any agreement contrary to the foregoing. In some states, the law requires that Brown's have my written permission before obtaining consumer reports on me, and I hereby authorize Brown's to obtain such reports.

Applicant's Signature _____ *Smith, Albert C.* _____

NOT TO BE FILLED OUT BY APPLICANT

(Store will enter dates as required.)

	Tested				REFERENCE REQUESTS		Mailed	Completed
	Physical examination scheduled for	*maybe*					*not yet*	
	Physical examination form completed	*I didn't get one*			CONSUMER REPORT	*my mom reads it*		
					With Tax (W-4)			
					State With Tax			
	Review Card prepared		Minor's Work Permit					
	Timecard prepared		Proof of Birth		*Can you take extra tax to get the IRS off my back?*			
			Training Material Given to Employee					

Unit Name and Number _____ *Albert Smith* _____

INTERVIEWER'S COMMENTS			
I really need a job now.	Date of Emp.	Regular _____ Part-time _____	
	Dept or Div.		
	Job Title		
	Job Title Code	Job Grade	
	Compensation Arrangement	*Maybe a offer*	
	Manager Approving		
Prospect for	Employee No.	Rack No.	
1.			
2.			

DATE: _____

JIST's Application for Employment

(PLEASE PRINT REQUESTED INFORMATION IN INK.)

JIST is an Equal Opportunity Employer and does not discriminate against any individual in any phase of employment in accordance with the requirements of local, state, and federal law. In addition, JIST has adopted an Affirmative Action Program with the goal of ensuring equitable representation of qualified women, minorities, Vietnam Era and disabled veterans, and other disabled individuals at all job levels.

Applicants may be subject to testing for illegal drugs. In addition, applicants for certain positions that receive a conditional offer of employment must pass a medical examination or meet other criteria prior to receiving a confirmed offer of employment.

PERSONAL INFORMATION

LAST NAME	FIRST NAME	MIDDLE INITIAL	SOCIAL SECURITY NO.

STREET ADDRESS OR RFD NO. (include apartment no., if any)	HOW LONG AT THIS ADDRESS?

CITY	STATE/PROVINCE	COUNTY/PARISH	ZIP CODE

HOME PHONE (include area code)	WORK PHONE (include area code) Ext.	SEX (for statistics only) ❏ Male ❏ Female	Other Last Names Ever Used

PREVIOUS ADDRESS (if less than one year)	HOW LONG AT THIS ADDRESS?

CITY	STATE/PROVINCE	COUNTY/PARISH	ZIP CODE

POSITION APPLIED FOR:

I AM AVAILABLE FOR: ❏ Part-time ❏ Full-time
Complete the hours available for work below.

HOW DID YOU HEAR OF THIS OPENING?

	Sun.	Mon.	Tues.	Wed.	Thurs.	Fri.	Sat.
FROM							
TO							

LOWEST RATE OF PAY YOU WILL ACCEPT:

WHEN WILL YOU BE AVAILABLE FOR WORK? (month and year)

ARE YOU AVAILABLE FOR TEMPORARY EMPLOYMENT?

	YES	NO

IF HIRED, CAN YOU FURNISH PROOF OF AGE?
❏ Yes ❏ No

A. Less than 1 month? ....
B. 1 to 4 months? ....
C. 5 to 12 months? ....

IF HIRED, CAN YOU FURNISH PROOF THAT YOU ARE LEGALLY ENTITLED TO WORK IN THE U.S.?
❏ Yes ❏ No

Answer the following only if the position for which you are applying requires driving.
Are you licensed to drive a car? ❏ Yes ❏ No   Is license valid in this state? ❏ Yes ❏ No

HAVE YOU EVER BEEN BONDED? ❏ No ❏ Yes - When?

DO YOU HAVE ANY PHYSICAL DISABILITIES PREVENTING YOU FROM DOING CERTAIN TYPES OF WORK?
❏ No ❏ Yes   If Yes, describe disabilities/limitations.

HAVE YOU HAD ANY SERIOUS ILLNESS IN THE PAST 5 YEARS? ❏ No ❏ Yes   If Yes, describe.

Please list any special skills, training, or experiences that qualify you for the position for which you are applying.

_____

_____

Please list any additional qualifications and skills (skills with machines, patents or inventions, your most important publication [do not submit copies unless requested], your public speaking and publications experience, membership in professional or scientific societies, etc.)

_____

Kind of license or certificate (pilot, registered nurse, lawyer, radio operator, CPA, etc.):	Latest license or certificate:		Approximate number of words per minute:	
	Year	State or other licensing authority	Word processing	Shorthand

ATTENTION — THIS STATEMENT MUST BE SIGNED

ead the following paragraph carefully before signing this statement.

provided by me in this application for employment is true and complete to the best of my knowledge. I understand that if I am employed, any false e considered as cause for possible dismissal. You are hereby authorized to conduct any investigation of my personal history and/or credit and employing investigative or credit agencies or bureaus of your choice subject to the provisions of the Fair Credit Reporting Act.

_____   _____
icant (sign in ink)   Date

APPLICANT — DO NOT WRITE IN THIS SECTION

	DATE	COMMENTS		
POSITION	WILL REPORT	LOCATION		SALARY
RSONNEL DEPARTMENT	DEPARTMENT MANAGER	GENERAL MANAGER		

EDUCATION

Did you graduate from high school or will you graduate within the next nine months, or do you have a GED high school equivalency certificate?
☐ Yes, month/year   ☐ No, highest grade completed:

Name and location (city and state) of last high school attended:

Name and location (city, state, ZIP code, if known) of college or university. (If you expect to graduate within nine months give MONTH and YEAR you expect to receive your degree.)	Dates Attended		No. of Credits Completed		Type of Degree (e.g. B.A.)	Year of Degree	GPA
	From	To	Semester Hours	Quarter Hours			

Chief undergraduate college subjects:	No. of Credits Completed		Chief graduate college subjects:	No. of Credits Completed	
	Semester	Quarter		Semester	Quarter

Major field of study at highest level of college work:

Other schools or training (for example, trade, vocational, Armed Forces or business). Give for each the name and location (city, state, and ZIP code, if known) of school, dates attended, subjects studied, number of classroom hours of instruction per week, certificate, and any other pertinent data.

Activities, honors, awards, and fellowships received:

Languages other than English. List the languages (other than English) in which you are proficient and indicate your level of proficiency by putting an (X) in the appropriate columns.

Name of Language	PROFICIENCY							
	Can Prepare and Deliver Lectures		Can Converse		Have Facility to Translate Articles, Technical Materials, etc.		Can Read Articles, Technical Materials, for Own Use	
	Fluently	With Difficulty	Fluently	Passably	Into English	From English	Easily	With Difficulty

REFERENCES

List three persons who are NOT related to you and who have definite knowledge of your qualifications and fitness for the position for which you are applying. Do not repeat names of supervisors listed under EXPERIENCE.

Full Name	Present Business or Home Address (Number, Street, City, State, and ZIP Code)	Telephone Number (Include Area Code)	Business or Occupation

NOTE: A conviction or a firing does not necessarily mean you cannot be hired. The circumstances of the occurrence(s) and how long ago it (they) occurred are important. Give all the facts so that a decision can be made.

	YES	NO
1. Within the last five years have you been fired from any job for any reason?		
2. Within the last five years have you quit a job after being notified you would be fired?		

If your answer to question 1 or 2 is "YES," give details in the space provided on the following page. Show the name and address (including ZIP Code) of employer, approximate date, and reasons in each case. This information should agree with your answers under EXPERIENCE.

(continues)

(continued)

	YES	NO
3. Have you ever been convicted, forfeited collateral, or are you now under charges for any felony or any firearms or explosives offense against the law? (A felony is defined as any offense punishable by imprisonment for a term exceeding one year, but does not include any offense under the laws of a state as a misdemeanor.)		
4. During the past seven years, have you been convicted, imprisoned, on probation or parole, or forfeited collateral, or are you now under charges for any offense against the law not included in the above question?		

NOTE: When answering the previous two questions, you may omit (1) traffic fines for which you paid a fine of $100.00 or less, (2) any offense committed before your 18th birthday which was finally adjudicated in a juvenile court or under a youth offender law, (3) any conviction the record of which has been expunged under federal or state law, and (4) any conviction set aside under the Federal Youth Corrections Act or similar state authority.

PERSONAL REFERENCES

NAME	ADDRESS	RELATIONSHIP	PHONE NUMBER

LIST ONLY PERSONS WE MAY CONTACT — BE SURE TO INCLUDE PHONE NUMBER

	YES	NO
5. While in the military service, were you ever convicted by a general court-martial? .... If your answer to question 3, 4 or 5 is "YES," give details in the space below. Show for each offense, (1) date; (2) charge; (3) place; (4) court; (5) action taken.		
6. Do you receive, or do you have pending, application for retirement or retainer pay, pension, or other compensation based upon military, federal, civilian, or District of Columbia government service? .... If your answer to this question is "YES," give details below. If military retired pay, include the rank at which you retired.		

Your statement cannot be processed until you have answered all questions, including questions 1 through 6 above.

QUESTION #	SPACE FOR DETAILED ANSWERS. BE SURE TO INDICATE QUESTION NUMBERS TO WHICH THE ANSWERS APPLY.

If more space is required, use full sheets of paper approximately the same size as this page. Write on each sheet your name and the announcement or position title. Attach all sheets to this page.

VETERAN PREFERENCES

Answer all parts. If a part does not apply to you, answer "No."

	YES	NO
Have you ever served on active duty in the United States military service? (Exclude tours of active duty for training in the Reserve or National Guard)		
Have you ever been discharged from the armed services under other than honorable conditions? (You may omit any such discharge changed to honorable or general by a Discharge Review Board or similar authority)		

If the above answer is "YES," you will be required to furnish records to support your claim at the time you are hired.

List dates, branch, and serial number of all active service (enter N/A, if not applicable).

FROM	TO	BRANCH OF SERVICE	SERIAL OR SERVICE NUMBER

BRANCH	RANK	DUTIES	SALARY		REASON FOR CHANGE IN RANK
			FROM	TO	

List any special school or skills acquired during your military service:

EXPERIENCE

Begin with current or most recent job or volunteer experience and work back. Account for periods of unemployment
residence address at that time.

May inquiry be made of your present employer regarding your character qualifications and record of employment?

1. NAME AND ADDRESS OF EMPLOYER'S ORGANIZATION

	Dates employed (month/year)
	From	To

Exact title of your position	Name of immediate supervisor	Area code Phone number

Kind of business or organization (manufacturing, accounting, social services, etc.)	Reason for leaving

Description of work. (Describe your specific duties, responsibilities and accomplishments in this job.)

2. NAME AND ADDRESS OF EMPLOYER'S ORGANIZATION

	Dates employed (month/year)
	From	To

Exact title of your position	Name of immediate supervisor	Area code Phone number

Kind of business or organization (manufacturing, accounting, social services, etc.)	Reason for leaving

Description of work. (Describe your specific duties, responsibilities and accomplishments in this job.)

3. NAME AND ADDRESS OF EMPLOYER'S ORGANIZATION

	Dates employed (month/year)
	From	To

Exact title of your position	Name of immediate supervisor	Area code Phone number

Kind of business or organization (manufacturing, accounting, social services, etc.)	Reason for leaving

Description of work. (Describe your specific duties, responsibilities and accomplishments in this job.)

(continued)

The information
statements will
financial record

Signature of ap

INTERVIEWER

DEPARTMENT

APPROVED: P

CHAPTER 9

JIST Cards®

A Powerful Mini-Resume That Gets Results

Imagine that you are an employer and are responsible for hiring workers for your auto shop. You may or may not have a job opening now. Read the information in the box below, and then answer the questions that follow it.

John Kijek
Phone Message: (219) 232-9213
Pager: (219) 637-6643

Position Desired: Auto mechanic

Skills: Over three years' work experience, including one year in a full-time auto mechanic's training program. Familiar with all hand tools and electronic diagnostic equipment. Can handle tune-ups and common repairs to brakes, exhaust systems, electrical and mechanical systems. Am a fast worker, often completing jobs correctly in less-than-standard time. Have all tools required and can start work immediately.

Prefer full-time work, any shift.

Honest, reliable, good with people.

How Did You React?

Please answer the questions that follow. Answer truthfully, but as if in the role of an employer who supervises auto repairs. Base your answers on your reaction to the information in the box on the previous page.

1. Do you feel good about this person—yes or no? _____

2. What were your emotions about this person and how did you feel about him? _____
_____

3. Would you be willing to interview him if you had a job opening—yes or no? _____
Why? _____
_____

4. Would you be willing to see him even if you did not have a job opening—yes or no?
Why? _____

It's a JIST Card!

The box you read at the chapter's beginning is a JIST Card. JIST stands for Job Information and Seeking Training. It is a name use to identify a whole series of job search techniques I began to develop years ago. I include many of those methods in this book. With more than twenty years of research and improvement, these job search techniques are among the most effective ever.

Most people can read a JIST Card in about thirty seconds. Yet in that very short time, the JIST Card often creates a positive impression! In fact, most people who read one say they would interview a person based on just that much information.

TIP

A JIST Card is the only job search tool that generates such an impression—and gets interviews—in such a brief time. A JIST Card can become very important to you in your job search.

JIST Cards are usually printed on 3-by-5-inch cards. They can also be done on smaller business card sizes and in other forms. JIST Cards are similar to a mini-resume or a business calling card. JIST Cards can be inexpensively printed in quantity on a desktop computer printer or at a quick-print shop so you will have plenty to use during your job search.

Some Uses for Your JIST Card

Here are some ways you can use your JIST Card in your job search:

- **Attach one to a completed application.** Employers can then separate it from the application and put it on their bulletin board or desk.

- **Give them to friends and relatives.** Ask them to keep you in mind if they hear of any job openings. Ask them to give the cards to others who might know of a job opening for you.

- **Send one to an employer before an interview.**

- **Enclose one in your thank-you notes.**

- **Give several to people who are willing to give them to others.** Everyone in your network should get some. Ask your network contacts to pass them on to others who might know of a opening for you.

- **Attach one to a resume.**

You may have other ideas on how to use JIST Cards. For example, they have been put on grocery store bulletin boards and under car windshield wiper blades in parking lots. The more JIST Cards you put into circulation, the better!

Why JIST Cards Work So Well

Employers love JIST Cards, and so do those who want to help you in your job search. JIST Cards are a very effective tool for several reasons:

- **JIST Cards are different.** People are interested in JIST Cards because they are unique and interesting. They attract positive attention and comments—good things to get when you are looking for a job.

- **JIST Cards quickly present the most important information employers want to know.** They very quickly give a lot of information, including your name, how you can be contacted, the job you want, and the key education, training, skills, and experience you have to support your job objective.

- **JIST Cards are less likely to get lost on a desk than other paperwork.** Resumes and applications tend to be put in piles and buried among other papers. But JIST Cards tend to get taped on a wall, put on a bulletin board, and left out in the open so that the employer can see them.

- **JIST Cards are great tools for people in your network.** Your friends and relatives may not know much about your skills, training, and experience. JIST Cards give them a tool they can use and pass along to others. Many job leads can come from putting hundreds of JIST Cards in use.

The Anatomy of a JIST Card

There is more to a well-written JIST Card than meets the eye. Look over the different sections of a JIST Card in the sample below. Additional details on each part of a JIST Card are provided after the card.

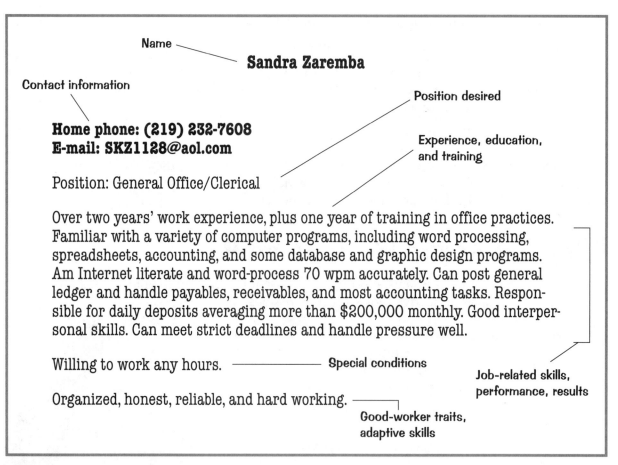

Name

Sandra Zaremba

Contact information

Position desired

Home phone: (219) 232-7608
E-mail: SKZ1128@aol.com

Experience, education, and training

Position: General Office/Clerical

Over two years' work experience, plus one year of training in office practices. Familiar with a variety of computer programs, including word processing, spreadsheets, accounting, and some database and graphic design programs. Am Internet literate and word-process 70 wpm accurately. Can post general ledger and handle payables, receivables, and most accounting tasks. Responsible for daily deposits averaging more than $200,000 monthly. Good interpersonal skills. Can meet strict deadlines and handle pressure well.

Willing to work any hours. ——————— Special conditions

Job-related skills, performance, results

Organized, honest, reliable, and hard working. ———

Good-worker traits, adaptive skills

3-by-5-inch pastel card

A JIST Card is small, so it can't contain many details. A JIST Card should list only the information that is most important to employers. For a simple card, consider all that Sandra's sample includes:

- **Identification.** Sandra gives her name.

- **Two ways to make contact.** Sandra lists two ways she can be reached: a home phone number and her e-mail address. Employers want to reach you quickly, so include at least two ways you can be contacted. Since employers usually won't write a letter, don't give your address. Instead, list two of these: a regular phone number, a cell phone number, a pager number, or an e-mail address. If you give a phone number, make sure the phone is answered professionally by a person, by voice mail, or by an answering machine.

- **Position.** Sandra includes a broad job objective. This will allow her to be considered for many jobs by an employer.

- **Length of experience.** Sandra lists her total length of work experience. Some of this experience was in part-time and volunteer jobs, something she can explain in an interview.

- **Education and training.** Sandra lists her total time spent in training.

- **Job-related skills, performance, and results.** This section tells a little about what Sandra can do and how well she can do it. She describes important job-related skills for this work. Sandra mentions the key adaptive and transferable skills she learned or used in her work and other experiences. Note that she includes several numbers. The first is "70 wpm," which means she word processes quickly at 70 words per minute. She states that she was responsible for $200,000 of cash deposits each month. This tells employers that she can be trusted with substantial responsibility.

- **Special conditions.** Sandra mentions that she is willing to work any hours. This shows that she is flexible and willing to work.

- **Good-worker traits/adaptive skills.** Sandra lists her key adaptive skills and personality traits that would be important to an employer.

All this on a 3-by-5-inch card that can be read in less than thirty seconds!

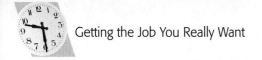

Sample JIST Cards

Following are some sample JIST Cards. They are for different jobs, from entry-level to those requiring more experience. Study them and use any ideas that help you write with your own JIST Card. While you can type or even handwrite your cards, most people use a desktop computer and laser printer.

Jonathan McLaughlin
Answering machine: (509) 674-8736
Cell phone: (509) 541-0981

Objective: Electronics—installation, maintenance, and sales

Skills: Four years of work experience, plus two years advanced training in electronics. AS degree in Electronics Engineering Technology. Managed a $500,000/year business while going to school full time, with grades in the top 25%. Familiar with all major electronics diagnostic and repair equipment. Hands-on experience with medical, consumer, communications, business, and industrial electronics equipment and applications. Good problem-solving and communication skills. Customer service oriented.

Willing to do what it takes to get the job done.

Self-motivated, dependable, learn quickly.

Jonathan is a new graduate from a two-year technical program. He was always interested in electronics but worked in construction jobs after high school. He then got a job helping the owner of a TV and electronics repair shop. His job was to answer phones, keep the place clean, and other simple tasks. But he volunteered to fix items, and the owner started to show him how to do more complex repairs and encouraged him to go back to school. Jonathan worked at the electronics shop for three years, and the owner let him schedule his work time around school. He eventually landed a job with a circuit board design and manufacturing company and now earns about three times more.

Andrea Scott   Answering machine: (639) 298-9704

E-mail: andys@hotmail.com

Position Desired: Warehouse Management

Skills: Three years' experience plus two years of formal business coursework. Have supervised a staff as large as eight people and warehousing operations valued at over $4,000,000. Automated inventory operations resulting in an estimated annual savings of over $25,000. Working knowledge of accounting, computer systems, and advanced inventory management systems.

Will work any hours.

Responsible, hard working, and can solve problems.

Andy got her work experience in the military, where she was responsible for warehouse operations for an infantry unit. Her business education includes high school courses, military training, and some college-level courses she took while in the military. It was enough for her to land a job with Federal Express, where she now supervises fourteen workers.

Maria Marquez

Home: (213) 432-8064
Messages: (213) 437-9836

Position Desired: Hotel Management

Two years' experience in sales, catering, and food service in a 300-room hotel. Associate degree in Hotel Management, plus one year with the Boileau Culinary Institute. Doubled revenues from meetings and conferences and increased dining room and bar revenues by 44%. Have been commended for improving staff productivity and courtesy and received several promotions. I approach my work with effort, imagination, and creative problem-solving skills.

Enthusiastic, well-organized, detail-oriented.

Maria took some college courses at night while she worked at a local hotel. She did not start with a goal of hotel management but ended up with a two-year degree in that field. She can't afford to go to school full time (she has family responsibilities), but wants to eventually get a four-year degree in business. She figures she can earn more money with her experience now and used this JIST Card to help her find a better job with the flexible schedule she needs to keep going to school.

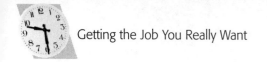

Jafar Browning

Home: (846) 299-3643
Pager: (846) 517-4525

E-mail: JMB0928@aol.com

Objective: Sales or business position requiring skills in problem solving, planning, organizing, and customer service.

Skills: Two years' experience, including coursework in business, sales methods, customer service, and business software. Promoted and received several bonuses for performance. Set record for largest single sale exceeding $130,000. Consistent record of getting results. Excellent communication skills. Familiar with database, word processing, and spreadsheet programs. Internet literate. Enjoy challenges and accept responsibility.

Willing to relocate.

Results-oriented, good problem-solving skills, energetic.

Jafar does not have formal education beyond high school but is smart and very good with people. He used these adaptive and transferable skills in sales, where he could earn good pay. He landed a position selling telecommunications services to businesses. His earnings have almost doubled from his previous job.

Lisa Marie Rhodes

E-mail: MLRhodes@earthlink.com
Phone: (424) 351-5935

Position desired: Internet startup or other Web-based business

Actively involved in intensive computer use and Web site development for more than four years. Familiar with all major software used in designing business-oriented Web sites, including graphics, interactive databases, credit card transactions, and security, firewall, virus, and other hacker-protection schemes. Excellent writing, grammar, and design skills. Did entire programming and design of a business-to-business e-commerce site and, over 12 months, grew it to annual sales of $620,000 before it went public.

Will consider contract work.

I work quickly and am persistent in finding solutions to complex problems.

Lisa is a recent high school graduate who learned most of her Web skills on her own. She did everything she says here by working at home on contract after school and in the summer. She wants to continue onto college and do Web design "on the side."

Tom Able

Cell phone at 872-924-6794 or e-mail at Tomable@juno.net

Job Objective: Responsible accounting or bookkeeping position

Skills: Four years of related work experience and training. Experienced with computerized accounting systems, spreadsheets, database programs, and report extraction programs. Practical experience in order entry, accounts payable, accounts receivable and collections, reconciling check and cash accounts, and posting to general ledger. Did full-service bookkeeping for small business with sales of $900,000 and handled a variety of accounting functions in a large manufacturing company.

Can work any hours.

Well-organized, problem solver, willing to relocate.

Tom is a high school graduate who took business courses in school and learned the rest on the job. He took several temporary accounting positions until one of them was offered to him as a full-time position. He accepted and has had several promotions since.

John Harold   Home: (619) 433-0040   E-mail: johnharold@easternair.com

Objective: Responsible Business Management Position

Skills: Over 7 years of management experience plus a degree in Business. Managed budgets as large as $5 million. Experienced in cost control and reduction, cutting more than 20% of overhead while sales increased almost 30%. Good organizer and problem-solver. Excellent communication skills.

Prefer responsible position in a medium-to-large business.

Cope well with deadline pressure, seek challenge, flexible.

John has lots of experience and great credentials. He accepted a job running a small window manufacturing company that is now growing rapidly.

The JIST Card Worksheet

This worksheet provides instructions to help you write your own JIST Card. Read the instructions carefully, then complete each section as well as you can. Later, you can use this worksheet to write your final JIST Card.

Your name _____

Tips. Keep this simple and professional. Don't use nicknames, middle names, or initials.

Contact information _____

Tips. Try to include two ways for an employer can contact you. Include a phone number that will be answered all the time. Always include your area code. If you use an answering machine or voice mail, make sure it does not have a silly greeting. If the phone is at home, make sure anyone who might answer it knows how to take accurate messages. Include a cell phone or pager number if you have one. Giving an e-mail address helps communicate that you are Internet literate.

Job objective _____

_____

Tips. Don't be too narrow in your job objective. Say "general office" rather than "receptionist" if you would consider a variety of office jobs. If you are specific in your job objective, try to avoid a narrow job title but give other details. For example, say "Management position in an insurance-related business" or "Working with children in a medical or educational setting."

Don't limit yourself to entry-level jobs if you have potential or interest in doing more. If you say "office manager" instead of "administrative assistant," you just might get a more responsible and higher-paying job. If you are not too sure of your ability to get a higher-paying job, it is still best to keep your options open if possible. Say "office manager or responsible secretarial position," for example.

Your Experience Statement

Writing your experience statement is a tricky matter for some people. I hope the following tips will help. The first set of tips will help you do the calculation that follows. Read those tips before adding up "your total experience."

Your total experience. Write years (or months, if you don't have much experience) in the spaces beside each question.

a. Total time paid work _____

b. Total time volunteer work + _____

c. Total time informal work + _____

d. Total time related education or training + _____

Your total experience = _____

Tips for adding up your total experience. In writing your JIST Card experience statement, take advantage of all the experience you have that supports your job objective. If you are changing careers, have been out of the work world for a while, or do not have much work experience, you will need to use other experiences to convince the employer you can do the job. Depending on your situation, you can include any or all of the following as part of your work experience:

- **Paid work.** You can list any work you were paid to do. The work does not have to be similar to the job you are looking for now. Baby-sitting and lawn-mowing jobs count. So can work at a fast-food place. If you worked part time, estimate the total number of hours you worked. Divide this total by 160 hours to get the number of months you worked. Of course, paid work directly related to your job objective is the best, if you have it.

- **Volunteer work.** You can include volunteer work as part of your total work experience. It counts, and you list it if you don't have much paid work experience.

- **Informal work.** Include work you did at home or as an unpaid hobby. It is best if this work relates to the job, but it doesn't have to. For example, if you worked on cars at home and want to be an auto mechanic, there is an obvious connection. You may have experience taking care of younger brothers or sisters. Or working in the family business. This is real experience and, if it can help you to use it, do so.

- **Related education and training.** If you took courses in high school or college that relate to the job you want, you can count this as part of your total experience. You can also count any courses or training you received in the military, business or technical school, or anywhere else. If they relate in some way to the job you want, they can count.

Now, go back and complete the information under "your total experience" above.

(continues)

(continued)

Tips for writing your experience statement. Because everyone has a different background, no single rule works. Here are some tips for writing your JIST Card experience statement.

- **If you have lots of work experience.** If some of this experience is not related to the job you want, you can leave it out. If you have twenty years of experience, say "over fifteen" or include just the experience that directly relates to the job you want. This keeps the employer from knowing how old you are. Your age is an advantage you will present in the interview!

- **If you don't have much paid work experience.** You need to include everything possible. If you have no paid work experience related to the job you now seek, emphasize your education, training, and other work. For example, "Nearly two years of experience, including one year of advanced training in office procedures." Remember to include the total of all paid and unpaid work as part of your experience! Include all those part-time jobs and volunteer jobs by writing "Over eighteen months' total work experience."

- **If your experience is in another field.** Mention that you have "Four years' work experience" without saying in what field.

- **Other.** If you won promotions, raises, or have other special strengths, this is the time to say so. For example: "Over seven years of increasingly responsible work experience, including three years as a supervisor. Promoted twice."

Look over the sample JIST Cards for additional ideas, then write your own statement below.

Your experience statement _____

_____

_____

_____

_____

Your Education and Training Statement

Depending on your situation, you can combine your education and training with your experience. Several of the sample JIST Cards do this. Or you can list your education and training as a separate statement.

Don't mention your education or training if it doesn't help you. If you have a license, certification, or degree that supports your job objective, mention it here. For example: "Four years of experience, plus two years of training leading to certification as an Emergency Medical Technician."

Look over the sample JIST Cards for more ideas and write your own education and training statement. If you want, you can revise your previous experience statement here to include your education and training.

Your education and training statement _____

_____

_____

_____

_____

Your Job-Related Skills Statement

In this section, you list the things you can do to support your job objective. If appropriate, mention job-related tools or equipment you can use. Use the language of the job to describe the more important things you can do.

Emphasize results! It is best to use some numbers to strengthen what you say. For example, instead of writing "can do word processing," state "accurately word-process eighty words per minute and am familiar with advanced graphic and formatting capabilities of Microsoft Word and PageMaker." It is too easy to overlook the importance of what you do. Add up the numbers of transactions you handled, the money you were responsible for, the results you got. Here are a few more examples:

- A person with fast-food experience might write, "Have handled over 50,000 customer contacts with total sales of over $250,000 quickly and accurately." While many think that a "lowly" job like those in fast food are not worthy ones, these jobs often require hard work, speed, and advanced skills. The figures are based on a five-day workweek, 200 customers a day for one year, and an average sale of $5. Impressive numbers, when presented in this way. The fact that this was done in a fast-food job does not have to be mentioned.

- Someone who ran a small store could say "Responsible for business with over $150,000 in sales per year. Increased sales by 35% within eighteen months."

- You could present a successful school fund-raising project as "Planned, trained, and supervised a staff of six on a special project. Exceeded income projections by 40%."

You should also include one or more of your transferable skills that are important for the job you want.

(continues)

(continued)

- Someone with receptionist, customer service, or sales experience might add "Good appearance and pleasant telephone voice."

- A warehouse manager might say "Well organized and efficient. Have reduced expenses by 20% while orders increased by 55%." It is certainly OK to give numbers to support these skills, too!

Think hard about your experiences and try to include numbers and results. Look over the sample JIST Cards for more examples of this and write your own statement below.

Your job-related skills statement _____

_____

_____

_____

Your Special Conditions or Preferred Working Conditions Statement

This section is optional. You can add just a few words—one or two lines at most—to let the employer know what you are willing to do. Do not limit your employment possibilities by saying "Will only work days" or "No travel wanted." It is better to not include this information than to state something negative.

Look at the sample JIST Cards for ideas. Then write your statement below.

Your preferred working conditions statement _____

_____

_____

Your Good-Worker Traits Statement

List three or four of your key adaptive skills. Choose skills that are most important in the job you are seeking. Be certain you do have them! Refer to Chapter 3 for your list of key adaptive skills. The sample JIST Cards also will give you ideas. Then list the skills you will include on your JIST Card.

Your good-worker traits statement _____

_____

_____

_____

The Final Edit

To fit all this information on a 3-by-5-inch card, you will probably need to edit what you've written. Here are some tips to help you write the final version of your JIST Card:

- **Make every word count.** Get rid of anything that does not directly support your job objective.

- **Use short phrases.** You don't have to use complete sentences. Remember, every word has to count, so cut unnecessary words.

- **Add more information if your JIST Card is too short.** But add things only if they make your statements stronger.

- **Cut anything that is not a positive.** Get rid of anything that does not present you in a positive way.

- **Handwrite or print your content on a 3-by-5 card.** This will help you see if you have included too much or too little information. Edit it again as needed to make it fit.

- **Read your JIST Card out loud.** This will help you to know how it sounds and may give you additional ideas to improve it.

- **Ask someone else to help you with the final version.** He or she may make some good suggestions, but make your own final decisions.

- **Check it one more time.** Make sure your final version does not have spelling, grammar, and other errors. One error can create a negative impression and undo all your hard work!

Tips to Produce and Reproduce Your JIST Card

Here are a few tips for getting your JIST Card produced in its final form.

- **You want to put lots of JIST Cards in circulation.** While you can type or even handwrite individual JIST Cards, it is best to have them printed in quantities of 100 to 500.

- **If you have a computer and a high-quality printer, it is probably best to print your own JIST Card.** If you don't have access to a computer and good printer, you can get this done at most print shops for a modest fee.

- **Be sure that no new errors were introduced in the final version.** Make sure that phone numbers, e-mail addresses, and other details are correct and that no new typographical errors have crept in.

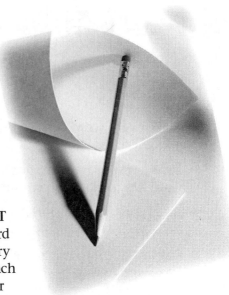

- **You can fit five copies of the same JIST Card on one standard sheet of stock.** Doing this allows you to copy or print multiple sheets in the most efficient way. Of course, you will need to cut the sheets to the size of the individual cards. Office supply stores also have regular-page-size sheets "micro-perforated" so that they can be easily torn into 3-by-5-inch cards. This lets you do the cards on your own computer without having to cut the sheets yourself.

- **Use "light card stock," not paper, for your JIST Card.** It is the same thickness used for a standard 3-by-5-inch card. Office supply stores often carry it in a range of colors in a standard 8½-by-11-inch size that works in most copy machines and laser printers.

- **I like off-white, ivory, or cream-color JIST Cards.** They give the cards a professional appearance. You can use other light pastel colors such as blue or gray. For most purposes, I do not suggest pink, red, or green.

- **A good-quality photocopy machine can make copies of your JIST Card.** Make sure that the copy quality is excellent and that it will handle light card stock without jamming.

- **Most good print shops can print your JIST Card (and resume) on high-quality printing equipment.** They usually have a selection of card stock and paper. They may also have matching paper to give a coordinated look to your resume, JIST Card, thank-you notes, and envelopes.

- **Look in the yellow pages for printing and word processing.** Check under headings such as Printers, Resume Service, Typing Service, and Secretarial Services. Call and ask for approximate prices for what you need to have done.

- **You often save time and money by having your resume and JIST Card prepared at the same time.** But do this only if writing your resume does not delay the start of your job search—and distribution of your JIST Cards. Resumes are covered in Chapter 13.

Get Your JIST Card in Circulation

Once you have your JIST Card, use it! Give hundreds away freely because they will not help you get a job if they sit on your desk. The more JIST Cards you have in circulation, the more people know about you and your skills. Try them, they work.

CHAPTER 10

Dialing for Dollars

Get Results with Telephone Contacts

Using the telephone is one of the most efficient ways of looking for work. You don't spend time traveling, and you can talk to a large number of people in a very short time. In one morning, for example, you can easily talk to more than twenty employers—once you learn how.

In fact, many job seekers get more interviews by using the phone than by any other method. You can call people you know to get referrals to employers, and then call the employers to request interviews. And you can make cold calls to employers whose names you get from the yellow pages and the Internet.

This chapter shows you some very effective ways to use the telephone to find job openings and set up interviews.

Overcome Phone Phobia

You may find it hard to use the phone in the way I suggest. Many people do. They think it is pushy to call someone and ask for an interview. Before you decide that this technique is not for you, think about why you are afraid. What is the worst thing that can happen to you?

Most calls take only a minute or so. And most employers don't mind talking to a person they might be interested in hiring.

> **TIP**
>
> *Making these calls requires you to overcome shyness. But once you get used to it, phone calls are quite easy to make.*

I suggest that you start by making calls to people you know—your warm contacts. Then call the people they refer you to. This network of people is often happy to help you. Even people you pick from the yellow pages will usually treat you well. The experience of thousands of job seekers is that very few people will be rude to you. And you probably wouldn't want to work for those who are rude.

Sample Phone Contact Based on JIST Card Content

You did a lot of work on your JIST Card in Chapter 9. Your JIST Card can be used as the basis for what you say in a phone call. Remember John Kijek's JIST Card from the last chapter? I used the content of his JIST Card to create the script for a phone call. As you read the text below, imagine you are an employer who hires people with these skills.

"Hello, my name is John Kijek. I am interested in a position as an auto mechanic. I have over three years of experience, including one year in a full-time auto mechanic's training program. I am familiar with all hand tools and electronic diagnostic equipment, and can handle common auto repair tasks, such as tune-ups, brakes, exhaust systems, and electrical and mechanical repairs. I also work quickly, often completing jobs correctly in less than the standard time. I have all the tools needed to start work immediately. I can work any shift and prefer full-time work. I am also honest, reliable, and good with people. When may I come in for an interview?"

How Did You React to This Phone Call?

If you were an employer, how would you feel about a person who called you with this approach? If you needed a worker like this, would you give him an interview?

_____

_____

_____

_____

_____

Just as with the JIST Card, most people say that this phone script makes a positive impression. Most people say they would give John an interview if they had an opening. Not everyone, but most. For this reason, reading a phone script based on your JIST Card is a very effective way to use the telephone.

Tips for Completing an Effective Phone Script

To help you write your phone script, I provide a worksheet on the next page. Read the tips that follow carefully. Then use the information on your JIST Card to help you fill in each section of "Your Telephone Contact Worksheet." Write with a pencil or erasable pen so that you can rewrite or make changes easily.

- **Write exactly what you will say on the phone.** A written script will help you present yourself effectively and keep you from stumbling for the right words.

- **Keep your telephone script short.** Present just the information an employer would want to know about you and ask for an interview. A good phone script can be read out loud in about 30 seconds or less. This is about the same time it takes to read a JIST Card. Short!

- **Write your script the way you talk.** Since you have completed your JIST Card, use it as the basis for your telephone script. But your JIST Card uses short sentences and phrases, and you probably wouldn't talk that way. So add some words to your script to make it sound natural when you say it out loud.

Anatomy of a Phone Script

Here is a sample phone script for a person with more experience and formal education. This one is a bit longer than the other sample but still can be read in about thirty seconds.

Like a JIST Card, your phone script can be separated into separate sections. The five parts of a phone script are pointed out in the sample below.

Your name statement   Your job objective statement

Hello, my name is Lisa Farkel. *I am interested in a management position in a small- to medium-size organization.* *I have a degree in business plus over five years' experience in increasingly responsible management positions. I have supervised as many as twelve staff whose productivity increased by 27 percent over two years. During a three-year period, I was promoted twice and have excellent references. I initiated a customer follow-up program that increased sales by 22 percent within twelve months. I get along well with others, am a good team worker, and am willing to travel or work any hours as needed.*

Your strengths statement

I am hard working, self-motivated, and willing to accept responsibility.

Your good-worker traits statement

When may I come in for an interview?

Your goal statement

Your Telephone Contact Worksheet

This worksheet includes tips for writing the five parts of a phone script. Read the tips for each part, and then complete that section of the worksheet. You will write your final phone script on the next worksheet. Refer to your JIST Card from the last chapter to help you complete each section of the worksheet.

1. **Your name statement.** This one is easy. Just fill in the blank.

   Hello, my name is _____

2. **Your job objective statement.** Always begin your statement with "I am interested in a position as." If you say you are "looking for a job" or something similar, you often will be interrupted and told there are no openings. It takes you only about thirty seconds to read your script, and you don't want to get rejected before you begin. So avoid the word "job" in your first sentence. After many years of experience, I know that this approach works! If the job objective from your JIST Card sounds good when you say it out loud, write it below. If it doesn't, change it around a bit. For example, if your JIST Card says you want a clerical/general office position, your phone script might say "I am interested in a clerical or general office position."

   I am interested in a position as _____

   _____

3. **Your strengths statement.** The experience and skills sections of your JIST Card list your length of experience, training, education, special skills related to the job, and accomplishments. Your phone script will use much of that same content. Rewriting the content from these parts of your JIST Card may take some time because your script must sound natural. You may find it helpful to write and edit this section on a separate piece of paper before writing it here.

   _____

   _____

   _____

   _____

   _____

   _____

4. **Your good-worker traits statement.** Simply take the last lines from your JIST Card and make these key adaptive skills into a sentence. For example, "reliable, hard working, learn quickly" from a JIST Card might be written in a phone script as "I am reliable and hard working, and I learn quickly."

_____

_____

5. **Your goal statement.** Your goal is to get an interview. The closing statement has been filled in for you because—that's right—it works! If you ask, "May I come in for an interview?," the employer could reply "No." Don't make it easy for them to say no! Once again, after many years of experience, this is how I suggest you handle the final line of your script:

When may I come in for an interview?

Your Final Phone Script Worksheet

When practicing a phone contact, it is important to have your script in front of you. Read it out loud until you know it by memory. Before you write your final script, you may want to read it to one or more people. This will allow you to make additional changes until it sounds right. It may take several drafts on separate sheets of paper before you think it is final. Once it is, write your final script below exactly as you will say it. Putting this information in one place will make it easier to read later.

Name. Hello, my name is _____

Job objective. I am interested in a position as _____

_____

Strengths. _____

_____

_____

_____

Good-worker traits. _____

_____

Goal. ___ _When may I come in for an interview?_ ___

Tips for Making Effective Phone Contacts

Now that you have developed your phone script, you need to know how to use it effectively. The tips that follow have been developed over many years, and they work!

Get to the Hiring Authority

You need to get directly to the person who is most likely to supervise you. Do not ask to speak with someone in human resources. Unless you want to work in the human resources department, you don't ask to talk to someone who does.

Depending on the type and size of the organization you're calling, you should have a pretty good idea of the title of the person who would supervise you. In a small business, you might ask to speak to the manager or person in charge. In a larger company, ask for the name of the person who is in charge of a particular department.

Get the Name of a Particular Person

If you don't have the name of the person you need to speak to, ask for it. For example, ask for the name of the person in charge of the accounting department if that is where you want to work. Usually, you will be given the supervisor's name, and your call will be transferred to him or her immediately.

When you get a name, get the correct spelling and write it down right away. Then you can use that person's name in your conversation.

Get Past the Receptionist

In some cases, receptionists or other staff will try to screen out your call. If they find out you are looking for a job, they may transfer you to the human resources department or ask you to send a resume or come by to complete an application. Here are some things you can do to keep from getting screened out:

- **Call back.** Call back a day later and say you are getting ready to send some correspondence to the manager of the department you're interested in. This is true, since you will be sending the manager something soon. Say you want to use the person's correct name and title. This approach usually results in the information you need. Say thank you and call back in a day or so. Then ask for the supervisor or manager by name—you will usually get through to the person.

- **Call when the receptionist is out.** You are likely to get right through if you call when that receptionist is out to lunch. Other good times are just before and after normal work hours. Less-experienced staff members are likely to answer the phones and put you through. Plus, the boss might be in early or working late, when the more experienced receptionist is not there to screen you out.

Dealing with Voice Mail

If you get a voice-mail message instead of an operator or receptionist, you can usually reach someone by pressing "0" or holding on the line. When a person answers, follow the previous points. If you get the voice mail of the person in charge, try calling back later.

Be Referred by Someone the Employer Knows

It is almost always better to be referred by someone the employer knows. If this is the case, immediately give the name of the person who suggested you call. For example:

"Hello, Ms. Beetle. Joan Bugsby suggested I give you a call."

If the receptionist asks why you are calling, say

"A friend of Ms. Beetle suggested I give her a call about a personal matter."

When a friend of the employer recommends that you call, you usually get right through. It's that simple.

When Calling Someone You Know

Sometimes using the telephone script on your worksheet will not make sense. For example, if you are calling someone you know, you would begin with some friendly conversation before getting to your call's purpose. Then you could use your phone script by saying something like this:

"The reason I called is to let you know I am looking for a job, and I thought you might be able to help. Let me tell you a few things about myself. I am looking for a position as. . ." (Continue with your phone script.)

You will encounter other situations that require you to adjust your script. Use your judgment. With practice, it becomes easier!

Your Goal Is to Get an Interview

The primary goal of a phone contact is to get an interview. To succeed, you must be ready to get past the first and even the second rejections. Here are some helpful ideas for reaching your goal of getting an interview.

Ask for an Interview Three Times If Needed

You must practice asking three times for the interview! Here is an example:

1. You: When may I come in for an interview?

   Employer: I don't have any positions open now.

2. You: That's OK, I'd still like to come in to talk to you about the possibility of future openings.

Employer: I don't plan on hiring in the next six months or so.

3. You: Then I'd like to come in and learn more about what you do. I'm sure you know a lot about the industry, and I am looking for ideas on getting into it and moving up.

Although this approach does not always work, asking the third time works more often than most people would believe. It is important to learn how to do this, since overcoming initial rejections is a very important part of getting to "yes."

Arrange a Specific Interview Date and Time

If the employer agrees to an interview, arrange a specific date and time. Send him or her a resume before the interview. If you are not sure of the employer's correct name or its spelling, call back later and ask the receptionist. Also be sure to have the company's correct address.

Sometimes Asking for an Interview Does Not Make Sense

Sometimes you will decide not to ask for an interview. The person may not seem helpful, or you may have caught him or her at a busy time. If so, you can take these approaches:

- **Get a referral.** Ask for names of other people who might be able to help you. Find out how to contact them. Then add these new contacts to your job search network!

- **Ask to call back.** If an employer is busy when you call, ask if you can call back. Get a specific time and day to do this, and add the call to your follow-up system described in Chapter 14. When you call back, the employer will be impressed. He or she may give you an interview for that reason.

- **Ask if you can keep in touch every week or so.** Maybe the employer will hear of an opening or have some other information for you. Many job seekers get their best leads from a person they have checked back with several times.

Follow Up and Send Thank-You Notes

It is important to follow up as promised with the people you contact in your job search. This effort can make a big difference in their remembering and helping you.

> *Some research suggests that following up with your contacts may be among the most effective step you can take.*

Send thank-you notes! It is good manners to thank people who help you. Send a thank-you note right after a phone call. When someone gives you a referral or suggestion, send another note telling him or her how things turned out. When you arrange an interview, send a note saying you look forward to your meeting. Enclosing a JIST Card or resume with your thank-you is often a good idea. I cover thank-you notes in more detail in Chapter 11.

Get Past Your Fear of Rejection— So You Can Get to "Yes"

Making phone calls takes work. It sets you up for some rejection and failure. But, as I suggested earlier, what is the worst thing that can happen? Think about it.

One way to look at the job search process is as a series of "no's." You need to get a lot of them before you finally get to "yes":

no no no no no no no no no no no no no no no no no no no no no no no no no no no
no no no no no no no no no no no no no no no no no no no no no no no no no no no
no no no no no no no no no no no no no no no no no no no **YES**

So, you could think of your phone contact task as getting quickly through the "no's" to get to the "yes."

So plan on making the calls and expecting many "no" and some "yes" responses. The important thing is to make the calls, so you can get to "yes" more quickly. You are more likely to make calls if you schedule them for a certain time each day (see Chapter 14). You should have a goal, so decide how many calls you will make. Most job seekers can make ten or more calls per hour and talk to twenty or more employers in a half day. And these job seekers often get one or more interviews by making that number of calls.
Not bad for a morning's work!

CHAPTER 11

The Seven Phases of an Interview— and How to Succeed in Each

What Employers Really Want to Know

Interviewing is one of the hardest parts of the job search. You may be a bit nervous about it. You may have had a bad interview experience, and you don't look forward to another. Most people end up getting rejected. And they don't like it.

But it doesn't have to be that way. You know what sort of job you want. You have the skills, experience, and training to do it. All you have to do is convince the employer that you can do the job. This chapter and the next will show you how.

Employers use an interview to evaluate you. Will you be able to do the job? Will you be a good employee? If they don't believe you are qualified and willing to work hard, you won't get a job offer. If you meet their expectations, you may get an offer. So you need to know what to do and say in a job interview. You need to meet an employer's expectations.

You looked at employer expectations in Chapter 2 in a section titled "What Employers Look For." These same expectations are very important to an employer in an interview. For this reason, I review these expectations here and add a few details.

Expectation 1: First impressions. The first impression you make in an interview is *very* important. If an employer has a negative first impression, it is not likely to change later. Here are some things that make the most difference in those first few minutes.

- Personal appearance and grooming. Do you look like the right person for the job?

- Manner and social skills. Do you behave well and seem right for the job?

- Paperwork, including application, resume, and JIST Card. Did they help make a good impression before the interview?

Expectation 2: Dependability and other personality traits. The employer wants to know if he or she can count on you. Anything you say or do can help or hurt you.

- Will you come in on time and not abuse days off?

- Can you be trusted?

- Will you get things done on time?

- Do you get along well with others?

- Are you productive and hard working?

Expectation 3: Skills, experience, and training. Can you do the job? The employer will want to find out if you have the needed background. Following are some of the points an employer will want to know. Do you have

- Enough work experience to do the job?

- The needed education and training?

- Interests and hobbies related to the job?

- Other life experiences to support your interest in the job?

- A record of achievement in school, work, or other activities?

- The ability to do the job, if given the chance?

In one way or another, interviewers must find out all these things. At every point in the interview process, they are evaluating you, even when you least expect it.

To help you do well in interviews, I've broken the process into seven parts or phases. As you learn to handle each one, you will be better able to meet an employer's expectations. When you do, you will be much more likely to get a job offer!

The Seven Phases of an Interview

No two interviews are alike, but there are similarities. If you look closely at the interview process, you can see separate phases. Looking at each phase will help you learn how to handle interviews well. Here are the seven phases of an interview that I have defined:

1. Before you go to the interview

2. Opening moves

3. The interview itself

4. Closing the interview

5. Following up

6. Negotiating salary

7. Making a final decision

Every phase is important. The following sections show you why and give you tips for handling each one.

Phase 1: Before You Go to the Interview

Before you even meet, the interviewer can form an impression of you.

How First Impressions Are Made Before an Interview

Write at least two ways you could make a good or a bad first impression before you even get to the interview.

1. _____

2. _____

An interviewer can make judgments about you in many ways before you meet. For example, you may have spoken to the interviewer or the receptionist on the phone. You may have sent a resume and other correspondence. Or someone may have told the employer about you. Be careful in all your early contacts with an employer. Do everything possible to create a good impression. Since your first impression is so important, consider the following points before an interview.

Dress and Groom Carefully

On a normal workday, you may not dress like the boss, but you should on the day you interview. Of course, different jobs and organizations require different styles of dress. For example, a person looking for a job as an auto mechanic would dress differently than one looking for an office job. You will have to make your own decisions about what is right for the jobs that interest you.

Rule for Interview Dress and Grooming

Dress (and groom) like the interviewer is likely to be dressed—but cleaner.

There are many dress and grooming differences for different jobs and in different parts of the country. So you will need to use good judgment in how to dress and groom for your situation. Here are a few tips that make sense in most situations:

- **Don't wear jeans, tank tops, shorts, or other very casual clothes.** Some clothing, even if it looks good on you, isn't good for a serious interview. If you are in doubt about anything you're thinking of wearing, don't wear it.

- **Be conservative.** An interview is not a good time to be trendy. Dressing in a conservative style is usually more important for office jobs and in large, formal organizations.

- **Details count.** One study found that employers reacted to the condition and style of a job seeker's shoes! Dirty or old shoes were an indication, they felt, of someone who was sloppy and would not work hard. Little things do count, so pay attention to everything you wear.

- **Cologne, aftershave, makeup, jewelry.** Again, be conservative. Keep your grooming simple and avoid too much of anything. Use perfume or cologne lightly or not at all.

- **Careful grooming is a must.** Get those hands and nails extra clean and manicured. Eliminate stray facial hairs. Get a simple hairstyle. Pay attention to the small details of your grooming. Employers notice.

- **Spend some money if necessary.** You don't need to spend a lot of money to dress well for an interview. Get your hair styled. Look a bit sharper than you usually do. If you have a limited budget, borrow something that looks good on you. Make sure you have at least one interview outfit that fits well and looks good. It's important.

- **Consider an interview "uniform."** Some styles are almost always acceptable in certain jobs. For men working in an office, a conservative approach might include slacks, a sports jacket, a solid-color shirt, and a conservative tie. Women have more alternatives, but a simple tailored skirt, matching jacket, and white blouse are safe choices.

- **Dress up, not down.** Many jobs, even many office jobs, don't require formal dress. But, for your interview, plan to dress a few notches above the clothing you might normally wear in that job. You can, of course, overdress for an interview too. That's why my "Rule for Interview Dress and Grooming" is so important.

- **Ask for advice.** If you are not sure how to dress and groom for an interview, discuss proper interview dress and grooming with friends and family members who have a good sense of style before you finally decide for yourself.

Your Interview Outfit

After you've thought about it, write how you plan to dress and groom for an interview in the space below.

_____

_____

_____

_____

Research the Employer Before the Interview

Learn as much as you can about the organization and the interviewer before an important interview. This will help you make a good impression! For example, knowing that the organization is expanding will help you emphasize the skills it needs. Or knowing the interviewer's hobby will help you make conversation at the interview's beginning. If the company has a Web site, check it out. A good research librarian can also help you get information from online databases, news stories, and other information sources. People who work for the company or who refer you to the employer are also excellent sources of inside information. You should try to find out the following points:

- **The organization**
  - ✔ Company size, number of employees
  - ✔ Major products or services
  - ✔ Competitors and the competitive environment
  - ✔ Major changes in policies or status
  - ✔ Reputation, values
  - ✔ Major weaknesses or opportunities

- **The interviewer**
  - ✔ Level and area of responsibility
  - ✔ Special work-related projects, interests, and accomplishments
  - ✔ Personal information (family, hobbies, and so on)
  - ✔ What sort of boss he or she is
  - ✔ Management style
- **The position**
  - ✔ Does an opening or similar job exist now?
  - ✔ What happened to others in similar positions?
  - ✔ Salary range and benefits?
  - ✔ Duties and responsibilities?

Other Things That Create a Positive First Impression

- **Get there early.** Allow plenty of time to get to the interview a few minutes early. If necessary, call the receptionist for directions.

- **Check your grooming and other details.** Before you go in for the interview, stop in a rest room. Look at yourself in a mirror and make any final adjustments to your hair and clothing. Get relaxed and mentally prepared. Check for extra resumes, JIST Cards, and a pen.

- **Remember that the receptionist's opinion of you matters.** Go out of your way to be polite and friendly to any employee who greets you. If you spoke to the receptionist on the phone, mention that and express appreciation for any help you were offered. Assume that interviewers will hear about everything you do in the waiting room. The interviewer may ask the receptionist how you treated him or her and how you conducted yourself.

- **Consider yourself fortunate if the interviewer is late.** He or she will probably feel bad about making you wait and may give you better-than-average treatment to make up for it. If you have to wait more than twenty minutes or so, ask to reschedule your appointment. You don't want to act as if you have nothing to do. Again, the interviewer will probably make it up to you later.

Some Self-Improvement Notes

Consider what you have learned about phase 1 of an interview and note specific ideas to improve your performance in this phase.

_____

_____

_____

_____

Phase 2: Opening Moves

The first few minutes of an interview are very important. Research indicates that employers quickly form a good or bad impression. If you make a bad impression during the first five minutes of an interview, you probably won't be able to change it.

Once Again, First Impressions Count

You already know how important your dress and grooming are. What else do interviewers react to? List three things that would affect an interviewer's impression of you when you first meet.

1. _____

2. _____

3. _____

What Interviewers React to in the First Few Minutes

Interviewers react to many things you say and do during the first few minutes of an interview. Here are some points they mention most often:

- **Initial greeting.** Be ready for a friendly greeting! Show you are happy to be there. Although this is a business meeting, your social skills will be considered. A firm but not crushing handshake is needed unless the interviewer does not offer to shake hands. Use the interviewer's last name in your greeting if possible, as in "It's good to meet you Ms. Kelly." Ask the receptionist in advance how to pronounce the interviewer's name and how the interviewer likes to be addressed.

- **Posture.** How you stand and sit can make a difference. You look more interested if you lean forward in your chair when talking or listening. If you lean back, you may look too relaxed.

- **Voice.** You may be nervous, but try to sound enthusiastic and friendly. Your voice should be neither too soft nor too loud. Practice sounding confident.

- **Eye contact.** People who don't look others in the eye are considered shy, insecure, and even dishonest. Although you should never stare, you appear more confident when you make eye contact while you listen or speak.

- **Distracting habits.** You may have nervous habits that you don't notice. Most interviewers find such habits annoying. For example, do you play with your hair or clothing? Do you say something like "You know?" or "Uhh" over and over? *("Uhh, you know what I mean?")* The best way to see yourself as others do is to have someone videotape you while you role-play an interview. If that is not possible, become aware of how others see you, and then try to change your negative behavior. Your friends and relatives can help you notice habits that could bother an interviewer.

Use the First Few Minutes to Establish the Relationship

Almost all interviews begin with informal conversation. Favorite subjects are the weather, if you had trouble getting to the office, and similar topics. This informal talk seems to have nothing to do with the interview, but it does. These first few minutes allow an interviewer to find out how well you relate to others socially. There are many steps you can take to improve the first few minutes of an interview. Here are some suggestions from experienced interviewers.

- **Allow things to happen.** Relax. Don't feel you have to start a serious interview right away. Follow the employer's lead.

- **Smile.** Look and sound happy to be there and to meet the interviewer.

- **Use the interviewer's name in a formal way.** Use "Mister Rogers" or "Miss Evans" unless you are asked to use another name. Say his or her name as often as you can in your conversation.

- **Compliment something in the interviewer's office or look for something you have in common with the interviewer.** Most offices have photographs or decorations you can comment on. Say how great her kids look or ask whether he decorated the office himself.

- **Ask some opening questions.** After a few minutes of friendly talk, you could ask a question to get things started. For example: "I'd like to know more about what your organization does. Would you mind telling me?" Or, "I have a background in _____, and I'm interested in how these skills might best be used in an organization such as yours."

Some Self-Improvement Notes

Consider what you have learned about phase 2 of an interview and note any specific ideas to improve your interview performance.

_____

_____

_____

_____

_____

Phase 3: The Interview Itself

Phase 3 is the most complicated part of the interview. This is when the interviewer tries to discover your strengths and weaknesses. Phase 3 can last from fifteen minutes to forty-five or more.

Interviewers may ask you almost anything during this time. They are looking for any problems you may have. They also want to be convinced that you have the skills, experience, and personality to do a good job. If you have made a good impression during the earlier phases of an interview, you can use this phase to talk about your qualifications for the job.

Key Steps You Can Take for This Phase

- **Know your key skills.** Select key skills you have to support doing the job the company is trying to fill. Then emphasize these skills in the interview.

- **Answer problem interview questions.** Every interviewer will ask you difficult questions. Be ready to answer them! In one survey, employers said that most of the people they interviewed could not answer one or more problem questions. More than 80 percent could not explain the skills they had for the job. Obviously, not being able to give good answers to basic interview questions is a big problem for most job seekers. The good news is that you can learn to answer most interview questions. This can make all the difference in getting a job offer. See the next section for more details.

- **Know something about the job.** Look up a description of the job in a reference such as the *Occupational Outlook Handbook* (available from JIST Works), and then emphasize why you are prepared to do that job well.

- **Ask good questions.** List points you want to know before you go to the interview. They may include information on job responsibilities, benefits, who you would report to, and office hours. Then ask these questions in the interview.

- **Show support documents.** Take extra copies of your resume, JIST Card, and letters of reference. If you have a portfolio with samples of your work and other useful items, have it on hand as well.

- **Give the employer a reason to hire you over someone else!** If you want the job, this is the most important point of all. Think about it in advance and give the employer one or more good reasons to hire you!

The Top Ten Tough Interview Questions

There are thousands of possible interview questions. That is too many to prepare for. So I've developed the ten questions that follow. Although the questions may be asked in different words, they represent the problem questions you are most likely to face during interviews. If you can learn to give good answers to these questions, you will be able to handle most others.

The Ten Most Frequently Asked Interview Questions

1. Why don't you tell me about yourself?

2. Why should I hire you?

3. What are your major strengths?

4. What are your major weaknesses?

5. What sort of pay do you expect to receive?

6. How does your previous experience relate to the jobs we have here?

7. What are your plans for the future?

8. What will your former employers (or references) say about you?

9. Why are you looking for this sort of position and why here?

10. Why don't you tell me about your personal situation?

The next chapter shows you how to answer these questions. It also shows you how to answer other difficult interview questions.

Some Self-Improvement Notes

Consider what you have learned about phase 3 of an interview and note any specific ideas to improve your interview performance.

_____

_____

_____

_____

_____

Phase 4: Closing the Interview

You can end an interview as effectively as you began it. While techniques for ending an interview are often overlooked, how you end it can make a big difference. Here are some tips.

- **Summarize at the end.** As an interview is about to close, take a few minutes to summarize your key strengths. Point out the strengths you have for the job and why you believe you can do it well. If any problems or weaknesses come up, state why they will not keep you from doing a good job.

- **If you want the job, ask for it.** If you are interested in the job, say so! If you want the job, ask for it! Many employers will hire one person over another because one candidate really wants it and says so.

- **Use the call-back close technique.** The call-back close is a technique that can end the interview to your advantage. You may not be comfortable with it at first. It takes some practice to use the call-back close technique, but it works!

Use the Call-Back Close Technique

1. Thank the interviewer by name.

2. Express your interest in the job and organization.

3. Arrange a reason and a time to contact the employer again.

4. Say good-bye.

A Sample Call-Back Close

Here's an example of a call-back interview close:

Thank the interviewer by name: While shaking hands, say *"Thank you, Mr. Williams, for your time today."*

Express interest: Tell the employer that you are interested in the position or organization (or both!). For example, *"The position we discussed today is just what I have been looking for. I am very impressed by your organization and believe I can make a contribution here."*

Arrange a reason and a time to call back: If the interviewer has been helpful, he or she won't mind your following up. It's important that you arrange a day and time to contact the interviewer again. Never expect the employer to contact you. Say something like *"I'm sure I'll have other questions. When would be the best time for me to get back to you?"*

Say good-bye: After you've set a time and date to contact the interviewer again, thank him or her by name and say good-bye. *"Thank you, Mrs. Mullahy, for the time you gave me today. I will contact you next Tuesday morning, between 9 and 10 o'clock."*

Some Self-Improvement Notes

Consider what you have learned about phase 4 of an interview and note any specific ideas to improve your interview performance.

_____

_____

_____

_____

_____

Phase 5: Following Up After the Interview

Once you've left the interview it's over, right? Not really. You need to follow up! This can make the difference between you and someone else getting the job. Here are some steps you should take.

- **Send a thank-you note.** As soon as possible after the interview—and no later than twenty-four hours—send a thank-you note. You can send your note by mail or by e-mail, although mailed thank-you notes are less likely to be "deleted." If by mail, enclose another JIST Card or resume or both. If by e-mail, include your JIST Card and resume as an attachment file.

- **Make notes.** Write yourself notes about the interview while it is fresh in your mind. This might include key responsibilities, benefits, and other details you may not remember in a week or so.

- **Follow up as promised.** If you said you would call back next Tuesday at 9 o'clock, do it. You will impress the interviewer with how well-organized you are.

More on the Importance of Sending Thank-You Notes

Sending a thank-you note is a simple act of appreciation. People who receive them appreciate them. And thank-you notes have practical benefits. People who receive your notes are more likely to remember you. Employers say they rarely get thank-you notes. They describe people who send them in positive terms, such as thoughtful, well-organized, and thorough.

A thank-you note won't get you a job you're not qualified for, but it will impress many employers. When a job you are qualified for opens up, they will remember you. People in your job search network will also be more interested in helping you when you thank them.

Tips for Preparing Thank-You Notes

As stated earlier, a paper thank-you note is more likely to be noticed by a busy employer who gets a lot of e-mail. You can also send a paper thank-you note after an e-mail note. Next are some tips for preparing thank-you notes in paper form. Many of these hints apply to e-mail notes as well.

- **Paper and envelope.** You can use note-size paper and smaller envelopes. Notes with a preprinted "Thank You" on the front are available at any stationery or office-supply store. Use good-quality paper with matching envelopes in white, off-white, or another conservative color.

- **Typed versus handwritten.** Handwritten notes are fine unless your handwriting does not look good. If so, you can word-process your notes on your computer.

- **Salutation.** Unless you are thanking a friend or relative, don't use first names. Write "Dear Ms. Krenshaw" or "Ms. Krenshaw" rather than "Dear Vera." Include the date.

- **The note itself.** Keep your note short and friendly. This is not the place to write, "The reason you should hire me is . . ." Remember that the note is a thank-you for a person's time and help. Do not make a hard-sell pitch for what you want to get from the person. As appropriate, be specific about when you will next contact him or her. If a meeting is planned, say you are looking forward to it and name the date and time.

- **Your signature.** Use your first and last name. Avoid initials. Make your signature legible.

- **When to send it.** As stated earlier, send your note no later than twenty-four hours after you make contact. Ideally, you should write it immediately after the contact while the details are fresh in your mind. Always send a note after an interview, even if things did not go well. The interviewer may feel badly, too, and give you another chance.

- **Enclosure.** Depending on the situation, a JIST Card is often the ideal enclosure. It's a soft sell and provides your contact information if the person should wish to reach you. ("Gosh, that job just opened up! Who was that person I spoke with last week?") Make sure your note cards are at least as big as the JIST Card so you don't have to fold the note card.

Sample Thank-You Notes

2244 Riverwood Avenue
Philadelphia, PA 17963
April 16, XXXX

Ms. Helen A. Colcord
Henderson & Associates, Inc.
1801 Washington Blvd., Suite 1201
Philadelphia, PA 17993

Dear Ms. Colcord:

Thank you for sharing your time with me so generously today. I really appreciated seeing your state-of-the-art computer equipment.

Your advice has already proved helpful. I have an appointment to meet with Mr. Robert Hopper on Friday. As you anticipated, he does intend to add more computer operators in the next few months.

In case you think of someone else who might need a person like me, I'm enclosing another JIST Card. I will let you know how the interview with Mr. Hopper goes.

Sincerely,

William Henderson

William Henderson

1030 College Avenue
Denver, Colorado 802
October 22, XXXX

Mr. Robert Hernandez
Manager, Data Processing Division
Harmon Enterprises
4648 Pearl Street
Denver, Colorado 80442

Dear Mr. Hernandez,

Thank you for meeting with me today. I'm impressed by the high standards your department maintains. The more I heard and saw, the more interested I became in working for your firm.

As we agreed, I will call you next Monday, October 28. In the meantime, I would be pleased to answer any additional questions you may have.

Sincerely,
Kay Howell

Some Self-Improvement Notes

Consider what you have learned about phase 5 of an interview and note any specific ideas to improve your interview performance.

_____

_____

_____

_____

_____

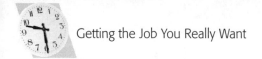

Phase 6: Negotiating Salary

Pay attention now. This information could end up being worth much more to you than the price of this book. Imagine that the job you are interviewing for sounds ideal. But you still have to answer some tough questions.

What Would You Say?

Suppose the interviewer asks, "What do you expect to get paid for this position?" What would you say? Write it here:

_____

_____

_____

_____

Whatever you say, you will probably lose—unless you are prepared. Suppose the employer was willing to pay $22,000 per year. If you say you will take $20,000, guess what you will be paid? At $200 a second, that may have been the most expensive ten seconds in your life!

There are other ways you can lose, too. The employer may decide not to hire you. He or she may think the company needs a person who is worth $22,000—which leaves you out. Or, you may have asked for $26,000 and hoped you would get it. You could lose here, too. Many employers will assume you'll be unhappy with the lower salary they had in mind, even if you would have been happy with it. So it is important to know how to answer questions about pay. Here is one important point to remember:

Salary Negotiation Rule
Never discuss salary until you are being offered the job.

Now you understand why. Many job seekers have trouble answering salary-related questions. Lots of trouble. I hope you can learn to do better than most job seekers. You will read more about negotiating salary in the next chapter.

Some Self-Improvement Notes

Consider what you have learned about phase 6 of an interview and note any specific ideas to improve your interview performance.

_____

_____

_____

_____

Phase 7: Making a Final Decision

The interview process is not over until you accept a job offer. Taking a job can sometimes be an easy decision. At other times, deciding can be very hard.

The sample worksheet that follows will help you put the positives and negatives of a difficult decision down on paper. People who use this process tend to make better decisions. Research shows these individuals tend to be happier with their decisions, even if it did not work out. You can use this example to help you make any decision.

The sample shows how one person considered a job offer. You can make your own worksheet on a blank sheet of paper. The final decision will always be yours, but this form can help you make a good decision.

A Sample Decision-Making Worksheet

Option Considered: <u>To accept or reject the job offer as Director of Sales, Farkel's Foods</u>

	Positives	Negatives
Tangible Things for Me	1. More money 2. Work I will like better. 3. An office of my own.	1. Lots of pressure and long hours. 2. Less job security. 3. My boss is known to have a bad temper.
Tangible Things for Others	1. Can move back to the country. 2. Can afford better clothes and more recreation for the family. 3. Can start a college fund for the kids.	1. I'll be away from home more often. 2. Less private time. 3. More driving. 4. Will be taking work home more often.
Self-Approval/ Disapproval	1. I get to set my own goals and timetables, at least to a point. 2. I'll have a chance to become better known in the field.	1. I may feel guilty about being on the road so much and away from the family.
Social Approval/ Disapproval	1. My friends and family will be impressed. 2. Professionally, this company is a leader.	1. I'll have to prove myself to some of our long-time sales reps and customers. 2. Other people in the firm may resent my status.

Some Self-Improvement Notes

Consider what you have learned about phase 7 of an interview and note any specific ideas to improve your interview performance.

_____

_____

_____

_____

Practice for Successful Interviews

You have now learned about the seven phases of an interview. I hope this information helps you understand and improve your interview performance. In the next chapter, you will learn to answer problem interview questions. Knowing how to answer these questions will help you get the job you want!

CHAPTER 12

Answering Problem Interview Questions

Don't Be Caught by Surprise

In the last chapter, you learned that an interview has seven phases. The third phase is the interview itself. This is the most complicated part of the interview. It can last fifteen to forty-five minutes or more.

An interviewer can ask you almost anything and is trying to find out about your strengths and weaknesses. He or she is looking for any problems you may have. The interviewer also wants to be convinced that you have the skills, experience, and personality to do a good job.

Answering Problem Questions

The biggest challenge most job seekers face in an interview is answering one or more problem questions. Write an answer to the problem question below. Keep your interview response short and positive.

Interview question: What are your plans for the future? _____

_____

_____

_____

Are you satisfied with what you wrote? Would your answer make a good impression on an interviewer? Would your answer meet one or more of an employer's expectations?

If you are like most job seekers, you can learn to do better. As I noted earlier, employers in one survey said that most of the people they interviewed could not answer one or more problem questions. More than 80 percent could not even describe the skills they had for the job. This is a serious problem for most job seekers. It keeps many of them from getting good jobs that use their skills. You will learn to do better.

The following list shows the ten questions you are most likely to be asked during an interview. This is the same list you saw in Chapter 11. While the questions may not be asked in these exact words, the interviewer is looking for answers to these questions.

The Ten Most Frequently Asked Interview Questions

1. Why don't you tell me about yourself?

2. Why should I hire you?

3. What are your major strengths?

4. What are your major weaknesses?

5. What sort of pay do you expect to receive?

6. How does your previous experience relate to the jobs we have here?

7. What are your plans for the future?

8. What will your former employers (or references) say about you?

9. Why are you looking for this sort of position and why here?

10. Why don't you tell me about your personal situation?

Besides these questions, there are hundreds of others that employers ask. So it is more important to learn a technique for answering any question than to memorize the answers to a few questions. Let's take some time now to learn a technique for answering all kinds of difficult questions.

Three Steps to Answering Problem Questions

The following approach gives you a simple way of looking at each question you are asked in an interview. With practice, you can use the steps to answer most interview questions.

Step 1. Understand what is really being asked. Most problem questions are about the employer's expectation of your dependability and other personality traits. The questions are often along these lines:

- Can we depend on you?

- Are you easy to get along with?

- Are you a good worker?

The question may also relate to another basic employer expectation: Do you have the skills, experience, and training to do the job?

Step 2. Answer the question briefly and in a non-damaging way.

- Acknowledge the facts.

- But present them as advantages, not disadvantages.

Step 3. Answer the real concern by presenting your skills. Once you know what the question is really asking, answer the question as it is asked. But add the information that will help you most:

- Mention one or more of your key skills, as listed on your JIST Card.

- Give examples to support your skills statements.

Notice how important it is to know what an employer expects. You can review this information in Chapter 2 under "What Employers Look For" or in Chapter 11.

Use the Three Steps to Answer a Problem Question

Let me give you an example of how to use the three-step technique. Here is one of the ten questions you are likely to be asked in an interview: *"What are your plans for the future?"* How would you answer this? Let's use the three steps to see how you could give an honest answer that meets the employer's expectations.

Step 1: Understand What Is Really Being Asked

What does the interviewer really want to know? Look at the three-step technique described above and decide what the employer is looking for with this question.

Write what you think is really being asked. _____

_____

_____

In this case, the interviewer probably wants to know if you are going to remain on the job long enough. And he or she probably wants to know that you *want* this particular kind of job in this type of organization. Saying that you hope to sail around the world may be interesting, but it would not be a good response.

Step 2: Answer the Question Briefly and in a Non-Damaging Way

First, answer the question as it is asked. For example, you could say *"There are many things I want to do over the next five years. One is to get settled into the career I have decided on and learn as much as I can."*

This is a brief answer to the question. It doesn't say much and it doesn't hurt you, but it allows you to begin answering the real question.

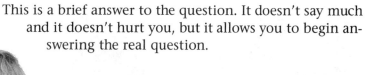

Step 3: Answer the Real Concern by Presenting Your Skills

Ask yourself what the employer really wants to know by asking this question. While it may not be obvious, the interviewer probably wants to know if he or she can depend on you. Knowing this, here is what you might say:

"I've had a number of jobs (or had one job, been unemployed, or had other experiences), and I have learned to value a good, stable position. My variety of experiences is an asset because I have learned so many things I can now apply to this position. I am looking for a position where I can get totally involved, work hard, and do well."

Depending on your situation, there are many other things you could say. This response emphasizes your stability. As brief as it is, this answer meets one of the major employer's expectations.

Early in this chapter you wrote an answer to the interview question, "What are your plans for the future?" Look at what you wrote there. Then use the three-step process to write a better answer below.

Interview question: What are your plans for the future? _____

_____

_____

_____

Good Answers to the Ten Most Frequently Asked Interview Questions

Now, let's look at some tips for answering the top ten interview questions. Your responses will be different from the examples I give here. But if you use the three steps to answering problem questions, you can learn how to answer these questions effectively. Then you'll be ready to do better than most of the job seekers who are competing with you.

Question 1: Why Don't You Tell Me About Yourself?

The interviewer does not want to know your life history! Instead, he or she wants you to explain how your background relates to doing the job. Following is how one person might respond:

"I grew up in the Southwest and my parents and one sister still live there. I always did well in school, and by the time I graduated from high school, I knew I wanted to work in a business setting. I had taken computer and other business classes and had done well in them. The jobs I've had while going to school have taught me how many small businesses are run. In one of these jobs, I was given complete responsibility for the night operations of a wholesale grocery business that grossed over $2 million a year. I learned there how to supervise others and solve problems under pressure."

This answer gives a brief personal history and then gets right into the job seeker's skills and experiences. A different job would require you to stress different skills. Your personal history is unique, but you can still use the three steps to answer the question for yourself.

Your Answer to Problem Question 1

How would you answer problem question 1 in an interview? Use the three-step process to write your own answer here.

_____

_____

_____

_____

_____

Question 2: Why Should I Hire You?

This is the most important question of all! If you don't have a good reason why someone should hire you, why will anyone? This question is not often asked so clearly, but it is "the" question behind many other interview questions.

The best answer shows how you can solve a problem for the employer, help the business make more money, or provide something else of value that the company needs. Think about the most valuable thing you can do for an organization. You should probably include that information in your answer. Here is a sample response from a person with recent training but little work experience:

"I have over two years of training in this field and know about all the latest equipment and methods. That means I can get right to work and be productive almost right away. I am also willing to work hard to learn new things. During the entire time I went to school, I held a full-time job to help earn the tuition and support myself. I learned to work hard and concentrate on what was important. I expect to do the same thing here. Since I won't be going to school now, I plan on putting in extra time after regular work hours to learn anything this job needs."

Your Answer to Problem Question 2

Now think about the job you want. What strengths can you bring to that job? Write your answer to the question here.

_____

_____

_____

_____

_____

Question 3: What Are Your Major Strengths?

This is a direct question with little hidden meaning. Answer it by emphasizing the adaptive skills you defined in Chapter 3. These are the skills employers are most concerned about. Here is one answer from a person who had little prior work experience:

"I think one of my strengths is that you can depend on me. I work very hard to meet deadlines and don't need a lot of supervision in doing so. If I don't know what to do, I don't mind asking. In high school, I got a solid B-plus average even though I was very involved in sports. I always got my assignments in on time and somehow found the time to do extra credit work, too."

Your Answer to Problem Question 3

Review Chapter 3 and use at least two of your top adaptive skills in answering this question.

_____

_____

_____

_____

Question 4: What Are Your Major Weaknesses?

This is a trick question. Most job seekers don't handle this one well. If you discuss what you don't do well, you may not get the job. If you say you have no weaknesses, the interviewer won't believe you. Ask yourself what the interviewer really wants to know. He or she wants to know that you are aware of your weaknesses. The interviewer wants to know that you have learned to overcome them so that they don't affect your work. Using the second step of the three-step process would result in a response like this:

"I do have some weaknesses. For example, in previous jobs I would get annoyed with coworkers who didn't work as hard as I did. I sometimes said so to them, and several times I refused to do their work when they asked me to."

You have answered the question, but the response should not end there! Using step three of the three-step process would result in a statement like this:

"But I have learned to deal with this better. I still work hard, but now I let the supervisor deal with another worker's problems. I've also gained some skills as a supervisor myself. I've learned to motivate others to do more because they want to, not because I want them to."

Did you notice that this weakness isn't such a weakness at all? Many of our strengths began in failure. We learned from them and got better. Your answer to any interview question should always present your positives.

Your Answer to Problem Question 4

List some weaknesses that you could use in your own answer. Then pick one that can be turned into a positive and use it to respond to the question. Remember to use the three steps!

_____

_____

_____

_____

_____

Question 5: What Sort of Pay Do You Expect?

This is another trick question. Knowing how to answer this question could be worth a lot of money! In the previous chapter, you learned that one of the interview phases is negotiating salary. This question deals with that issue. In that chapter, you learned this important rule in salary negotiation:

Farr's Salary Negotiation Rule 1
Never discuss salary until you are being offered the job.

Before you continue, it might be helpful to review why this is so. Let's review that I said in the previous chapter to refresh your memory:

Whatever you say, you will probably lose. Suppose the employer was willing to pay $22,000 per year. If you say you will take $20,000, guess what you will be paid? That may have been the most expensive ten seconds in your life!

There are other ways you can lose, too. The employer may decide not to hire you. He or she may think the company needs a person who is worth $22,000—which leaves you out.

Or, you may have asked for $26,000 and hoped you would get it. You could lose here, too. Many employers will assume you'll be unhappy with the salary they had in mind, even if you would have been happy with it.

Good advice. But you didn't really learn how to answer the salary question. For this question, you need to remember three additional rules.

Farr's Salary Negotiation Rule 2

Know the probable salary range in advance.

Before the interview, you need to know what similar jobs in similar types of organizations pay. To find out, ask others in similar jobs. The library and the Internet are other good sources of salary information. At the library, ask the research librarian to help you. You also can call your state employment service's statistical office. It is required to keep this information for each area. This research will give you an idea of the pay for the position you're seeking.

Farr's Salary Negotiation Rule 3

Bracket your salary range.

If you think the employer pays between $20,000 and $25,000 per year, state your range as "low to mid-twenties." That covers the amount the employer probably had in mind and gives you room to get more. Bracketing will not get you screened out, and it leaves open the possibility of getting more than your minimum.

Look over the examples below. The principles apply for any salary range, so simply translate the concept and apply it to the salary range that makes sense for you.

Some Examples of Salary Brackets

If the Job Pays	You Say
$9/hour	$8 to $11 per hour
$15,000/year	mid- to upper teens
$18,000/year	upper teens to low twenties
$22,000/year	low to mid-twenties
$27,500/year	upper twenties to low thirties
$90,000/year	high five-figure to low six-figure

OK, that last entry was for fun. But I hope you get the idea. Bracketing keeps your options open. It won't get you screened out, and it may allow you to get a higher offer than you might have otherwise. Which brings us to my next rule.

Farr's Salary Negotiation Rule 4

Never say no to a job offer before it is made or until twenty-four hours have passed.

Remember, the objective of an interview is to get a job offer. Many job seekers get screened out early in the interview by discussing salary. If you give the impression that the job doesn't pay what you had hoped, or that it pays more, you could get screened out. The best approach is to avoid discussing salary until you are offered the job. If the money is not what you had in mind, say you want to consider the offer and will call back the next day. You can always turn it down then.

You may also say that if the salary were higher you would take the position. Perhaps you could be given more responsibility to justify a higher wage? Or you could negotiate an increase after a certain period of time? Do not negotiate like this unless you are willing to give up the job offer. But you just might be able to get a counteroffer that you would accept.

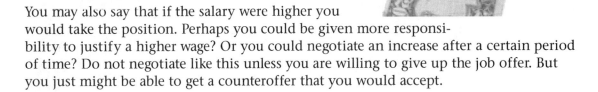

Your Answer to Problem Question 5

Now, using the bracketing technique, answer the salary question.

_____

_____

_____

_____

_____

Question 6: How Does Your Previous Experience Relate to the Jobs We Have Here?

This one requires a direct response. The employer is really asking, "Can you prove you have the experience and skills to do the job?" The question is directly related to the employer's expectation on skills and training. In some cases, other people with better credentials than yours will want the job you're after. You can even mention this, and then explain why you are a better choice. Here is an example of how one person answered this question:

"As you know, I have over five years of experience in a variety of jobs. While this job is in a different industry, it will also require my skills in managing people and meeting the public. In fact, my daily contact with large numbers of people on previous jobs has taught me how to work under pressure. I feel very able to deal with pressure and to get the job done."

One of the jobs this person had was waitress. She had to learn to handle people under pressure in such a job. By presenting the skills she used, her answer tells the employer that she could use the same skills in another job.

Your Answer to Problem Question 6

Be sure to mention any specific skills and training you have that will help you do the job. Include your greatest job-related strengths in your answer.

_____

_____

_____

_____

_____

Question 7: What Are Your Plans for the Future?

As you may recall, I cover this question earlier in this chapter. The interviewer is really asking whether you are likely to remain on the job. But an employer has many concerns, depending on your situation, including

- Will you be happy with the salary? (If not, you may leave.)

- Will you leave to raise a family or relocate because of a spouse's job transfer?

- Do you have a history of leaving jobs after a short stay? (If so, it seems likely you will do so again.)

- Are you overqualified? (And likely to be unhappy in this job—and eventually leave?)

Depending on the situation, there may be other concerns, too. You may wish to practice answering this question again. If so, put yourself in an employer's place. Then answer the real question.

Your Answer to Problem Question 7

Try to bring up anything in your life situation that employers might be concerned about. Then write a response to the question that will put them at ease. Of course, whatever you say should be true.

_____

_____

_____

_____

_____

Question 8: What Will Your Former Employers (or References) Say About You?

This question again concerns the employer's expectation regarding dependability and other adaptive skills. Are you easy to get along with? Are you reliable?

Many employers will call your references and former employers. If you are less than honest about problems in previous jobs, you could get caught! If everyone you ever worked for thinks you are great, answering this question will be easy. But almost everyone has had some problem. If the interviewer is likely to find out about your problem by checking with previous employers, honesty could be the best policy. Consider telling it like it was and accept responsibility for being part of the problem. If you learned something from the experience, say so. Many employers have been fired at some point. It's no sin and often has little to do with being a good worker.

In a way, this question is similar to asking about your major weakness. A good answer can help you get the job—even if you have to reveal some negative information. Here is an example:

"If you check with my two previous employers, they will tell you that I am a good worker and that I do things right. But you may find out that one of them is not too enthusiastic about me. I really can't explain why we did not get along. I tried to do my best, but she passed me over for merit raises twice.

"She will tell you that I got the work done, but she may also tell you that I was not willing to socialize with the other workers after hours. I had a new baby and I was working full time. I was very reliable, but it was true that I didn't go out two or three times a week with the others. I felt uncomfortable on that job and eventually left on my own. My next job was with a boss who will say wonderful things about me. But I thought you might want to know."

It is better to know in advance what a previous employer will say about you. If you do expect a problem from a previous employer, try to find out exactly what will be said. If possible, talk it over with the former employer so you know exactly what he or she will say. Sometimes, you can get your past employer to agree to avoid being negative. Ask the employer to write you a letter of reference. Usually it will not be too negative, and your new employer may accept the letter and not call.

TIP

> *If you know that this employer will give you a negative reference no matter what, think of someone else you worked with closely in the same organization. Ask that person to write you a letter of reference instead.*

Some organizations do not allow their supervisors to discuss previous employees. They are afraid of being sued. If someone calls the organization for a reference, managers or human resources staff give out only your employment dates and nothing else. Since a new employer can't find out about you, he or she may not take a chance on hiring you. This situation makes it even more important for you to get letters of reference from those employers, if they are positive.

Your Answer to Problem Question 8

Go ahead and answer the question now. Try to address any problems you may have had with previous bosses that will be revealed if your references are checked or past employers are called.

_____

_____

_____

_____

_____

Question 9: Why Are You Looking for This Sort of Position and Why Here?

Employers know that you will do better in a job you really want. Employers want to make sure you know what you want. They also want you to tell them what you like about the job, and what you like about doing the job in their organization. The closer you come to wanting what they have, the better.

The best answer for this is the truth. You should have a clear idea of the type of job you want before the interview. You should also know the sort of organization and the type of people you want to work with. You gathered all of this information earlier in this book. If you are interviewing for a job you want, in a place where you think you would enjoy working, answering this question should be easy.

Your Answer to Problem Question 9

Consider your reasons for wanting the type of job you're seeking. Select your top two reasons and include them in your answer. Since you don't yet have a particular employer to respond to, use your imagination to decide what the organization you're interviewing with is like. Then explain what you like about the organization and the job.

_____

_____

_____

_____

_____

Question 10: Why Don't You Tell Me About Your Personal Situation?

Very few interviewers will ask this question so directly. But they want to know the answer. They will often try to find out in casual conversation. While you may feel that this is none of their business, they may not hire you unless they feel comfortable about you and your personal situation.

If you follow the three-step process, you should first ask yourself what employers are really asking. Their concern is whether you can be counted on. Interviewers will look for signs that you are unstable or unreliable.

Laws restrict the types of questions an employer may directly ask without risk of a lawsuit. Even so, most employers want to know enough about you to feel comfortable. They are, after all, people.

Following is a list of points related to your personal situation that an employer might wonder about. You could argue that interviewers would be unfair and biased if they asked these questions. But you must understand employers want to know that you can be counted on. Even if you just moved here, even if you have kids, even if you are single.

Some Things an Employer Might Wonder About Your Personal Situation

The Question	An Employer's Real Concern
Are you single?	Will you stay?
Are you married?	Will you devote the time needed?
Do you have marital or family problems?	Missed work, poor performance, or poor interpersonal skills?
How do you handle money or personal problems?	Theft, irresponsible?
Have you moved recently?	Will you move again?
How do you spend your free time?	Alcohol or substance abuse; other socially unacceptable behavior?
Do you have children?	Child-care problems and days off?

Some Sample Responses to Question 10

Following are some sample responses to direct or indirect questions about your personal situation. If one or more of these life situations are true for you, and they do not limit your ability to work, consider telling the interviewer (even if the employer doesn't directly ask).

When answering a question about your personal life, be friendly and positive. The message to give is that your personal situation will not hurt your ability to do a good job. Instead, suggest that your situation could offer some advantage to the employer! The responses that follow are simple, direct, and positive. Each one also allows you to quickly move to presenting the skills you have to do the job.

- **Young children at home.** *"I have two children, both in school. Child care is no problem since they stay with a good friend."*

- **Single head of household.** *"I'm not married and have two children at home. It is very, very important to me to have a steady income, and so child care is not a problem."*

- **Young and single.** *"I'm not married, and if I should marry, that would not change my plans for a full-time career. Since I don't have any distraction now, I can devote my full attention to my career."*

- **Just moved here.** *"I've decided to settle here in Depression Gulch permanently. I've rented an apartment, and the six moving vans are unloading now."*

- **Relatives, childhood.** *"I had a good childhood. Both of my parents still live within an hour's flight from here, and I see them several times a year."*

- **Leisure.** *"For relaxation I grow worms in my spare time and am a member of the American Worm Growers Association."* OK, that one may not be the best of responses, let's try another one. *"My time is family-centered when I'm not working. I'm also active in several community organizations and spend at least some time each week in church activities."*

All these responses could be expanded, but they should give you ideas on how you might answer personal questions. The responses follow the principles presented in the three steps to answering problem questions.

Your Answer to Problem Question 10

Think about your personal situation and what an employer might want to know about it. If you have more than one issue to explain, list them here. Then write an answer for each one. Remember, you want an employer to know that you will be a responsible, reliable worker. Keep your response positive and mention your skills!

_____

_____

_____

_____

_____

Quick Answers to Other "Problem" Questions

Most people feel that employers will hold one particular point against them. It may be something obvious, like age (being "too old" or "too young"). Or it may be something not so obvious, like not having certain training or work experience.

But employers are also people. They generally try to be fair. And as employers, they are very interested in getting a good worker.

Your job is to make it easy for an interviewer to find out you *can* do the job. The problem is that many interviewers may *assume* you have a problem. They may not ask you directly if their assumption is true for you. And you won't have a chance to tell them that, in your case, their assumption is not true.

For example, if you are more than a little overweight, some employers may feel you will be sick often or be slow in your work. The interviewer will probably not bring it up. But this assumption can affect the employer's opinion, unless you convince him or her that you are healthy, reliable, and quick. You can bring up your weight or not. It is up to you. But it would be wise, if you do not bring it up directly, to emphasize that you do not fit any stereotype.

In almost all cases, the employer's assumptions have to do with, once again, employer's expectation of dependability. Employers need to know that they can depend on you to do the job. If they don't ask, and you don't tell them, who will?

Here are sample statements and recommendations covering typical "problems" that may concern an employer. Some are not fair or accurate assumptions. As a job seeker, though, you need to deal with what is real. Once you have the job, you can show them what is true for you.

- **Too old.** *"I am a very stable worker requiring very little training. I have been dependable all my life, and I am at a point in my career where I don't plan on changing jobs. I still have ten years of work until I plan on retiring, which is probably longer than the average young person stays in a position these days."* (This last statement is quite true, as most employers know.)

- **Too young.** *"I don't have any bad work habits to break, so I can be quickly trained to do things the way you want. I plan on working hard to get established. I'll also work for less money than a more experienced worker. I will prove that I am worth more than I am paid."*

- **Prison or arrest record.** *"You need to know that I've spent time in jail. I learned my lesson and paid my debt to society for a mistake I have not repeated. While there, I studied hard and earned a certificate in this trade. I was in the top one-third of my class."*

- **Unemployed.** *"I've been between jobs now for three months. During that time, I've carefully researched what I want to do and now I'm certain. Let me explain."*

- **Overweight.** *"You may have noticed that I am a tad overweight. Some people think that overweight people are slow, won't work hard, or will be absent frequently. But let me tell you about myself."*

- **Gender.** *"Not many women (or men) are interested in these kinds of positions, so let me tell you why I am."*

- **Race.** Race should not be an issue. Present your skills, do your best, rest your case, and send a thank-you note. This advice is the same for all job seekers.

- **National origin.** A lack of English language skills is a real limitation in getting many jobs. If you are not a citizen of this country, employers will be concerned about your stability on the job—and they may be legally restricted in their ability to hire you. These are specialized problems where you may need help from the agencies who provide assistance to immigrants. Even so, many employers will consider hiring you if you can present a good argument.

- **Physical limitations or disability.** Don't be defensive or clinical. If your disability is obvious, consider mentioning it in a matter-of-fact way. People will want to know that your disability will not be a problem, so explain why it won't be. Then emphasize why you can do the job better than the next job seeker. For example: *"Thank you for the job offer. Before I accept, you should know that I have a minor physical limitation, but it will not affect my performance on the job."*

Illegal Questions

Some people argue that questions on the issues I mention in the previous section are illegal for an employer to ask. I agree that these questions would be in poor taste. But this is a free country. Anyone can ask anything he or she wants. It is what an interviewer *does* with the information that can be a problem. Hiring or not hiring people based on certain criteria is illegal. A number of laws protect people with certain characteristics from being kept out of jobs for those reasons alone. These laws require that people be considered for their ability to do the job and no other criteria.

For example, a woman should be considered fairly for a job as a carpenter based on her ability, not on her gender. A person in a wheelchair should be considered fairly for a job as an accountant based on his or her accounting skills alone. A manager should be hired on his or her management skills and credentials, without race or ethnic background as an issue. This is our right, to be treated fairly. And there is no question in my mind that this should be so.

The problem is that most interviewers will not ask these questions as clearly as they are stated above. But they most likely will wonder how these issues may affect your ability to do the job. You don't have to answer a question if you don't want to. It's a free country for you, too. But you should understand by now that most questions are intended to find out if you will be a good employee. So why not say that, yes, there are good reasons that employers can count on you to do a good job.

Fortunately, most employers are just like you are. They will be sensitive to your feelings and will treat you as an adult. They want to hire someone they believe will do a good job. There is a lot at stake for them, too, in making a hiring decision. So, ultimately, it is your responsibility to convince them you will be a good employee. Do not leave their impressions to chance. Tell them why they should hire you!

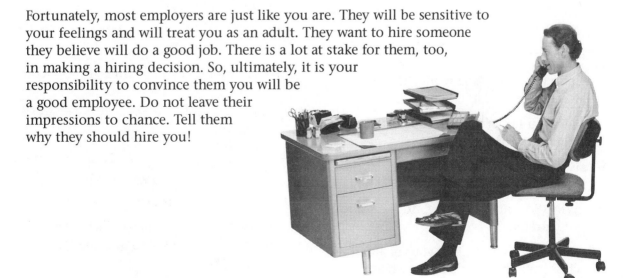

Fifty More Questions

Here is a list of fifty interview questions. It came from a survey of ninety-two professional interviewers who interviewed students for jobs after graduation. Most of the questions are those asked of any adult. Underline the questions you would have trouble answering. These are the ones you need to practice answering! In doing so, remember to use the three-step process.

1. In what school activities have you participated? Why? Which did you enjoy the most?

2. How do you spend your spare time? What are your hobbies?

3. Why do you think you might like to work for our company?

4. What jobs have you held? How were they obtained, and why did you leave?

5. What courses did you like best? Least? Why?

6. Why did you choose your particular field of work?

7. What percentage of your school expense did you earn? How?

8. What do you know about our company?

9. Do you feel that you have received good general training?

10. What qualifications do you have that make you feel that you will be successful in your field?

11. What are your ideas on salary?

12. If you were starting school all over again, what courses would you take?

13. Can you forget your education and start from scratch?

14. How much money do you hope to earn in five years? Ten years?

15. Why did you decide to go to the school you attended?

16. What was your rank in your graduating class in high school? Other schools?

17. Do you think that your extracurricular activities were worth the time you devoted to them? Why?

18. What personal characteristics are necessary for success in your chosen field?

19. Why do you think you would like this particular type of job?

20. Are you looking for a permanent or temporary job?

21. Are you primarily interested in making money or do you feel that service to your fellow human beings is a satisfactory accomplishment?

22. Do you prefer working with others or by yourself?

23. Can you take instructions without feeling upset?

24. Tell me a story!

25. What have you learned from some of the jobs you have held?

26. Can you get recommendations from previous employers?

27. What interests you about our product or service?

28. What was your record in the military service?

29. What do you know about opportunities in the field in which you are trained?

30. How long do you expect to work?

31. Have you ever had any difficulty getting along with fellow students and faculty? Fellow workers?

32. Which of your school years was most difficult?

33. Do you like routine work?

34. Is the stability of your employment important to you?

35. What is your major weakness?

36. Define cooperation.

37. Will you fight to get ahead?

38. Do you have an analytical mind?

39. Are you willing to go where the company sends you?

40. What job in our company would you choose if you were free to do so?

41. Have you plans for further education?

42. What jobs have you enjoyed the most? The least? Why?

43. What are your special abilities?

44. What job in our company do you want to work toward?

45. Would you prefer a large or a small company? Why?

46. How do you feel about overtime work?

47. What kind of work interests you?

48. Do you think that employers should consider grades?

49. Are you interested in research?

50. What have you done that shows initiative and willingness to work?

Plus, One More Question

What is the one question you are most afraid an employer will ask? Write it here. Then use the three-step process to give a positive answer that an employer could accept.

The question: _____

_____

The answer: _____

_____

_____

_____

_____

There you have it. You are now better prepared for a job interview than most other job seekers. If you do well, you will be considered for jobs over people with better credentials. The more interviews you have, the better you will get at handling them. And you will get job offers.

CHAPTER 13

How to Write Resumes and Cover Letters

Use Resumes and Cover Letters to Get Interviews!

Many resume books and job search "experts" tell you that a good resume is important. They say that a well-done resume will help you get an interview over others whose resumes are not as good.

While it is true that a poorly done resume can get you screened out, a resume alone is usually not a good tool for getting an interview. The best way to get an interview is through direct contact with people. As you learned in earlier chapters, most people find their jobs through one of two techniques. They get leads from people they know (warm contacts) or by making direct contacts with employers (cold contacts).

Why Even a "Great" Resume Probably Won't Get You a Job

Sending out lots of resumes is not an effective way to get a job. Posting your resume on job-related Internet sites may not get you much response—unless your skills are very much in demand. While almost any job search technique works for some people, the odds are not in your favor. Mass distribution of your resume often delays direct contact with potential employers. Your resume gets put on a pile or into a database of other resumes from people who are competing for the same job. Even with a good resume, you are far more likely to get screened out in such circumstances.

Resume experts who tell you to create a great resume and then send it to lots of people are giving old-fashioned advice. They assume that the way to get a job is to deal with human resources offices, go after publicly advertised jobs, and use passive job search methods. Instead, this book teaches you to use techniques that are effective with large as well as smaller employers (that may not have a human resources office), to go after the hidden market of jobs that are not advertised (where most jobs are found), and to use active techniques.

Why You Need a Resume

While a resume may not be the best tool to get you an interview, you need one for several reasons.

- Employers expect you to have one.
- A good resume will help you present what you have to offer an employer.
- Using the Internet in your job search requires one.

Employers use resumes to find out about your credentials and experience. Covering these details in an interview is not the best use of that valuable time. A well-written resume forces you to summarize the highlights of your experience. Once you've done this, you are better able to talk about yourself during the interview. If you want to use the Internet to help you look for a job, you need a resume in an electronic format to transmit to employers and to post in searchable databases.

While many books continue to tell job seekers to send out lots of resumes or to post resumes on the Internet in hopes of getting interviews, here is better advice.

The Five Most Effective Ways to Use a Resume

Even an excellent resume won't get you interviews unless you use it effectively. Following are some details on how to best use your resume to get more interviews.

1. **Get the interview first.** It is almost always better to first contact employers by phone, by e-mail, or in person before you send a resume. If possible, get a referral from someone you know. Or make a cold contact directly to the employer. In either case, ask for an interview. If no opening is available now, ask to come in and discuss the possibility of future openings.

2. **Then send your resume.** Whenever possible, send or e-mail your resume after you schedule an interview, so the employer can read about you before your meeting. Valuable interview time can then be spent discussing your skills rather than details that are best presented in a resume.

3. **Follow up with a JIST Card and thank-you note.** Immediately after an interview, send a thank-you note. Even if you use e-mail to communicate with employers, most appreciate a mailed thank-you note. And a mailed note allows you to enclose your JIST Card or another copy of your resume.

4. **Send your resume and JIST Card to everyone in your growing job search network.** This is an excellent way for people in your network to help you find unadvertised leads. They can pass or e-mail information to others who might be interested in a person with your skills.

5. **Send your resume in the traditional way if you can't make direct contact.** In some situations, you can't easily make personal contact with an employer. This is true, for example, if you want to post your resume on the Internet. Another example is when responding to a want ad that gives only a box number. Go ahead and do these things; just plan on using more active job search methods, too.

Some Tips on Writing an Effective Resume

There are no firm rules for writing a good resume. Every resume is different. But here are some tips that I have learned are important in writing any resume.

- **Write it yourself.** Look at the sample resumes in this book and elsewhere, but don't use their content in your resume. If you do, your resume will sound like someone else's. Many employers will know you didn't write it—and that will not help you.

- **Make every word count.** Most resumes should be limited to one or two pages. After you have written a first draft, edit it at least two more times. If a word or phrase does not support your ability to do the job, cut it out. Short is often better.

- **Make it error free.** Just one error on your resume can create a negative impression. It could be enough to get you screened out. So ask someone else to check your resume for grammar and spelling errors. Check each word again before you print a final version. You can't be too careful.

- **Make it look good.** Appearance, as you know, makes a lasting impression. For this reason, your resume must look good, with good design and format. Later in this chapter I give you more tips on producing a good-looking resume in paper and electronic forms.

- **Stress your accomplishments.** A resume is no place to be humble. Emphasize results. Give facts and numbers to support your accomplishments. Instead of saying that you are good with people, say "I supervised and trained five staffers and increased their productivity by 30 percent." The sample resumes and JIST Cards often include numbers. They make a difference.

- **Don't delay.** Don't delay your job search while working on a "better" resume! Many job seekers spend time improving their resume when they should be out looking for a job. A better approach is to quickly do a simple, error-free resume. Then actively look for a job. You can work on a better version at night and on weekends.

- **Keep it lively.** Keep your resume short. Use action verbs and brief sentences. Keep it interesting.

The Three Basic Types of Resumes

Resume styles vary. The two most common types are "chronological" and "skills" resumes. I show you how to develop these types and give samples. I also include samples of a third resume type, the "combination" resume. A combination resume combines parts of the chronological and the skills resumes. Each resume style has advantages and disadvantages. The best resume type for you depends on your situation.

Let's look at each resume type and learn more about its advantages and disadvantages for different situations.

The Chronological Resume

"Chronology" refers to time. A chronological resume begins with your most recent work or other experiences and moves back in time. Two sample resumes for the same person follow. Both use a chronological format.

Look at the first resume. It is a simple one. Notice the job objective and how the job seeker's experience is organized. While this resume could be improved, it presents the facts and would be an acceptable resume for many employers.

It works well because Judith is looking for a job in her present career field. She has a good job history plus related education and training. Note that Judy wants to move up in responsibility. She emphasizes the skills and education that will assist her in doing so. One nice feature is that she put her business schooling in both the education and experience sections. Doing this fills a job gap and allows her to present her training as equal to work experience. This resume also includes a "Personal" section. Here Judy lists some of her strengths, which are often not included in a resume. This resume would work fine for most job search needs—and it could be completed in about an hour.

This same resume is improved in the second example. The improved resume features a more thorough job objective, a "Special Skills and Abilities" section, and more accomplishments and skills. Notice, for example, the impact of the numbers she adds. For example "top 30 percent of my class" and "decreased department labor costs by over $30,000 a year." This resume will take an extra hour or two to write. The first resume is fine, but most employers will like the additional positive information in the improved resume.

A Basic Chronological Resume Example

Judith J. Jones

115 South Hawthorne Avenue
Chicago, Illinois 66204
(312) 653-9217 (home)
email: jj@earthlink.com

JOB OBJECTIVE

Desire a position in the office management, accounting, or administrative assistant area. Prefer a position requiring responsibility and a variety of tasks.

EDUCATION AND TRAINING

Acme Business College, Lincoln, Illinois
Graduate of a one-year business program.

U.S. Army
Financial procedures, accounting functions.

John Adams High School, South Bend, Indiana
Diploma, business education.

Other: Continuing education classes and workshops in business communication, computer spreadsheet and database programs, scheduling systems, and customer relations.

EXPERIENCE

2001-present—Claims Processor, Blue Spear Insurance Co., Wilmette, Illinois. Handle customer medical claims, develop management reports based on spreadsheets I created, exceed productivity goals.

2000-2001—Returned to school to upgrade my business and computer skills. Took courses in advanced accounting, spreadsheet and database programs, office management, human relations, and new office techniques.

1998-2000—E4, U.S. Army. Assigned to various stations as a specialist in finance operations. Promoted prior to honorable discharge.

1996-1998—Sandy's Boutique, Wilmette, Illinois. Responsible for counter sales, display design, cash register and other tasks.

1994-1996—Held part-time and summer jobs throughout high school.

PERSONAL

I am reliable, hard working, and good with people.

An Improved Chronological Resume Example

Judith J. Jones

115 South Hawthorne Avenue • Chicago, Illinois 66204
(312) 653-9217 (home)
email: jj@earthlink.com

JOB OBJECTIVE

Seeking position requiring excellent business management skills in an office environment. Position should require a variety of tasks, including office management, word processing, and spreadsheet and database program use.

EDUCATION AND TRAINING

Acme Business College, Lincoln, Illinois.
Completed one-year program in Professional Office Management. Grades in top 30 percent of my class. Courses included word processing, accounting theory and systems, advanced spreadsheet and database programs, time management, and basic supervision.

John Adams High School, South Bend, Indiana.
Graduated with emphasis on business courses. Excellent grades in all business topics and won top award for word-processing speed and accuracy.

Other: Continuing education programs at my own expense, including business communications, customer relations, computer applications, sales techniques, and others.

EXPERIENCE

2001-present—Claims Processor, Blue Spear Insurance Company, Wilmette, Illinois. Handle 50 complex medical insurance claims per day, almost 20 percent above department average. Created a spreadsheet report process that decreased department labor costs by over $30,000 a year (one position). Received two merit raises for performance.

2000-2001—Returned to business school to gain advanced skills in accounting, office management, sales and human resources. Computer courses included word processing and graphics design, accounting and spreadsheet software, and database and networking applications. Grades in top 30 percent of class.

1998-2000—Finance Specialist (E4), U.S. Army. Responsible for the systematic processing of over 200 invoices per day from commercial vendors. Trained and supervised eight employees. Devised internal system allowing 15 percent increase in invoices processed with a decrease in personnel. Managed department with a budget equivalent of over $350,000 a year. Honorable discharge.

1996-1998—Sales Associate promoted to Assistant Manager, Sandy's Boutique, Wilmette, Illinois. Made direct sales and supervised four employees. Managed daily cash balances and deposits, made purchasing and inventory decisions, and handled all management functions during owner's absence. Sales increased 26 percent and profits doubled during my tenure.

1994-1996—Held various part-time and summer jobs through high school while maintaining good grades. Earned enough to pay all personal expenses, including car and car insurance. Learned to deal with customers, meet deadlines, work hard, handle multiple priorities, and develop other skills.

SPECIAL SKILLS AND ABILITIES

Quickly learn new computer applications and am experienced with a number of business software applications. Have excellent interpersonal, written, and oral communication and math skills. Accept supervision well, am able to supervise others, and work well as a team member. Like to get things done and have an excellent attendance record.

Advantages and Disadvantages of a Chronological Resume

This resume format has both advantages and disadvantages.

- **Advantages.** This resume is the simplest and quickest one to write. Many employers want to know details about where you have worked, including dates employed. This is a good resume style to use if you have a solid work history in jobs similar to those you want now.

- **Disadvantages.** A chronological resume may display your weaknesses. It quickly shows an employer your employment gaps, frequent job changes, lack of work experience related to your job objective, recent graduation, and other potential problems. If you are in one or more of these situations, a traditional chronological resume may not be best for you.

TIP

Here's a humble suggestion. A chronological resume is simple and quick to do. For this reason, I suggest you create a simple chronological resume before making a "better" one. You might even get a job offer before you finish an improved version.

The Skills Resume

The skills resume is sometimes called a "functional resume." In this format, your experience is organized under key skills. A well-done skills resume emphasizes skills that your job objective requires. These should also be the same skills that you are good at and want to use.

Look at the resume that follows and notice how it emphasizes skills rather than employment dates and job titles. It is an example of a simple skills resume. Andrea is a recent high school graduate. All of her work experience is in part-time and summer jobs. The skills format allows her to emphasize what she has to offer. It allows her to present her job-related training and experience in a positive way.

A Skills Resume Example

ANDREA ATWOOD
3231 East Harbor Road
Grand Rapids, Michigan 41103
Message: (303) 447-2111
E-Mail: aatwood@arrow.com

Objective: A responsible position in retail sales or marketing.

Areas of Accomplishment:

Customer Service
- Communicate well with all age groups.
- Able to interpret customer concerns to help them find the items they want.
- Received six Employee-of-the-Month awards in 3 years.

Merchandise Display
- Developed display skills via in-house training and experience.
- Received Outstanding Trainee Award for Christmas toy display.
- Dress mannequins, arrange table displays, and organize sale merchandise.

Inventory Control
- Maintained and marked stock during department manager's 6-week illness.
- Developed more efficient record-keeping procedures

Additional Skills
- Operate cash register and computerized accounting systems.
- Willing to work evenings and weekends.
- Punctual, honest, reliable and hard working.

Experience:
Harper's Department Store
Grand Rapids, Michigan
Two years' total experience

Education:
Central High School
Grand Rapids, Michigan
3.6 on a 4.0 grade point average
Honor Graduate in Distributive Education

Two years' retail sales training in Distributive Education. Also courses in Business Writing, Computerized Accounting, and Word Processing.

Advantages and Disadvantages of a Skills Resume

As with a chronological resume, the skills resume has good and not-so-good points.

- **Advantages.** A skills resume allows you to present accomplishments from all your life experiences. It is a good format when you need to hide problems that a chronological resume might show. For example, Andrea's resume does a good job of presenting what she can do, without making it obvious that her work experience is limited to part-time and summer jobs. Nor does it say that she is a recent graduate.

  A well-written skills resume presents your strengths and avoids showing your weaknesses. For example, it can hide limited paid work experience, gaps in your job history, and little or no paid work experience in the field you want to get into now.

- **Disadvantages.** Because a skills resume can hide details that can be used to screen people out, some employers don't like them. A skills resume can also be harder to write than a chronological resume.

The Combination Resume

A combination resume includes elements of both the chronological and skills formats. For example, a new graduate might use the combination style to first list key skills and related school, work, and life experiences. The resume would then give a brief chronological list of jobs.

A combination resume allows you to use resume features that fit you best. I include several samples of this resume type at the end of this chapter. Look them over for ideas to use in your resume.

Tips for Writing Each Section of Your Resume

Whatever type of resume you choose, you can do many things to make it stand out. Use the following tips to write any style of resume. As you look over the sample resumes later in this chapter for ideas, notice how each resume handles these issues.

- **Your name and address.** It is often best to use your formal name instead of a nickname. On your address, avoid abbreviations and include your zip code. If you might move, arrange with the post office to forward your mail to your new address or use a relative's address on your resume.

- **Telephone numbers and e-mail address.** It's important for employers to be able to reach you, even if only to leave messages. If your home phone is not always answered during the day, use an answering machine or voice mail. Make sure it has a professional-sounding message! If you have a pager or cell phone, you can list those numbers as well. Always give your area code. Include an e-mail address if you have one. You can get a free e-mail address from providers such as Yahoo and then check your e-mail on a library computer.

- **Job objective.** Include your job objective in all but the most basic resume. Look at the examples to see how others have handled this. Notice that Judith didn't narrow her options by using a specific job title or by using terms such as "clerical," which might keep her out of the running for more responsible jobs.

- **Education and training.** List job-related training and education, including military training. If your education and training are important parts of your credentials, put them at the top. However, people with five or more years of work experience usually place this information at the end of their resumes.

- **Previous experience.** List your most recent job first, then work your way back. Show promotions as separate jobs. Cluster jobs held long ago or not related to your present objective. These could include the part-time jobs you had while going to school.

  If you have little work experience, list unpaid work, such as helping with the family business, and volunteer jobs. Always emphasize the skills you used in these experiences that will help you in the job you want now. There is no need to mention that this work was unpaid.

- **Job gaps.** Your list of work experiences may have gaps. You may have been going to school, having a child, working for yourself, or had other reasons for not being traditionally employed. Present this time positively. Saying "self-employed" or "returned to school to improve my business skills" is better than saying "unemployed."

  You can avoid showing that you did not have a job at certain times by listing years or seasons. For example, if you didn't work from late January to early March, write your years of employment and not the months. No one will be able tell that you had a two-month space between jobs. For example: Job A. 2000-2001; Job B. 2001-2002.

- **Job titles.** Many people have more responsibilities than their job titles suggest. Some titles are unusual and won't mean much to most people. In these cases, use a title that more accurately tells what you did. For example, say "shift manager" rather than "waiter" if you were in charge of things. Of course, make sure that you don't misrepresent your responsibilities.

- **Accomplishments.** An employer wants to know about the work you did well and other experiences you had. As you would in an interview, describe some of your best accomplishments. Emphasize the number of people you served, units produced, staff trained, sales increased, and other measurable achievements. You should include special activities or accomplishments from other life activities, such as your school club roles.

TIP

If you have access to a computer and a good-quality printer, you can customize your resume for specific employers by changing your job objective and emphasizing certain experiences and skills.

- **Personal data.** This information is optional. Who cares how tall you are or that you like to read romance novels? Include personal details only if they support your job objective.

- **References.** Don't list references on your resume. If employers want them, they will ask. Saying "references available on request" at the end of your resume adds nothing an employer does not know. If you have good references, you can say something like "excellent references from previous employers are available." This sentence can be in the personal section.

A Few Words on Honesty

A good resume presents your strengths and not your weaknesses. But this does not mean that you should misrepresent yourself. Do not claim you have skills you do not have or a degree you did not earn, or make any other claim that is not true. It is not the right thing to do. Many employers will fire you for lying, should they find out. This, of course, would serve you right.

Resume Design and Production Tips

What you say in your resume is very important. How you present it is just as important. So here are some brief tips that will help you create a superior resume after the writing is done.

- **Make your resume look good.** Make sure your resume looks good. Word-processing software and laser printers allow you to create a professional-looking resume. All major word processors have resume-writing templates and "wizards" that make designing your resume simple.

  If you don't have access to a computer and a high-quality printer, most small print shops and resume-writing services can produce a professional-looking resume for a modest cost. Unless you need help in writing your resume, they should charge no more than $50 to format a one- or two-page resume.

TIP

If you are not experienced in using word-processing software, now is not the time to learn. Trust me on this.

- **Get lots of copies.** Earlier in this book, you learn how you can develop hundreds of job leads through networking and cold contacts. It is to your advantage to give each contact one or more copies of your resume. So plan on having lots of copies available. You may go through several hundred before you land your job.

  If you have access to a computer and a good laser printer, you can print excellent quality copies. If you don't have regular access to a computer system, you can get good photocopies made at most quick-print shops. Look in the yellow pages for listings.

- **Use good paper and matching envelopes.** Most office supply stores and print shops have good-quality papers and matching envelopes for use with resumes and cover letters. The best papers have a rich look and texture. They cost more but are worth every penny. Ivory, white, and off-white are conservative colors that look professional.

Electronic and Scannable Resumes

A traditional resume is printed on paper. The Internet and other technology now often require resumes to be in electronic form. If you plan to use the Internet in your job search, you will need to submit your resume in electronic form. Once you do so, your resume is entered into a data-base that might be searched by many employers.

Even if you don't plan on using the Internet, you need to understand how electronic resumes work. This is because more and more employers are scanning the resumes they receive. Scanners are machines that convert your resume into electronic text. This allows employers to use a computer to quickly search hundreds or thousands of resumes to find qualified applicants. Many larger employers use scanning technology. But your paper resume is likely to be scanned into a database without your knowing it.

Since electronic resumes are used differently than those on paper, it is important to understand how you can increase their effectiveness.

TIP

As electronic resumes and scanning increase, it makes sense to have two resumes—one on paper that looks good to humans and another that scans and e-mails well. Having both, for use in different situations, gives you a competitive edge.

Needs of One Large Employer Are Typical

Employers want resumes in electronic or scannable form to save time. It's not practical to look through hundreds or thousands of paper resumes. For this reason, Internet resume sites and many employers require you to submit your resume in a way that can be easily put into their databases. To show you how this works, I include the instructions from one large employer's Web site on how to submit a resume. I've deleted references to the specific employer.

Instructions from a Large Employer on How to Submit Your Resume

We are employing a new electronic applicant tracking system that uses the latest in document-imaging/scanning technology. The system allows us to receive your resume by e-mail, direct line fax, or hard copy. This system will enhance your exposure to a wider variety of employment opportunities at all sites within our company. The one-time submission of your resume makes you eligible for consideration of any openings for which you meet the minimum qualifications.

As your resume is input into our system, you receive an acknowledgment and your resume is kept active in our database for one year. As openings occur, our recruiters search the database for individuals whose qualifications and skills match the criteria needed for the open positions. If a match occurs, you receive further notification regarding the specific opening.

To increase the effectiveness of your resume, be sure to clearly state your skills and experiences, educational background, work history, and specific salary information. In addition, please follow these directions when preparing your resume:

- Prepare your resume on white or light-colored 8½-by-11 paper (for hard copy or faxing).

- Use a standard paper weight so that the system will produce a quality image (for hard copy or faxing).

- Avoid fancy treatments such as italics, underlining, and shadowing. Bold-faced type and capital letters are acceptable.

- Place your name at the top of the page on its own line, use a standard address format below your name, and list each phone number on a separate line.

You may submit your resume by one of the following methods:

- **Electronic mail.** The e-mail address is resume@bigcompany.com. You must put the word resume in the subject or reference line when e-mailing and submit it in ASCII text format. All information must be contained in the body of the message. We cannot accept attachments into this system.

- **FAX.** You may fax your information to 866-244-3325 (too-big-deal). Please fax in fine mode.

- **Postal mail.** You may mail a hard copy of your resume to Corporate Recruitment, Big Company, Corporate Center, Big City, ST 90214.

While these instructions aren't friendly, the methods for submitting a resume are pretty clear: No matter how you get your resume to the company, it converts your resume into a simple text file.

For an Electronic Resume, a Simple Design Is Best

The databases that your resume go into want only text, not design. Scanners introduce fewer errors when the text is simple. What this means is that your resume's carefully done format and design elements need to be taken out, and your resume reduced to the simplest text format:

- No graphics
- No lines
- No bold, italic, or other text variations
- Only one easy-to-scan font

- No tab indentations
- No line or paragraph indents
- No centering

This may be discouraging, but it's the way it is.

Quick Tips to Reformat Your Resume

Fortunately, you can easily take your existing resume and reformat it for electronic submission. Here are some quick guidelines for doing so:

1. Cut and paste your resume text into a new file in your word processor.
2. Eliminate any graphic elements such as lines or images.
3. Limit your margins to no more than 65 characters wide.
4. Use an easy-to-scan font, such as Courier, Arial, Helvetica or Times Roman. Eliminate bold, italic, and other font styles.
5. Introduce major sections with words in all uppercase letters, rather than in bold or a different font.
6. Keep all text aligned to the left and eliminate centering, unless you use the space key to do so.
7. Instead of using bullets, use a standard keyboard character such as the asterisk.
8. Instead of using the tab key or paragraph indents, use the space key to indent.
9. When done, click the File menu, choose the Save As command, and select the Plain Text, ASCII (American Standard Code for Information Interchange), or Text Only option. Then name the file and click Save or OK. Then reopen the file to see how it looks. Make additional format changes as needed.

While this may undermine your creative side, think of it as mashed potatoes: It can be very good if you do it right. Try to take satisfaction from that thought, OK?

An Electronic Resume Should Have Lots of Key Words

Employers using electronic databases search for "key words" in resumes. So, the more key words you include, the more likely your resume will be selected. Key words are words and phrases specific to the job you want. Here are some ways to find and handle key words on your resume:

- **Add a key word section.** A simple technique is to add a section to your resume titled "Key Skills." You can then add key words not included elsewhere in your resume.

- **Include all your important skill words.** If you completed Chapters 3 and 4, include the key skills documented there.

- **Think like a prospective employer.** List the jobs you want. Then think of the key words employers are likely to use when searching a database.

- **Review job descriptions.** Carefully review descriptions for jobs you seek in major print references like the *Occupational Outlook Handbook* and the *O*NET Dictionary of Occupational Titles.* Most large Web sites that list job openings have lots of employer job postings and job descriptions to review. Corporate Web sites often post information on job openings, another source of key words. Make a list of key words in descriptions of interest and include them in your resume.

- **Be specific.** List certifications and licenses, name any software and machines you can operate, and include special language and abbreviations used in your field.

An Electronic Resume Example

The following sample resume has been redone for scanning or e-mail submission. It has a plain format that is easily read by scanners. It also has lots of key words that increase its chances of being selected when an employer searches a database. This resume is based on one from *Cyberspace Resume Kit* by Mary Nemnich and Fred Jandt and published by JIST Works.

RICHARD JONES

3456 Generic Street

Potomac MD 11721

Phone messages: (301) 927-1189

E-mail: richj@riverview.com

SUMMARY OF SKILLS

Rigger, maintenance mechanic (carpentry, electrical, plumbing, painting), work leader. Read schematic diagrams. Flooring (wood, linoleum, carpet, ceramic and vinyl tile). Plumbing (pipes, fixtures, fire systems). Certified crane and forklift operator, work planner, inspector.

+++

EXPERIENCE

Total of nine years in the trades—apprentice to work leader.

* MAINTENANCE MECHANIC LEADER, Smithsonian Institution, Washington, DC, April 2001 to present: Promoted to supervise nine staff in all trades, including plumbing, painting, electrical, carpentry, drywall, flooring. Prioritize and schedule work, inspect and approve completed jobs. Responsible for annual budget of $750,000 and assuring that all work done to museum standards and building codes.

* RIGGER / MAINTENANCE MECHANIC, Smithsonian Institution, February 1998 to April 2001: Built and set up exhibits. Operated cranes, rollers, forklifts, and rigged mechanical and hydraulic systems to safely move huge, priceless museum exhibits. Worked with other trades in carpentry, plumbing, painting, electrical and flooring to construct exhibits.

* RIGGER APPRENTICE, Portsmouth Naval Shipyard, Portsmouth, NH, August 1996 to January 1998: Qualified signalman for cranes. Moved and positioned heavy machines and structural parts for shipbuilding. Responsible for safe operation of over $2,000,000 of equipment on a daily basis, with no injury or accidents. Used cranes, skids, rollers, jacks, forklifts and other equipment.

+++

TRAINING AND EDUCATION

HS graduate, top 50% of class.

Additional training in residential electricity, drywall, HV/AC, and refrigeration systems. Certified in heavy crane operation, forklift, regulated waste disposal, industrial blueprints.

A Few Final Words on Resumes

Before you write and use your resume, here is some advice that applies to both paper and electronic resumes.

- **Even the best of resumes will not get you a job.** You have to do that yourself. To do so, you have to get interviews and do well in them. Interviews are where the job search action is, not resumes.

- **Don't listen to resume experts.** If you ask ten people for advice on your resume, they will all be willing to give it—yet no two will agree. You have to make up your own mind about your resume. Feel free to break any "rules" if you have a good reason. It's your resume.

- **Don't avoid the job search by worrying about your resume.** Write a simple and error-free resume, and then go out and get lots of interviews. Later, you can write a better resume—if you want or need to.

- **Look over the sample resumes.** I include several sample resumes at the end of this chapter. Some break "rules" and none is perfect. However, all are based on real resumes written by real people, though the names and other details have been changed. So look them over, learn from them, and then write your own.

How to Write Effective Cover Letters

A cover letter is sent with and "covers" a resume. Different situations need different types of letters. The sample cover letters in the next section deal with a variety of typical situations. Look them over for ideas to use when writing your own letters. As always, make certain that your correspondence makes a good impression.

You may find that you don't need to send many formal cover letters. Job seekers using the approaches I recommend get by with informal thank-you notes sent with resumes and JIST Cards. But certain types of jobs and some organizations require a more formal approach. Use your judgment.

Here are some suggestions to help you create and use superior cover letters.

- **Send it to someone by name.** Get the name of the person who is most likely to supervise you. Call first to get an interview. Then send your letter and resume.

- **Get it right.** Make sure you get the person's name, organization name, and address right. Include the person's correct job title. Make sure that your letter does not contain grammar and other errors, since this creates a poor impression.

- **Be clear about what you want.** If you want an interview, ask for it. If you are interested in the organization, say so. Give clear reasons why the company should consider you.

- **Be friendly and professional.** A professional, informal style is usually best. Avoid a hard-sell "hire me now!" approach. No one likes to be pushed.

- **Make it look good.** Just as with a resume, correspondence to an employer must look good. Use good-quality paper and matching envelopes. A standard business format is good for most letters.

- **Target your letter.** Typical reasons for sending a cover letter include responding to an ad, preparing an employer for an interview (the best reason!), and following up after a phone call or interview. Each of these letters is different. Samples for each situation are included with the sample letters.

- **Follow up.** Remember that contacting an employer directly is much more effective than sending a letter. Don't expect letters to get you many interviews. They are best used to follow up after you have contacted the employer.

Samples for You to Study

The samples that follow give you content, style, and format ideas for cover letters and resumes. Space limited the number of samples I could include. The ones I do include use pretty simple formats. Some resumes were submitted by professional resume writers, and their names are noted. You can find professional resume writers in your area through the Professional Association of Résumé Writers at www.parw.com and the National Résumé Writers' Association at www.nrwa.com.

If you want to see more cover letters and resumes, many good books and Web sites provide samples. JIST publishes excellent collections written by professional resume writers. And I've written several books that provide lots of examples.

Sample Cover Letter After an Interview

The writer uncovered a problem during an interview and afterward offers to solve the problem when no job exists. Many job seekers never think of scheduling an interview when there is no job opening, but many jobs are created this way to accommodate a good person.

Sandra A. Zaremba

115 South Hawthorn Drive
Dunwoody, Georgia 21599

April 10, XXXX

Ms. Christine Massey
Import Distributors, Inc.
417 East Main Street
Atlanta, Georgia 21649

Dear Ms. Massey:

I know you have a busy schedule so I was pleasantly surprised when you arranged a time for me to see you. While you don't have a position open now, your organization is just the sort of place I would like to work. As we discussed, I like to be busy with a variety of duties and the active pace I saw at your company is what I seek.

Your ideas on increasing business sound creative. I've thought about the customer service problem and would like to discuss a possible solution. It would involve the use of a simple system of color-coded files that would prioritize correspondence to give older requests priority status. The handling of complaints could also be speeded up through the use of simple form letters similar to those you mentioned. I have some thoughts on how this might be done too, and I will work out a draft of procedures and sample letters if you are interested. It can be done on the computers your staff already uses and would not require any additional cost to implement.

Whether or not you have a position for me in the future, I appreciate the time you have given me. An extra copy of my resume is enclosed for your files—or to pass on to someone else.

Let me know if you want to discuss the ideas I presented earlier in this letter. I can be reached at any time on my cell phone at (942) 267-1103. I will call you next week, as you suggested, to keep you informed of my progress.

Sincerely,

Sandra A. Zaremba

Sample Cover Letter for a Specific Opening

This new graduate called first and arranged an interview—the best approach of all. She mentions specifically how she changed procedures for a business and saved money. Note how she includes skills such as working hard and dealing with deadline pressure.

113 S. Meridian Street
Greenwich, Connecticut 11721

March 10, 20XX

Ms. Willa Hines
New England Power and Light Company
604 Waterway Boulevard
Parien, Connecticut 11716

Dear Ms. Hines:

I am following up on the brief chat we had today by phone. After getting the details on the position you have open, I am certain that it is the kind of job I have been looking for. A copy of my resume is enclosed providing more details of my background. I hope you have a chance to review it before we meet next week.

My special interest has long been in the large-volume order processing systems that your organization has developed so well. While in school I researched the flow of order processing work for a large corporation as part of a class assignment. With some simple and inexpensive procedural changes I recommended, check-processing time was reduced by an average of three days. For the number of checks and dollars involved, this one change resulted in an estimated increase in interest revenues of over $135,000 per year.

While I have recently graduated from business school, I have considerable experience for a person of my age. I have worked in a variety of jobs dealing with large numbers of people and deadline pressure. My studies have also been far more hands-on and practical than those of most schools, so I have a good working knowledge of current business systems and procedures. This includes a good understanding of various computer spreadsheet and application programs, the use of automation, and experience with cutting costs and increasing profits. I am also a hard worker and realize I will need to apply myself to get established in my career.

I am most interested in the position you have available and am excited about the potential it offers. I look forward to seeing you next week.

Sincerely,

Wendy Presson

Sample Cover Letter Following Up on a Cold Call

This person made contact with the office manager by phone and set up an interview for his upcoming visit to the area.

1768 South Carrollton Street
Nashville, Tennessee 96050
May 26, XXXX

Ms. Karen Miller
Office Manager
Lendon, Lendon, and Sears
Suite 101, Landmark Building
Summit, New Jersey 11736

Dear Ms. Miller:

Enclosed is a copy of my resume that describes my work experience as a legal assistant. I hope this information will be helpful as background for our interview next Monday at 4 p.m.

I appreciate your taking time to describe your requirements so fully. This sounds like a position that could develop into a satisfying career. And my training in accounting—along with experience using a variety of computer programs—seems to match your needs.

Lendon, Lendon, and Sears is a highly respected name in New Jersey. I am excited about this opportunity and I look forward to meeting with you.

Sincerely,

Richard Wittenberg

Sample Cover Letter from a Network Contact

The person uses names from a professional association to conduct a long-distance job search. He explains the end of his old job, indicates certain skills, and mentions the availability of positive references.

July 10, XXXX

Mr. Paul Resley
Operations Manager
Rollem Trucking Co.
I-70 Freeway Drive
Kansas City, Missouri 78401

Mr. Resley:

I obtained your name from the membership directory of the Affiliated Trucking Association. I have been a member for over 10 years, and I am very active in the Southeast Region. The reason I am writing is to ask for your help. The firm I had been employed with has been bought by a larger corporation. The operations here have been disbanded, leaving me unemployed.

While I like where I live, I know that finding a position at the level of responsibility I seek may require a move. As a center of the transportation business, your city is one I have targeted for special attention. A copy of my resume is enclosed for your use. I'd like you to review it and consider where a person with my background would get a good reception in Kansas City. Perhaps you could think of a specific person for me to contact?

I have specialized in fast-growing organizations or ones that have experienced rapid change. My particular strength is in bringing things under control, then increasing profits. While my resume does not state this, I have excellent references from my former employer and would have stayed at its similar position existed at its new location.

As a member of the association, I hoped that you would provide some special attention to my request for assistance. I plan on coming to Kansas City on a job-hunting trip within the next six weeks. Prior to my trip I will call you for advice on who I might contact for interviews. Even if they have no jobs open for me now, perhaps they will know of someone else who does.

My enclosed resume lists my phone number and other contact information should you want to reach me before I call you. Thanks in advance for your help on this.

Sincerely,

John B. Goode
Treasurer, Southeast Region
Affiliated Trucking Association

John B. Goode

312 Smoke Way   Nashville, Tennessee 3201

Sample Chronological Resume Emphasizes Results

A simple format focuses on accomplishments through the use of numbers. While her resume does not say so, it is obvious that she works hard and that she gets results.

A simple chronological format with few but carefully chosen words. It has an effective summary at the beginning, and every word supports her job objective.

She emphasizes results!

Maria Marquez

4141 Beachway Road
Redondo Beach, California 90277

Messages: (213) 432-2279
E-mail: mmarq@msn.net

Objective: Management Position in a Major Hotel

Summary of Experience: Four years' experience in sales, catering, banquet services, and guest relations in 300-room hotel. Doubled sales revenues from conferences and meetings. Increased dining room and bar revenues by 44%. Won prestigious national and local awards for increased productivity and services.

Experience:
Park Regency Hotel, Los Angeles, California
Assistant Manager
1999 to Present

- Oversee a staff of 16 including dining room and bar, housekeeping, and public relations operations.
- Introduced new menus and increased dining room revenues by 44%. Gourmet America awarded us their first place Hotel Haute Cuisine award as a result of my efforts.
- Attracted 28% more diners with the first revival of Big Band Cocktail Dances in the Los Angeles area.

Kingsmont Hotel, Redondo Beach, California
Sales and Public Relations
1997 to 1999

- Doubled revenues per month from conferences and meetings.
- Redecorated meeting rooms and updated sound and visual media equipment. Careful scheduling resulted in no lost revenue during this time.
- Instituted staff reward program, which resulted in an upgrade from B- to AAA+ in the *Car and Travel Handbook*.

Education: Associate Degree in Hotel Management from Henfield College of San Francisco. One-year certification program with the Boileau Culinary Institute, where I won the Grand Prize Scholarship.

Notice her use of numbers to increase impact of statements.

Bullets here and above increase readability and emphasis.

While Maria had only a few years of related work experience, she used this resume to help her land a very responsible job in a large resort hotel.

Sample Chronological Resume Stresses Technical Credentials

This resume emphasizes the candidate's technical qualifications. The "Additional Qualifications" section highlights statements that do not fit into a traditional chronological form.

Chronological resume with some nice features that make it very effective.

Simple but attractive use of bold, centering, and lines.

Jack B. Harris

12 Browertown Road
Little Falls, NJ 07424
e-mail: jbquick@autonet.com
Messages: (201) 785-3011

Class A Automotive Mechanic
Specializing in complete engine overhaul and front end repair work

Education & Training

Graduate of Rockford Community College, 1998
Basic and Advanced Automotive Technology courses. Top 20% of class.
ASE Certified in repair of:

- Engines
- Suspensions
- Steering
- Cooling systems
- Brakes
- Electrical systems

GM training on the job:

- Use of computerized engine analyzers and other electronic test devices.
- Diagnostics and service to electronic fuel injection, ignition, and emission control components.

Additional Qualifications

- Experience with foreign and domestic late model cars, vans and light trucks.
- Stay current on new technology; understand and act on instructions from repair manuals and manufacturers' bulletins.
- Very service oriented, hard working and cooperative.
- Own power and hand tools for most applications; able to do heavy lifting.

Work Experience

2000–Present **Master Automotive Technician**
DRISCOLL CHEVROLET, South Caldwell, NJ

- Attained highest status at dealership employing 12 technicians because of ability to quickly diagnose troubles and make accurate repairs.
- Kept track of recurring problems in certain models for manufacturer notification. Shared information with other mechanics.
- Increased department profitability by consistently performing most services in 10-20% less time than allowed by industry standards.
- Contributed to 29% increase in customer satisfaction levels over the last year.

1997-2000 **Automotive Mechanic**
SEARS AUTO CENTER, Clairmont, NJ

- Started with basic tune-ups and tire service, advancing after 2 months to brake, general repair, radiator and air conditioning repairs.
- Was often assigned to customers with complaints of unsatisfactory original service. Corrected problems and maintained good relationships.
- Trained 6 newly hired mechanics in shop procedures.

Submitted by Melanie A. Noonan

This section includes details that would not be easy to list in a typical chronological format.

Strong direct words emphasize effectiveness and results.

Numbers support his results and skills.

Chronological section - notice the use of check marks. Much better than a paragraph of text!

Sample Combination Resume for a Career Changer

Because this job seeker has no work experience in the field, this resume emphasizes her relevant education and transferable skills.

Writer's comments: This client was finishing computer programming school and had no work experience in the field. After listing the topics covered in the course, I summarized her employment experience, specifying that she earned promotions quickly. This Mary Beth Kurzak would be attractive to any employer.

Mary Beth Kurzak
2188 Huron River Drive • Ann Arbor, MI 48104 • 734-555-4912

Profile

▶ Strong educational preparation with practical applications in computer/internet programming.
▶ Highly motivated to excel in new career.
▶ A fast learner, as evidenced by success in accelerated training program.
▶ Self-directed, independent worker with proven ability to meet deadlines and work under pressure.
▶ Maintain team perspective with ability to build positive working relationships and foster open communication.

Education/Training

ADVANCED TECHNOLOGY CENTER • Dearborn, MI — xxxx-Present
Pursuing Certification in **Internet/Information Technology** — *Anticipated completion: Aug. xxxx*
An accelerated program focusing on computer and internet programming

Highlights of Training:

(Important to include specific things learned)

- Networking Concepts — - Client Server — - UNIX
- Programming Concepts — - Visual Basic — - IIS — - VB/ASP
- Programming in Java/Java Script — - OC++ — - Oracle — - CGI
- Web Authoring Using HTML — - DHTML, XML — - Perl
- Photoshop

Highlights of Experience and Abilities

(Experiences selected to support job objective)

Customer Service
▶ Determined member eligibility and verified policy benefits.
▶ Responded to customer questions; interpreted and explained complex insurance concepts.
▶ Collaborated with health care providers regarding billing and claim procedures.

Leadership
▶ Creatively supervised 30 employees, many of whom were significantly older.
▶ Motivated employees and improved working conditions, resulting in greater camaraderie.
▶ Trained coworkers in various technical and nontechnical processes.

Analytical/Troubleshooting
▶ Investigated and resolved computer system errors.
▶ Researched discrepancies in claims and identified appropriate actions.
▶ Compiled and analyzed claims statistics.

Administrative Support and Accounting
▶ Managed and processed medical, mental health and substance abuse claims.
▶ Oversaw accounts receivable; reconciled receipts and prepared bank deposits.
▶ Coordinated 50+ line switchboard; routed calls as appropriate.

Employment History

MEDICAL SERVICES PLUS [Contracted by Health Solutions - Southfield, MI] — xxxx-xxxx
Promoted within eight months of hire.
Claims Supervisor / Claims Adjudicator

HANSEN AGENCY OF MICHIGAN • Ann Arbor, MI — xxxx-xxxx
Earned two promotions in one year.
Claims Adjudicator / Accounting Clerk / Receptionist

FORD WILLOW RUN TRANSMISSION PLANT • Ypsilanti, MI — Summer xxxx
Temporary Production Worker

PEARL HARBOR MEMORIAL MUSEUM • Pearl Harbor, HI — xxxx-xxxx
Assistant Crew Manager

References available on request

Submitted by Janet L. Beckstrom

Sample Skills Resume for Someone with Limited Work Experience

This sample is for a recent high school graduate whose only paid work experience was at a fast-food place!

A skills resume where each skill directly supports the job objective of this recent high school graduate with very limited work experience.

Lisa M. Rhodes
813 Lava Court • Denver, Colorado 81613
Home: (413) 643-2173 (leave message)
Cell phone: (413) 442-1659
Email: lrhodes@netcom.net

Position Desired

Sales-oriented position in a retail sales or distribution business.

Skills and Abilities

(key skills)
Support for the skills comes from all life activities: school, clubs, part-time jobs.

Communications — Good written and verbal presentation skills. Use proper grammar and have a good speaking voice.

Interpersonal — Able to get along well with coworkers and <u>accept supervision</u>. Received positive evaluations from previous supervisors.

Flexible — <u>Willing to try new things</u> and am interested in improving efficiency on assigned tasks. *(Good emphasis on adaptive skills.)*

Attention to Detail — Concerned with quality. My work is typically orderly and attractive. Like to see things completed correctly and on time.

Hard Working — Throughout high school, worked long hours in strenuous activities while attending school full-time. Often handled as many as 65 hours a week in school and other structured activities, while maintaining above-average grades. *(Very strong statement)*

Customer Contacts — Routinely handled as many as 500 customer contacts a day (100,000 per month) in a busy retail outlet. Averaged lower than a .001% complaint rate and was given the "Employee of the Month" award in my second month of employment. Received two merit increases. Never absent or late. *(Good use of numbers)*

Cash Sales — Handled over $2,000 a day ($40,000 a month) in cash sales. Balanced register and prepared daily sales summary and deposits.

Reliable — Excellent attendance record, trusted to deliver daily cash deposits totaling over $40,000 a month.

Education

Franklin High School. Took advanced English and other classes. Member of award-winning band. Excellent attendance record. Superior communication skills. Graduated in top 30% of class.

Other

Active gymnastics competitor for four years. This taught me discipline, teamwork, how to follow instructions, and hard work. I am ambitious, outgoing, reliable, and willing to work.

Lisa's resume makes it clear that she is talented and hard working.

Sample Combination Resume in a Two-Page Format

This sample for a recent graduate emphasizes applicable education and skills as real experience and relates all sections back to the applicant's job objective. Key adaptive and transferable skills are highlighted throughout.

A two-page combination format for a soon-to-graduate student

Emphasizes what he can do and not just what he wants!

Jonathan McLaughlin

6926 Mapleton Court (602) 298-9704 cell phone

Phoenix, AZ 85009 jafar@quickwit.com e-mail

JOB OBJECTIVE

Position in the electronics industry requiring skills in the design, sale, installation, maintenance, or repair of computer, audio, video, and other advanced electronics. Prefer tasks needing creative problem-solving skills and customer contact.

EDUCATION

PHOENIX TECHNICAL INSTITUTE
Phoenix, AZ, Graduating in June with AS Degree in Electronics Engineering Technology, top 25% of class.

Completing a comprehensive, two-year curriculum, including over 1,000 hours of classroom instruction and advanced laboratory experience. Theoretical, practical, and hands-on knowledge of audio and RF amplifiers, AM/FM transmitter-receiver circuits, circuit board theory and practice, PC and network systems and maintenance, microwave and radar communications, digital circuits, and much more. Excellent attendance while working two jobs to pay tuition.

These statements show he is responsible, hard working, motivated.

PLAINS JUNIOR COLLEGE
Phoenix, AZ.

Courses included digital electronics, programming, computer software applications, and business topics. Worked full time and maintained a B+ average.

DESERT VIEW HIGH SCHOOL
College prep courses, including advanced math, business, marketing, merchandising, computer software applications, and computer programming. Very active in varsity sports and National Honor Society for two years.

Gives lots of emphasis to recent and past education, including specific things he learned that relate to his job objective.

This section allows him to emphasize the skills from school, work, and life that support his job objective.

SKILLS

PROBLEM-SOLVING: Familiar with the underlying theory of most electronic systems and am particularly good at isolating problems by using logic and persistence. I enjoy the challenge of solving complex problems and will work long hours, if necessary, to meet a deadline.

Explains important adaptive skills

INTERPERSONAL: Have supervised five staff and trained many more. Comfortable with one-to-one and small group communications. Can explain technical issues simply to staff and customers of varying levels of sophistication. Had over 10,000 customer contacts and several written commendations.

TECHNICAL: Background in a variety of technical areas, including medical equipment, consumer electronics, computers, automated cash registers, photocopiers, and standard office and computer equipment and peripherals. Have designed special applications using sequential logic circuits and TTL logic. Constructed a microprocessor and wrote several machine language programs for this system. Can diagnose and repair problems in digital and analog circuits.

ORGANIZATIONAL: Have set up and run my own small business and worked in another responsible job while going to school full-time. Earned enough money to live independently and pay all school expenses during this time. I can work with minimal supervision and have learned to use my time efficiently.

EXPERIENCE

While 2 of his 3 jobs are not related to his current objective, he uses them to support skills that will help him do his next job.

BANDLER'S INN: 2000–present. Waiter, promoted to night manager. Complete responsibility for all operations of a shift grossing over $500,000 in sales per year. Supervised five full-time and three part-time staff. Business increased during my employment by 35% and profits by 42%, much of it due to word-of-mouth advertising of satisfied customers.

Uses numbers to reinforce his skills.

FRANKLIN HOSPITAL: 1999–present. Electronic Service Technician Assistant. Work in General Medicine, Diagnostic Labs, and radiology departments. Assisted technicians in routine service and maintenance of a variety of hospital equipment. Left to attend school full time but continue to work weekends while attending school.

JON'S YARD SERVICE: 1998-1999. Set up a small business while in school. Worked part time and summers doing yard work. Made enough money to buy a car and save for tuition.

More examples of his willingness to work hard and meet goals.

Sample Combination Resume with Matching JIST Card

This resume showcases the job seeker's substantial work experience. He emphasizes skills related to his job objective in the first section and then includes his work history in chronological form later. I include Peter's JIST Card here to show you how these two job search tools can relate to each other effectively.

Peter Neely

Messages: (237) 649-1234
Pager: (237) 765-9876

Position: Short- or Long-Distance Truck Driver

Background and Skills: Over fifteen years of stable work history including no traffic citations or accidents. Formal training in diesel mechanics and electrical systems. Familiar with most major destinations and have excellent map-reading and problem-solving abilities. I can handle responsibility and have a track record of getting things done.

Excellent health, good work history, dependable

Carefully written combination resume includes both skills and chronological sections.

Peter Neely
203 Evergreen Road
Houston, Texas 39127
Messages: (237) 649-1234   Pager: (237) 765-9876

POSITION DESIRED: Short- or Long-Distance Truck Driver

Summary of Work Experience: Over fifteen years of stable work history, including substantial experience with diesel engines, electrical systems, and driving all sorts of trucks and heavy equipment.

Skills format allows him to stress experiences that are important for the job

SKILLS

Driving Record/ Licenses: Have current Commercial Driving License and Chauffeur's License and am qualified and able to drive anything that rolls. No traffic citations or accidents for over 20 years.

Vehicle Maintenance: I maintain correct maintenance schedules and avoid most breakdowns as a result. Substantial mechanical and electrical systems training and experience permit many breakdowns to be repaired immediately and avoid towing.

Record Keeping: Excellent attention to detail. Familiar with recording procedures and submit required records on a timely basis.

Lots of emphasis on reliability and results.

Routing: Thorough knowledge of most major interstate routes, with good map reading and route planning skills. I tend to get there on time and without incident.

Other: Not afraid of hard work, flexible, get along well with others, meet deadlines, excellent attendance, responsible.

Key adaptive skills

WORK EXPERIENCE

Short chronological listings reinforce his good work history

1999—Present CAPITAL TRUCK CENTER, Houston, Texas
Pick up and deliver all types of commercial vehicles from across the United States. Am trusted with handling large sums of money and handling complex truck purchasing transactions.

1995–1999 QUALITY PLATING CO., Houston, Texas
Promoted from production to Quality Control. Developed numerous production improvements resulting in substantial cost savings.

1992–1995 BLUE CROSS MANUFACTURING, Houston, Texas
Received several increases in salary and responsibility before leaving for a more challenging position.

Prior to 1992 Truck delivery of food products to destinations throughout the South. Also responsible for up to 12 drivers and equipment maintenance personnel.

No dates on older military experience, but emphasizes related skills

OTHER Four years' experience in the U.S. Air Force, driving and operating truck-mounted diesel power plants. Responsible for monitoring and maintenance on a rigid 24-hour schedule. Stationed in Alaska, California, Wyoming, and other states. Honorable discharge.

Summarizes "old" experience

High school graduate plus training in diesel engines and electrical systems. Excellent health, love the outdoors, stable family life, nonsmoker and nondrinker.

Sample Chronological Resumes with Unique Graphic Touches

These two resumes show how simple graphic images can convey a job objective and make a resume stand out in a crowd! Both also feature lots of white space for easy reading.

Writer's comments: The graphic tells you that this trim resume is about food—the serving or preparation of it—before you have a chance to read one word.

Good design, lots of white space, and few but well-chosen words make this an effective resume

88 Harbor Place
Rock Cove, ME 00000   (207) 555-5555

François J. Boudreau

Objective: Assistant or Sous Chef

Summary of Qualifications:
- Associate's Degree in Culinary Arts with training in American and International Cuisines
- Restaurant experience has included broiler, grill, sauté, fryer, expo, breakfast and salads
- Able to handle a multitude of tasks at once, meeting deadlines under pressure
- Demonstrates ability to respond with speed and accuracy in a highly productive setting
- Works cooperatively and harmoniously with coworkers and supervisors
- Dedicated to quality in service and product

Experience:

Broiler/Prep Cook — Jacques Restaurant, West Cove, Maine (9/94 to Present) 200-seat Four Diamond restaurant featuring an extensive menu of French and American cuisine

Fry Cook — The Lobster Net, Port Hancock, Maine (1992-94) Indoor and outdoor dining, specializing in fresh lobsters and seafood; take-out and banquet service

Fry/Prep Cook — The Weathervane, Rocky Coast, Maine (1991) Traditional New England seafood served in a casual setting

Education:

Associate's Degree in Culinary Arts – Newbury College, Brookline, Massachusetts (1992)
Curriculum and Training Included:
- Soup, Stock and Sauces
- Breads and Rolls
- Desserts
- Classical Bakeshop
- American Cuisine
- International Cuisine
- Yarde Manger
- Sanitation and Dining Room

Submitted by Becky J. Davis

Writer's comments: Skip has limited broadcasting experience, so the challenge was to demonstrate his potential for success. The resume emphasizes Skip's production and on-air experience, stressing high-quality production, audience appeal, and broad knowledge of many kinds of music. The graphic and font gave the resume the desired funky look.

A very clean format with good use of white space

44 Buckingham Road • Allston, MA 02132 • (617) 555-5555

Daniel "Skip" Norton

Summary

Over 5 years in broadcasting, including production, engineering, and on-air experience. Knowledge of extensive variety of music with appeal to broad range of listeners. Expertise in state-of-the art technology, including 24-track recording and digital editing. Ability to work well under pressure. Commitment to high standards of quality.

Related Experience

WZZX 92.9 FM Boston, MA   xxxx–present
Host, Producer, Engineer of six-hour weekly show called Daydream. Freeform format consisting of music from station's playlist and from extensive personal library and combining alternative and popular material.
- Expanded audience size by encouraging and increasing listener feedback.
- Successfully modified format to appeal to broader audience.
- Serve as substitute host for other shows, as needed.
- Maintain consistent, high standards of production by reviewing program tapes and responding to listener feedback.
- Introduce and feature new local artists.
- Produce promotional spots.

Boston Audio, Allston, MA   xxxx–present
Producer, Manager of my own project studio.
- Archive rare and odd records.
- Record material for promotions, including sound effects and music.
- Produce and record local artists for demos and release material.

Other Experience

Head Barista, Coffee Brewers, Newton, MA   xxxx–present
Assistant Manager, Coffee Specialties, Needham, MA   xxxx–xxxx

Education

Full Sail Center for the Recording Arts, Winter Park, FL   xxxx
Associate's Degree in Audio Engineering

Submitted by Wendy Gelberg

CHAPTER 14

Getting a Job Is a Job

Organize Your Time to Get Results

If you've read this book to this point, you now know more about finding a job than most people in North America. But knowing about effective job search methods will not help unless you use what you have learned. This chapter helps you put these job search methods to work. It helps you organize your time so that you get more interviews, get the job you want, and get it in less time.

The More Interviews You Get, the Less Time It Takes to Get a Job

The average job seeker gets just a few interviews a week. At that rate, it takes an average of three to four months to find a job. Anything you can do to increase the number of interviews you get is likely to decrease the time it takes to land a job. It's that simple.

Look at the chart that follows. It shows the number of interviews the average job seeker needs to get a job.

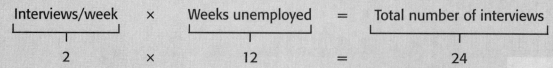

How Many Interviews It Takes to Get a Job

The Average Job Seeker Gets About

Interviews/week	×	Weeks unemployed	=	Total number of interviews
2	×	12	=	24

So, it takes about twelve weeks and twenty-four interviews to get a job.

The More Time You Spend Looking, the More Interviews You Are Likely to Get

The average job seeker takes about twelve weeks and twenty-four interviews to get a job. Many people find jobs in less time, but some take much longer. The average time goes up and down with the unemployment rate. People tend to take longer to find jobs when the unemployment rate is high. But, whatever the unemployment rate, people who get more interviews tend to get their jobs in much less time than average.

The key to getting a job in less time is to get more interviews per week. Doing this requires you to work harder and spend more hours on your job search. The average job seeker only spends about fifteen hours a week looking for a job and remains unemployed longer than needed. Are you willing to spend more than fifteen hours a week looking for your next job? If so, this chapter shows you how to organize your time to get more interviews. It shows you how to turn your job search into a job itself. In a sense, getting a job is your job. So let's get to it.

Set Up Your Job Search Office

To organize your job search as if it were a job, you need a place to work. Usually, this is a spot in your home set aside as your job search office. Following are some ideas to help you set up this office.

The Basics

- **A telephone.** A telephone is an essential tool. If you don't have one, ask to set up your office in the home of a friend or relative who does.

- **Basic furniture.** You will need a table or desk to write on, a chair, and enough space to store your materials.

- **A quiet place.** As on a job, you must have a place where you can concentrate. If you have children, arrange for someone to care for them during your "office" hours. Ask family or friends not to contact you on personal matters during these hours. It is best to select a place where your materials will be undisturbed.

- **A computer, if you have one.** More on this later.

Other Materials You Will Need

- Several good blue or black ink pens
- Pencils with erasers
- Lined paper for notes, contact lists, and other uses
- Three-by-five-inch cards for use as job lead cards
- Three-by-five-inch card file box with dividers
- Thank-you notes and envelopes

- Copies of your resume and JIST Card
- Business-sized envelopes
- Stamps
- Yellow pages phone book
- Daily newspaper
- Calendars and planning schedules
- Career references and other books
- A copy of this book, of course

- What else do you need? Continue your list here:

_____

_____

_____

_____

_____

Using a Computer to Help Organize Your Job Search

Depending on your situation, having access to a computer can be very important. As you actively look for a job, it will help you create professional-looking cover letters, customize your resume, write thank-you letters, and handle other correspondence. I discuss using the Internet in your job search in earlier chapters and, of course, a computer is essential for it. If you don't have a home computer, you can find computers at public libraries, quick-print shops, and coffeehouses with Web access.

A computer can also help you organize your search. You can use scheduling or contact management software to remind you of tasks, appointments, and follow-up activities. If you have one, pocket-sized electronic schedulers and assistants can be of great help in taking notes and setting follow-up times.

If you have access to a computer, use it when it makes sense. The simple paper-based techniques presented in this chapter work very well. Their simplicity gives you an advantage since you can use them right away.

Set Up a Weekly Job Search Schedule

What will you do on the first Tuesday morning of your job search? Do you have a schedule for each day of your job search? Most job seekers don't have a plan, and this is one reason that they don't get much done.

Remember that looking for a job is your job. If you want to get a good job in less time, you should make a daily and weekly schedule—and stick to it. Take the following steps to create your own weekly job search plan. It will make a difference.

Step 1: How Many Hours Per Week?

Think about how many hours per week you are willing to spend looking for a job. I recommend you spend at least twenty-five hours per week in your job search. Since the average job seeker spends about fifteen hours a week looking for work, twenty-five hours is much more than the average. People who spend more hours looking are likely to find their jobs before those who spend fewer hours. However many hours you decide to spend is fine—just remember that the more hours you can spend, the more likely you are to find a job.

If You Can't Look for Work Full Time

This chapter assumes you will look for work more or less full time. If you already have a job, go to school, and have other responsibilities, this obviously reduces the time you can spend looking for a job. You will have to do the best you can, so adapt the techniques I present here to your situation. And be creative: Tell more people you are looking for a job; get more JIST Cards and resumes in circulation; and set interviews for early mornings, lunch times, and other times you can squeeze into your schedule.

Write the number of hours per week you plan to spend looking for work: _____

Step 2: Which Days of the Week Will You Look?

Decide which days each week you will use to look for work. Since most organizations are open Monday through Friday, these are usually the best days to conduct your search. In the first column of the following form, check the days you plan to use for your job search. Don't mark in the other columns yet.

Job Search Days, Hours, and Times Worksheet

Days	Number of Hours	Times
_____ Sunday	_____	From _____ to _____
_____ Monday	_____	From _____ to _____
_____ Tuesday	_____	From _____ to _____
_____ Wednesday	_____	From _____ to _____
_____ Thursday	_____	From _____ to _____
_____ Friday	_____	From _____ to _____
_____ Saturday	_____	From _____ to _____
Total number of hours per week _____		

Step 3: How Many Hours Will You Look Each Day?

How many hours will you look for work on each day you have selected? Write the number of hours in the second column of the worksheet. For example, if you selected Monday as a day you would look for work, you may decide to spend six hours looking on that day. You would then write "6" in the "Number of Hours" column. Do this with each day you checked. Total that column at the bottom of the worksheet. It should equal the number of hours you listed in Step 1. It's OK if you want to spend more hours than you listed in Step 1. If so, go back and change the number of hours you wrote in Step 1.

Step 4: What Times Each Day?

If you plan to look for work for six hours on each Monday, which hours? For example, you may decide to begin at 8 a.m. and work until noon (four hours), take an hour off for lunch, and then work from 1 to 3 p.m. (two hours). Complete the third column with this information for each day you selected.

Step 5: Set Goals for Your Daily Job Search Schedule

Now you have decided which days and hours to spend on your job search. But what will you do each day? You need a daily plan to get the most out of each hour. Look at the following "Sample Daily Job Search Schedule." Your schedule may look different, but you should use many of the same ideas in your daily schedule.

Sample Daily Job Search Schedule

7:00 to 8:00 a.m.	Get up, shower, dress, eat breakfast, get ready to go to work.
8:00 to 8:15 a.m.	Organize my workspace. Review schedule for interviews and promised follow-ups. Update schedule as needed.
8:15 to 9:00 a.m.	Review old leads for follow-up. Develop new leads (want ads, yellow pages, networking lists, Internet exploration, and so on.
9:00 to 10:00 a.m.	Make phone calls. Set up interviews.
10:00 to 10:15 a.m.	Take a break.
10:15 to 11:00 a.m.	Make more calls. Set up more interviews.
11:00 to noon	Make follow-up calls and send follow-up notes.
Noon to 1:00 p.m.	Lunch break.
1:00 to 3:00 p.m.	Go on interviews. Make cold contacts in the field. Research potential employers at the library, on the Internet, and at the local bureau of employment services.
Evening	Read job search books, make calls to warm contacts you could not reach during the day, work on a "better" resume, spend time with friends and family, exercise, relax.

This schedule is based on years of research into what gets the best results. I tested many schedules in job search programs I ran. Some had more hours, some less. Some had different activities or times spent on those activities. Those who used this schedule got jobs in less time than any other schedule I tried.

Tips for Your Daily Job Search Schedule

- **Set a daily goal for number of interviews.** Use the form later in this chapter to create your job search schedule. I suggest you set a goal of getting at least one or two interviews per day. Many people who use the methods I present in this book get two (or more) interviews per day. Remember to think of an interview as seeing people who hire people like you but who don't necessarily have an opening now. Increasing the number of interviews you get is a simple step that can make a big difference in getting a job in less time.

Your Daily Interview Goals Add Up!

Getting one interview a day equals twenty interviews a month. Getting two interviews a day equals forty interviews a month.

Compare this to the average job seeker, who gets fewer than eight interviews a month. Getting just one interview a day is more than double that average. And getting two interviews a day is more than five times what the average job seeker gets. If you get more interviews, you are likely to get a job in less time. And you are more likely to find the job you really want. It is that simple.

- **Expect to get rejected.** Most people make ten to fifteen phone calls to get one interview. Most people can make that many calls in an hour, so two hours of calls will often result in two interviews. Making fifteen calls to get one interview sounds like a lot of rejection. But the calls that don't get you an interview are often friendly, so the rejection you experience is really no big deal. So get ready for some rejection. The more the better, since the more you get, the closer you are to your objective. Don't stop calling until you meet your daily objective!

- **Make phone calls and be active, not passive.** You won't get interviews or job offers by reading job search books or working on your resume during the day. Save those activities for other times. During the day, concentrate on active methods!

- **Stick to your daily job search schedule.** Approach your job search like a job. Like a job, you have certain things to get done. This is why you should create a daily schedule and stick to it. That way you are more likely to do the things you don't like to do, such as making phone calls. If possible, arrange interviews at times other than those you planned to spend in your job search office. Plan to take care of your personal business after your office hours.

Step 6: Create Your Own Job Search Schedule

Now you need to put together your own job search schedule and stick to it. The best way to do this is to write down your schedule in advance. The completed sample "Job Search Schedule Worksheet" that follows shows how one person created a daily and weekly schedule that made sense for her. Look it over carefully for ideas on completing your own worksheet.

Consider what you have learned so far when completing your own "Job Search Schedule Worksheet." Make several copies of the blank worksheet and use one for each week during your job search. Or you may want to use a computer scheduler or schedule book. These are great for organizing your time. I use my schedule book every day and like it better than a computer scheduler because it's portable.

Getting the Job You Really Want

Job Search
Schedule Worksheet–Sample

	DAYS OF THE WEEK						
TIME	Sunday	Monday	Tuesday	Wednesday	Thursday	Friday	Saturday
8:00		Organize day	→				→	Day off
9:00	Read want ads	Gather old and new leads	→				→	
10:00		Make phone contacts	→				→	
11:00		Follow up. Get 2 interviews	→				→	
noon	Lunch	Write/send follow-up correspondence	→				→	
1:00	Explore Internet	Plan afternoon. Lunch	→				→	
2:00			Leave for interview	Drop off resume at printer	Appt. with Lisa at Whitman Co.	Afternoon off!	
3:00		Work on resume	Interview at Fischer Brothers	→	Pick up resume		
4:00	↓	↓	Make final revisions on resume	→	Drop by state employment office	↓	
5:00	Dinner	→				→	
6:00	Read job search books	→				→	↓

218

© JIST Works

Job Search
Schedule Worksheet

TIME	DAYS OF THE WEEK						
	Sunday	Monday	Tuesday	Wednesday	Thursday	Friday	Saturday
8:00							
9:00							
10:00							
11:00							
noon							
1:00							
2:00							
3:00							
4:00							
5:00							
6:00							

More Forms and Filing Systems to Help You Organize Your Search

Here are a few more forms and ideas to help you organize your job search. Use the ideas to create systems and forms that work for you. Many of these ideas can be adapted for use on a computer.

Job Lead Cards

By using the job search methods you have learned in this book, you can develop hundreds of contacts. Keeping track of them is more than any person's memory can handle. Look at the following 3-by-5-inch card. It shows the kind of information you can keep about each person who helps you in your job search. (If desired, you can list the same kind of information on your computer instead.)

Buy a few hundred 3-by-5 cards to start with. Create one card for each person who gives you a referral or is a possible employer. Keep brief notes each time you talk with that person to help you remember important details for your next contact. Here is an example of one job lead card. Notice that the notes are brief but contain enough to remember what happened and when to follow up.

Organization: _Mutual Health Insurance_

Contact person: _Anna Tomey_

Phone number: _(555) 555-2211_

Source of lead: _Aunt Ruth_

Notes: _4/10 called. Anna on vacation. Call back 4/15. 4/15 Interview set 4/20 at 1:30. 4/20 Anna showed me around. They use the same computers we used in school. Sent thank-you note and JIST Card. Call back 5/1. 5/1 Second interview 5/8 at 9 a.m._

Set Up and Use the Job Search Follow-Up Box

Most department and office-supply stores have small file boxes made to hold 3-by-5-inch cards. Also available are tabbed dividers for these boxes. Everything you need will cost you about $10.

Set up file box dividers for each day of the month, numbering them 1 through 31. Once this has been done, file each completed job lead card under the date you want to follow up on it. Here are some ways you can use this simple follow up system to get results.

- **Example 1.** You get the name of a person to call, but you can't get to this person right away. Create a job lead card and file it under tomorrow's date.

- **Example 2.** You call someone from a yellow pages listing, but she is busy this week. She tells you to call back in two weeks. You file this job lead card under the date for two weeks in the future.

- **Example 3.** You get an interview with a person who doesn't have any openings now, and he gives you the name of someone who might have an opening. After you send a thank-you note and JIST Card, you file his job lead card under a date a few weeks in the future.

As you contact more and more people in your job search, the number of cards you file for future follow-up will increase. You will find more and more new leads as you follow up with people you've contacted one or more times in the past. Following up with past contacts is one of the most effective ways of getting a job!

Every Monday, simply review all the job lead cards filed for the week. On your weekly schedule, list any interviews or follow-up calls you promised to make at a particular date and time. At the start of each day, pull the job lead cards filed under that date. List appointments and calls on your "Daily Job Search Contact Sheet," which is described next. The job search follow-up box is a simple, inexpensive system that works very well. You can do the same thing with computer scheduling software, but it doesn't work any better than the box.

Is a Computer Better Than 3-by-5 Cards?

Maybe not. If you already use scheduling or time management software, go ahead and use it to manage your job search contacts. If you don't use such software now, you will probably be better off trying the card system I suggest. The reason is simple: It works. Instead of spending your time messing with new software, you can go right to work making contacts and getting results.

Daily Job Search Contact Sheet

If you do what I suggest, you will try each day to set up one or two interviews. To get this done, you will have to contact a lot of people. Some you will contact for the first time; others you will follow up from earlier contacts.

To get you started now, I suggest you begin each day by completing a "Daily Job Search Contact Sheet." Use it to list at least twenty people or organizations to call. Use any source to get these leads, including people you know, referrals, yellow page leads, Internet leads, and want ads. Feel free to make copies of the form, or make your own on lined paper. An example of a contact sheet follows.

TIP

This is a good time to review Chapter 7. There I cover networking and how to develop lists of people to contact. That chapter also discusses how to use the yellow pages to generate contacts. Reviewing this information will remind you of how you can generate the contacts you need.

Daily Job Search Contact Sheet–Sample

	Contact Name/Organization	Referral Source	Job Lead Card?	Phone Number/E-Mail Address
1.	Manager/The Flower Show	Yellow pages	Yes	897-6041
2.	Manager/Rainbow Flowers	Listed on Rainbow's Web site	Yes	admin@rainbowflowers.com
3.	Joyce Wilson/Hartley Nurseries	John Lee	Yes	892-2224
4.	John Mullahy/Roses, Etc.	Uncle Jim	Yes	299-4226
5.	None/Plants to Go	Want Ad	Yes	835-7016

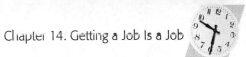

Daily Job Search Contact Sheet

	Contact Name/Organization	Referral Source	Job Lead Card?	Phone Number/E-Mail Address
1.				
2.				
3.				
4.				
5.				
6.				
7.				
8.				
9.				
10.				
11.				
12.				
13.				
14.				
15.				
16.				
17.				
18.				
19.				
20.				

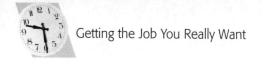

A Few Final Words on Being Organized

Most people don't enjoy the job search experience. It is true that lots of rejection is involved. To avoid failure, people find many ways to avoid looking for work.

Of course, delaying your job search just leaves you unemployed longer than you need to be. Or it keeps you from getting the job you really want just that much longer. So don't get discouraged. The best way to shorten your job search is to structure your time as if your job search is your job.

Looking for a job is hard work, so take time for breaks. And take time to take care of yourself. There is a job out that that is just what you are looking for, or very close. And there is someone out there who wants just what you have to offer. But you will not find those opportunities unless you go out and look for them.

CHAPTER 15

Tips for Long-Term Career Success

Planning Is Important

Most people work for forty or more years. Some work in one job after another, without a plan. Others plan ahead and work toward long-term career and life goals. Since a bit of luck is involved in career success, either approach can work out well. But people who plan and work toward their objectives are more likely to end up with satisfying careers—and lives.

Most people have more control over their lives than they realize. What we do, and how we do it, often sets us up for what happens next. For example, what you learn in one job can prepare you for the next. You can either let things happen to you, or you can get involved and *make* things happen.

This last chapter presents steps you can take to increase your chances of job success. It also covers details on how and when to leave a job in a positive way.

To Get Ahead, You Need to Exceed an Employer's Expectations!

In the second chapter, you learned about the three major employer expectations. These are the points that are most important to an employer in deciding to hire one person over another. In case you don't remember, here are the expectations:

- First impressions
- Dependability and other personality traits
- Skills, experience, and training

An employer will not hire someone unless the person meets his or her expectations in these areas. Once you have the job, you must continue to meet your employer's expectations. Meeting minimum expectations may keep you from getting fired. But, to get promotions or pay increases, you need to do *more* than the minimum.

The Skills Employers Want

Way back in Chapter 3, you identified some of your key skills. At the end of that chapter, I include a list of skills that came from an employer survey. It includes skills employers said are most important for success on the job. Let's take another look at the skills on that list:

1. Learning to learn
2. Basic academic skills in reading, writing, and computation
3. Listening and oral communication
4. Creative thinking and problem solving
5. Self-esteem and goal setting
6. Personal and career development
7. Interpersonal skills, negotiation, and teamwork
8. Organizational effectiveness and leadership

Employers say these skills are most important for success on the job. The tips that follow cover these skills and provide other steps you can take to get ahead.

Twelve Extra Steps You Can Take to Get Ahead

You have to do the minimum to keep from getting fired. But, if you want pay increases and promotions, you have to do more. There are no guarantees of success, but the tips that follow will help. Each tip is followed by space for you to write notes on how you can apply the information to your own situation. Use extra paper if needed.

To give you an example, here is what one person wrote after the first tip:

I don't write all that well and make mistakes in grammar and spelling. My job now doesn't need much writing but the technician job I want requires lots of reports sent to customers. I will look into a remedial writing class at the junior college and sign up for the next class. I am also using the spell and grammar checking features on everything I write. This helps me see my errors and correct them. I am writing more e-mails to friends at home to practice writing. I first write on the word processor so I can check spelling and grammar, then cut and paste that text into e-mail. I plan to keep writing more and get better at it.

1. Correct Weaknesses in Your Basic Skills

Employers expect you to have good basic academic skills. If, for example, you don't write well or don't have good language skills, this can keep you from getting ahead. While the skills needed for different jobs vary, consider weaknesses you have and decide to make improvements. This may include taking courses or learning and practicing on the job and in other ways.

How might you use this tip in your next job? _____

_____

2. Dress and Groom for a Promotion

If you want to get ahead in an organization, dress and groom as if you work at the level you hope to reach next. This is not always possible, but at the very least, be clean and well-groomed. Wear clothes that fit well and look good on you. Copy the grooming and dress of others in the organization who are successful. Even when your coworkers see you away from work, present the image you want for yourself at work.

How might you use this tip in your next job? _____

_____

3. Arrive Early and Stay Late

Get to work a little early each day. Use the time to list what you plan to get done. Always be at your workstation at the time work begins, so your coworkers and boss know you are there. At the end of the day, leave at least a few minutes after quitting time. Let the boss know that you are willing to stay late to meet an important deadline. If you do stay late, let the boss know!

Some employers may not want you to work beyond their regular hours. They fear problems with governmental agencies that may force them to pay overtime wages. If this is so, do what your employer wants you to do, but make it clear that you are willing to help in any way needed.

How might you use this tip in your next job? _____

_____

4. Be Positive and Enthusiastic

Go out of your way to enjoy your job. Tell others, particularly your boss and those you work with, what you like about it. Emphasize those parts of your job that you like and do well. It will help others notice what you do. Enthusiasm also encourages teamwork and can improve how you feel about your work and yourself. Share this enthusiasm with your friends. Being positive will help you overcome problems and be more effective.

How might you use this tip in your next job? _____

_____

5. Set Clear Goals

Many tips in this section assume you want to get ahead. It is up to you to set your own goals in your career and personal life. The clearer your goals, the more likely you will reach them. If, for example, you want to get promoted, it may be clear to you that you will need to supervise others or learn new skills. If your goal is important to you, you are more likely to do what is needed to meet it. So spend some time writing down your key goals, and then write down what you have to do to get there.

How might you use this tip in your next job? _____

_____

6. Ask for More Responsibility

Let the boss know you want to move up and are willing to take on more responsibility. Ask for advice about what you can do to be more valuable to the organization. As soon as you begin a new job, look for ways to learn new things. Volunteer to help out in ways you feel will make you more valuable to the organization. For example, go out of your way to help solve a problem. If you are willing to supervise others, let your boss know.

How might you use this tip in your next job? _____

_____

7. Ask for Advice in Getting a Pay Increase or Promotion

In your first few weeks on the job, ask your supervisor for about thirty minutes of private time. When you have your boss's attention, say that you want to be more valuable to the organization. Ask what you can do to get a raise within a reasonable time. Make sure you know what you have to do to get the raise. Before you leave the meeting, ask for a specific future date to go over your progress. Ask the boss to give you feedback on your progress from time to time. Don't push too hard for an increase. Just letting your boss know about your ambitions can help him or her see you as someone to develop for the future.

How might you use this tip in your next job? _____

_____

8. Ask for Training

Get as much training as possible! Take any training that is available from your employer. Even if the training is not in your area of responsibility, it may help you gain new skills. Define what training you need to do your job better. If it is not available through your employer, explain to your supervisor how the training will help the organization. Ask for help in finding the best training source.

How might you use this tip in your next job? _____

_____

9. Learn More on Your Own Time

Decide what you need to learn to get ahead in this or a future job you want. Take evening classes instead of watching TV and read books and magazines on related subjects. Stay up-to-date on your field and identify skills you need to learn to get ahead. Computer and technical skills are very important for many jobs, so pay special attention to these. If your job does not require you to develop technical skills, it is most important that you learn them outside of your job. As you learn new skills, look for ways to use them in your present job.

How might you use this tip in your next job? _____

_____

10. Volunteer for Difficult Projects

You won't get much positive attention unless you do more than is expected of you. Look for projects you think you can do well and that would benefit the organization in some clear way. Don't promise too much, and keep a low profile while you do the work. If no one expects much, it is easier to be seen as successful—even if your results are not as good as you had hoped. If you succeed, your boss will often appreciate what you did and is more likely to reward you in the future.

How might you use this tip in your next job? _____

_____

11. Get Measurable Results

Look for some way to measure the results of your work. Keep records of what you do. Compare your results to past performance or the average performance of others in similar situations. If your results look good, send a report to your supervisor. For example, if orders went up 40 percent over the same month last year with no increase in staff, that's a big accomplishment. Look for ways to present what you do in numbers: dollars saved, percent of increased sales, number of persons served, number of units processed, budget size.

How might you use this tip in your next job? _____

_____

12. Keep Planning

You can take many steps to succeed on the job. The tips I gave you here will help you learn and use many of the skills that employers say are most important to them. Getting ahead does require some luck, but it also requires hard work. The important point to remember is to plan ahead, set goals, and work toward what you want to accomplish.

How might you use this tip in your next job? _____

_____

Why People Get Fired

To get ahead on a job, you first have to understand what will get you in trouble. Here is a list of points often mentioned in employer surveys as top reasons for firing workers.

- Unable to get along with other workers.

- Was dishonest: lied or stole things.

- Poor dress or grooming.

- Unreliable, too many times late or absent.

- Used work time for personal business.

- Was unable or unwilling to do the work.

- Worked too slowly or made too many mistakes.

- Would not follow orders, did not get along with supervisor.

- Abused alcohol or drugs.

- Misrepresented their skills, experience, or training.

- Too many accidents, did not follow safety rules.

How to Leave a Job in the Right Way

Too many people leave their jobs for the wrong reasons or in the wrong way. Some jobs just don't work out. It may be that you don't get along with your supervisor or coworkers. Maybe you don't see a way to advance to a job you want. There are many reasons why you may want to leave a job. But, before you do, you should consider a few points. This section gives tips to help you to decide to stay or leave. If you decide to leave, the tips here will help you do so in a professional way.

- **Don't just quit!** If you quit suddenly and without notice, your boss and coworkers will not have time to cover your job. This can hurt you later, since you will not be able to use them as references to help get another job. While this may not seem important to you now, many employers will not hire you unless they can verify your employment history.

  Exceptions: There are some situations where you should leave a job right away. For example, if you feel threatened by coworkers or a supervisor, you should leave as soon as possible. If you are asked to do something dishonest or "wrong" and don't think you can safely report this to a supervisor, consider leaving right away.

- **Clearly define why you are not happy.** If you are not satisfied in a job, it is important to know why. If you are thinking about quitting, take some time to write down why you are not satisfied. Doing this will help you know what to avoid in your next job and point out things you can change on your present job.

- **Before you give up, consider something different.** Once you define why you want to quit, ask yourself if you can change it. Be creative—what do you have to lose? Consider asking for a job change within the organization before you give up. Or be more assertive in asking your boss for more responsibility or different assignments. At this point, you have nothing to lose by trying something different.

- **Don't tell anyone you are thinking of leaving.** Many people tell coworkers that they are unhappy and thinking of leaving. The problem is that others, including the boss, often find out. If the boss hears about your plans, he or she may start looking for someone to replace you and then fire you when a replacement is found. Even if the boss doesn't know about your thoughts, others will begin to take you less seriously or not give you the help and training you need to succeed.

- **Get a new job before you leave your old one.** The best way to leave a job is to resign to go to a better one. Once you decide to leave a job, start actively looking for a new one. Since you are still working, you will have to use job search methods that don't interfere with your work. For example, use the Internet to post your resume and search for openings. Set up interviews over lunch or outside of regular work hours. Use vacation or personal time as needed.

- **Stay positive and productive.** Most people who are unhappy with their jobs develop a negative attitude. They complain more, blame others, and often don't perform as well as they used to. If this keeps up, many employers will notice the poor performance and bad attitude. This can lead to being fired for poor performance, even though the employer never knew that the person wanted to leave. So, if you are looking for another job, it is important to keep a positive attitude and to keep doing your job well. Doing so will allow you to leave on your own terms.

- **Give plenty of notice before you leave.** Once you find a new job, you will need to resign. The best way to do so is in a letter to your supervisor. Keep it positive, say you appreciate your boss's help, and mention other good points about your experience there. Offer to remain on your job for at least two weeks—more if you can. This will allow the company to find someone to replace you and make a smooth transition.

- **Leave on good terms with everyone.** Remember that your next employer will want to contact your previous ones, so be as friendly and as productive as possible in your final days on a job. Get your projects and work area organized so someone else can quickly understand what to do. Help train the person who will take over. Say positive things about your experience to coworkers and supervisors.

And Now, in Conclusion

This book now comes to an end. But, for you, there is so much more to come. The final lessons I can offer are these:

- **Trust yourself.** No one can know you better than you do.

- **Decide to do something worthwhile.** Whether it is raising a family or saving the whales, believe in something you do as special, as lasting, as valuable.

- **Work well.** All work is worth doing, so put your energy into it and do it as well as you are able.

- **Enjoy life.** It's sort of the same as having fun, but lasts longer and means more.

- **Send thank-you notes.** Many people will help you throughout your life in large and small ways. Let them know you appreciate them. The more you give, the more you are likely to get in return.

Thank you for using this book. I wish you good fortune in your job search and your life.

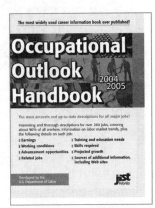

Enhanced Occupational Outlook Handbook,
Fifth Edition

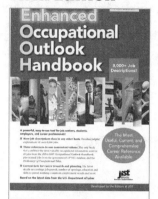

Based on data from the U.S. Department of Labor
Compiled by Editors at JIST

This award-winning book combines the best features of America's three most authoritative occupational references—the *Occupational Outlook Handbook*, the *Dictionary of Occupational Titles*, and the O*NET (the Department of Labor's Occupational Information Network). This is a huge reference with more than 8,000 job descriptions. It helps readers identify major jobs of interest and then obtain information on these jobs and the many more-specialized jobs related to them.

ISBN 1-59357-030-9 / Order Code LP-J0309 / **$39.95** Softcover
ISBN 1-59357-031-7 / Order Code LP-J0317 / **$49.95** Hardcover

Guide for Occupational Exploration, Third Edition

J. Michael Farr; LaVerne L. Ludden, Ed.,D.; and Laurence Shatkin, Ph.D.

The first major revision since the *GOE* was released in 1979 by the U.S. Department of Labor! It still uses the same approach of exploration based on major interest areas but is updated to reflect the many changes in our labor market. The new *GOE* also uses the recently released O*NET database of occupational information developed by the U.S. Department of Labor. An essential career reference!

ISBN 1-56370-636-9 / Order Code LP-J6369 / **$39.95** Softcover
ISBN 1-56370-826-4 / Order Code LP-J8264 / **$49.95** Hardcover

Career Guide to America's Top Industries,
Sixth Edition

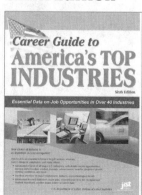

U.S. Department of Labor

This information-packed review of 42 top industries discusses careers from an industry perspective and covers employment trends, earnings, types of jobs available, working conditions, training required, and more. Helps the reader see that choosing the right industry is as important as choosing the right occupation.

This valuable companion reference to the *Occupational Outlook Handbook* includes cross-references to jobs listed there.

ISBN 1-59357-032-5 / Order Code LP-J0325 / **$13.95**

6074